WATCHING
GOD
WORK

MINISTRY AMONG THE MACUSHI

Miriam Abbott and Jane Burns

Selected and Edited with Commentary by Stephanie Smith

LUCIDBOOKS

Watching God Work
Ministry among the Macushi

By Miriam Abbott and Jane Burns

Selected and Edited with Commentary by Stephanie Smith

To those God used to make it possible, the individuals and churches who supported me for years. Many have already received their "Well done!" from the Lord. To the First Baptist Church of Collingdale, PA, for their efforts and generosity to raise the funds to publish the Macushi New Testament. And to my most faithful prayer supporter, my mother, to whom I addressed these letters of many years. Mother, your prayers are still being answered.
—Miriam Abbott

To the many of Covenant Community Church who prayed and supported me throughout these years. And to the Women's Missionary Society for their faithfulness. To my family who were always ready to lend a hand, from packing to printing, from computer help to sending out prayer letters, and more.
—Jane Burns

To Miriam and Jane, who allowed me the privilege of telling their story. To my husband, Mike, and my children, Rachel, Sarah, Bethany, Drew, and Katelyn, who were so patient with me during the writing of this book. And to my precious Lord, Jesus Christ, who makes the story worth telling.
—Stephanie Smith

Table of Contents

Part Two: God at Work: Providing

Part Three: God at Work: Producing

Introduction

Marriage joins more than just two people; marriage joins families. I knew that when I married my husband, I would be gaining another set of parents and siblings, which I loved. I didn't realize that I would also be gaining aunts and uncles, cousins and grandparents, and the history that each of these possess.

In exploring and learning about this big-hearted family, I became acquainted with Aunt Miriam and her ministry in Brazil. Occasionally when traveling, our family would stop in for a visit with Aunt Miriam and Aunt Jane. ("Aunt" Jane is not actually related. It's just our way of letting her know that we count her as family and love her the same.) Both ladies regaled our children with stories of Brazil's people, animals, and adventures, careful to include the ways that they witnessed God's work there. And always, we would leave their house with the same sentiment: "Someone really needs to write their story. It should be preserved at least for the family."

Eventually, we began to ask Aunt Miriam and Aunt Jane about it, and they agreed to let us try. Aunt Miriam told us that she had written hundreds of letters to her mother, detailing nearly every aspect of her life in Brazil. Little did Miriam know until Grandmom's last weeks, that all of the letters had been kept! What a treasure! And what a perfect resource.

Aunt Miriam allowed me to have copies of the letters, which I then read straight through. I took notes and prepared to write their story in my own words. It didn't take long to realize, though, that my words fell flat compared to Aunt Miriam's way of telling things. Of course, she had first-hand experiences!

So, through trial and error and many revisions, we have attempted to tell the story of Aunt Miriam and Aunt Jane and their years living in South America as missionaries. Of the two, Miriam was the writer. Jane stayed busy with many things, but she didn't write much. We don't have as much information about her because of this. However, that doesn't mean we hold her in less esteem or think her role to be less important. No, we understand that neither of them could have had the ministry they did without the other. God knew what He was doing!

Through the last four and a half years, I have had the privilege of traveling to Florida to visit Aunt Miriam and Aunt Jane three times. Each time has been for the primary purpose of interviewing them, gleaning information from them, and working through the details of this book. We always have many things to discuss, a few things to weep over, much to laugh about, and such a precious time together. I have come to respect their wisdom, appreciate their advice, and treasure their friendship. Their deep knowledge of God comes from a lifetime of walking with and depending upon Him. Perhaps their eager submission to Him—even when His plan did not match their own—is why their ministry was so effective.

As we worked and prayed toward the completion of this book, the Lord impressed on my heart that this story is not meant to be shared with just family. This is a story for Christians. Through

Introduction

it, we see God's sovereignty, His protection, His goodness, His faithfulness, and His grace. This book is also for those interested in missions. It will inspire, convict, and motivate you to further service for the King. Above all, we want to bring glory to God as the true Author of these events.

Several things will help you better understand as you read. I am the narrator of the book. Most of the story is told in the words of Aunt Miriam through her letters to Grandmom. There are a few excerpts of letters written to Aunt Miriam's own Aunt Miriam (her mother's sister), as well as prayer letters written to all of the churches and individuals that supported Aunt Miriam and Aunt Jane. In several places, I have interviewed the ladies, and their responses are included for you to read. This is especially true with Aunt Jane, as we only had a few of her letters to glean from.

There are several passages that are notes sent to me by coworkers, friends, and family of the ladies. These are meant to be a commentary on the nature of the work done in Brazil and on the character of Aunt Miriam and Aunt Jane. Although I tried to organize these into logical places within the narrative, they are separate and independent from it.

At the beginning of each chapter, we have included a Bible verse. Each verse is written two times. The first time is what we call a "back translation." This means that Aunt Miriam read the Macushi version of each verse, and then told it back to me in English. While this is not an actual translation, we thought it would be fun for the readers to hear a bit of how the Macushi think and speak.

Originally, we planned to write the story in chronological order. We quickly discovered that 50 years of ministry made the book much too long! Therefore, Parts One and Two are primarily in chronological order, but Part Three is organized topically. You may see some shifting back and forth in time, which was unavoidable due to this arrangement. To help you see the big picture, we have included a timeline of important dates and events. Along those lines, we have also included a map of the immediate area in which Aunt Miriam and Aunt Jane lived and ministered. Finally, we have included a list of people that you will read about. Each person is categorized and briefly defined to help you remember their role in Aunt Miriam's and Aunt Jane's lives.

If you are a family member or someone close to the family, you will likely enjoy every word of the book and wish for more. We had to eliminate so many funny, interesting stories because the book was just too long. If you possess a particular interest in missions, not necessarily these specific missionaries, you will find portions of Part Two and all of Part Three more helpful. They include the methods and results of the ministry itself.

May the Lord bless and encourage your heart as you learn of His working in Brazil among the Macushi through the efforts of Miriam Abbott and Jane Burns. To God be the glory!

Stephanie Smith

Important People

Missionaries Who Worked with Jane during Her First Term:

Jean Bradshaw and Phyllis McLean	Missionaries on the Belém field. Jane lived with them in order to improve her Portuguese. Phyllis was severely injured in the Portel house fire.
Durval and Miriã Uchoa	Brazilian missionaries at Gorotire, the Kayapo village where Jane first worked.
Beth Ann Smith	Came to work with Jane at Gorotire among the Kayapo.

UFM/CrossWorld Missionaries:

Pat and June Foster	Missionaries at Parishara, the first to do an analysis of the Macushi language. He translated the books of Mark, epistles of John, and several chapters of the Gospel of John. They moved to Brazil after the revolt and worked in the village of Manoá and in administration in Boa Vista.
Bob, Neill, and Radar Hawkins	Three brothers who originally began missionary work among the indigenous tribes of Guyana and northern Brazil (continued on next page).

5

Bob and his wife, Florene, translated the whole Bible into the Wai Wai language. They worked in Kanashen, Guyana, and then moved to Anaua, Brazil, after the revolt.

Neill and his wife, Mary, founded MEVA, the Brazilian arm of UFM. They started the work among the Macushi in Brazil. He was also responsible for bringing in Brazilian missionaries João Batista and Paulo Silas to work among the Macushi.

Radar and his wife, Ann, worked in Guyana in Georgetown. They moved to Lethem and started a church there. He was captured during the Guyanese revolt and subsequently moved to Brazil.

Lib Weeks	Taught literacy to adult Macushi at Parishara, where Miriam lived with her. After the Guyanese revolt, she taught in the mission school in Georgetown.
Dave and Grace Crompton	Missionaries to the Macushi. Dave helped check the Macushi New Testament translation and helped with the dictionary.
Dan and Marge Teeter	Missionaries to the Macushi. Serving currently in administration and producing material to teach Indian leadership.
Don and Barb Borgman	Missionaries to the Sanuma tribe (a Yanomami group). He translated the New Testament into that language. They lost their son to a snake bite in the jungle.

Fran Tracy	Missionary among the Wapishana. She started the work in the south Rupununi district. After the revolt, she remained in Guyana and worked with Wycliffe missionary Bev Dawson.
Joe and DiAnne Butler	Served in Guyana and Brazil. Frequently worked with the Macushi.
Flo Riedle	Nurse among the Wai Wai in Kanashen, Guyana, and Anaua, Brazil. Gave Miriam her orientation to missionary nursing.
Carole Swain and Carol James	Serve the Yanomami at Mucajai. Miriam continues to serve as Carole's translation consultant for the Yanomami New Testament.
Eric and Donna Shrift	Came to Brazil first as short-term missionaries to help at Serra Grande. Eric discovered that he could teach and serve in many ways on the field, so they stayed. He currently produces the Macushi radio broadcasts.
Irene Benson	School teacher among the Wai Wai in Guyana and Brazil.

Other Missionaries:

John Gaunt	Missionary Aviation Fellowship pilot who was captured during the Guyanese revolt.

Doris Wall	A Pilgrim Holiness (Wesleyan) missionary nurse and midwife. She did some translation and started a Bible school among the Patamona Indians. Miriam was visiting her during the Guyanese revolt. Doris stayed in Guyana until her retirement.
Catherine Rountree	Wycliffe missionary in Surinam. She was the consultant who checked the Macushi New Testament before publication.
Marge Crofts	Wycliffe consultant who helped Miriam train Macushi to do translations. She came to Boa Vista to help with the Macushi New Testament.

Personal Long-time Friends:

Ruth Sharp Cochrane	Miriam's roommate in nursing and Bible schools. Served as a missionary in Chad, Africa.
Elizabeth Kereji	Jane's friend, a pharmacist from Jane's home church. She visited Brazil three times and helped Miriam and Jane find medications for use on the clinic trips.
Carol Morrill	Jane's friend, whose mother was one of Jane's supporters. Carol and Jane share a birthday!

Brazilian Missionaries:

João Batista	The first Brazilian missionary with UFM. He traveled and worked in Macushi villages, teaching in Portuguese. He later pastored in the south of Brazil.
Julieta Souza and Isabel Rocha de Carvalho	Both were Miriam's coworkers early in her ministry in Brazil.

Macushi:

Waldemar and Josefa	Assisted at Serra Grande. Waldemar was the main translation assistant for the Macushi New Testament and the best Macushi preacher for many years. He often accompanied Jane on the clinic trips, he translated many of the songs and hymns that the Macushi sing, and he recorded messages on tape and eventually for the radio broadcasts.
Domingos and Iracema	Helped Miriam and Jane learn the Macushi language and also assisted with the New Testament translation. Iracema taught women's classes, and they both helped at Serra Grande in the Bible school.

Sebastiao and Luciola	A young, Macushi couple that Jane worked with. Luciola became a medical attendant and midwife.
Jose Carlos and Auxiliadora	Worked at Serra Grande. He is Brazilian, and she is half Macushi.
Francisco, Raimundo, Odilon, Adolfo	The first four Macushi medical attendants trained by Jane. Adolfo was the chief of Macedonia.

Part One

God at Work: Preparing

"Get Involved"

Get involved in the lives of others; do it now for Jesus's sake.
Put aside all of your "druthers," for the many hearts that ache.
Cross the seas to distant nations, that the Savior do not know;
Do it not for man's ovations, but because Christ loved you so.
Say a word to mend the broken heart, that feels it has reached
the end.
To those who feel lonely and apart, be a blessing and a friend.
When one is down and in despair, to defeat do not give in.
Lift him up to God in prayer, never let Satan win.
Don't pass by a soul in need, as the Levite did and the Priest;
Be as the Samaritan in his deed; be mindful of the least.
"Why get involved in another's strife?" I might in selfishness
whine.
Jesus Christ for me gave His life. Thank God He got involved
in mine.

Mr. Jim Bjur
Missionary to Chile

How does a child grow up to become a faithful, committed missionary? The path for each is different, and yet, the same. The outward circumstances, the family dynamics, the education and experiences all vary. But each servant of God must learn the same lessons in faith, submission, trust, and patience.

God beckons; she responds. God instructs; she learns. God tests; she trusts. God blesses; she marvels. And day by day, through hardships and blessings, in times of monotony and adventure, a rock is polished into a beautiful diamond of God's grace.

Macushi Background

As God was making us to search, in order that we all find Him in our searching, because He is not far from every single one of us.

—Acts 17:27, Macushi Back Translation[1]

So that they should seek the Lord, in the hope that they might grope for Him and find Him, though He is not far from each one of us.

—Acts 17:27

Near the dawn of the 20th century, the Alleluia religion came to the Patamona Tribe of South America. Although they had no written Scripture, the people orally shared Bible stories, prayed, sang, and practiced various forms of worship. They wanted to learn and know of God, and they diligently searched for Him.

In the 1950s, God answered their prayers by sending missionaries to them. Rev. Maxie Walton, Rev. J. C. Garth, Rev. Clifton Berg, and others came to share the gospel with the Patamonas. The Word was received with joy, and many were saved. It didn't take long for these eager new believers to recognize that it was their responsibility to

---

1. Note: The Macushi Back Translation is Aunt Miriam's wording of a verse by reading the Macushi Version and then translating it back into English. I wanted to use this method to help the readers "hear" how Macushis talk and think.

13

share God's love with their neighbors.

Among these neighbors were the Macushi tribe. A few Macushi heard the gospel message and accepted Christ as their own. They traveled to the Patamona village, learned the Patamona language, and grew in their knowledge and walk with God. They then returned to their homes, where they lived out their Christian faith among their families and friends.

Thus it was that the villages and hearts of the Macushi Indians had been fertilized to receive the seed of God's Word. And in His perfect time, in just His perfect way, God sent two ladies to reap a great harvest among the spiritually hungry Macushis.

Miriam

Chapter One

God Begins

God is working good in all your hearts like that. He will continue His work up until its finish, until Jesus Christ comes. That I know.
　　　　　—Philippians 1:6, Macushi Back Translation

Being confident of this very thing, that He who has begun a good work in you will complete it until the day of Jesus Christ.
　　　　　　　　　　　　　—Philippians 1:6

Miriam Abbott was born into a Christian heritage that was generations deep. She made her debut on December 6, 1942, in Laurel, Delaware. Her parents, Edward Mitchell Abbott, Jr. and Maude Smith Abbott were hardworking, God-fearing farmers. Miriam was the third of seven children in the Abbott family: Edward, Johnny, Miriam, Arthur (Butch), Sue, Bill, and Nancy. God had a plan.

Miriam was taught the importance of God and His Word from a young age.

Philippians 1:6 says, "For I am confident of this very thing, that He who began a good work in you will perfect it until the day of Christ Jesus." I chose this verse as my life verse. It is still the one I believe day by day as I marvel at what God is doing.

How and when did it begin? From the time I was born, I was taken to church on a regular basis - Sunday mornings, Sunday evenings, and Wednesday evenings. God gave me a real love for His Word. Mother made it come alive to me as she taught us each evening in our "Bible Times." She was quite dramatic as she told of David and his victory over Goliath. And the stories in the book of Judges were among my favorites. She had us acting out the Bible stories, and we were great actors!

Scripture memory was a big part of our training; we would often learn a Psalm together. Psalm 1, 2, 23, 24, 100, and others that I memorized as a child have stayed with me throughout my life. The emphasis put on the Word of God left the distinct impression that whatever problem I was to face in life, the answers were there for me to search out. God was teaching me the importance of His Word.

Missions was also a part of our family life. Mother put up a big map of the world on our dining room wall and put up pictures of various missionaries, showing where they were serving. We prayed faithfully for them. One was a childhood friend of Mother's who went to Guatemala. She visited our home when she came on furlough and told me of a Guatemalan girl my age that shared my name. She gave me her address and promised she would interpret my letters to this Miriam.

We were pen-pals for several years. (That's what we did in the "old days" before Facebook!) God was enlarging my world.

We prayed for a Chinese seminary student who often visited our church and our home. His wife and family were in China and couldn't get out, and he couldn't return to them. We had a "penny" bank on our table, and we saved up change to give him and help him. All that he earned, he sent to his family. We prayed for seven years that God would enable his family to join him in the US, and how we rejoiced when the miracle happened! This answer to prayer really encouraged me through the years to not give up praying for people. God was teaching me perseverance in prayer!

Mother conducted a Good News Club in our home during the school year. Neighborhood children would crowd on our school bus to be dropped off at our home for the club. I was involved in the preparation. Mother gave out "favors," a small, cut-out figure with the memory verse written on the back, to remind the children of the Bible story. She used a flannel graph to illustrate the stories, and we helped in coloring and cutting out the figures and gluing the flannel on the back so they would stick to the flannel board.

Once a year, Mother gave a party! She told us there were too many of us to each have an individual birthday party, so she gave an annual Halloween party for all of us and invited all the Bible Club children, too. What fun we had going through our costume box in the attic (a big box of old clothes, hats, shoes, etc.) to come up with our latest costume for that year's party. We planned the decorations and games, and, of course, *chose the refreshments! Mother always made the highlight of the party her story time, where she told a Bible story and gave the gospel so that children could understand it. My favorite "Halloween" story was the one where Israel's neighbors put on costumes to fool Joshua, pretending to be people from a far country, wearing old, worn-out clothes and shoes, so that Joshua would sign a peace treaty with them. Deceit was a tool of the enemy, and Joshua learned the hard way (like we often do) that it doesn't pay. It is best to trust the Lord and not believe the lies of Satan! God was continuing my training.*

Vacation Bible School was also a much-celebrated event as summer rolled around. We all participated in that, and when I was older, I still helped Mother in her preparations. I would stay at home and prepare our noon meal so that she could continue to teach. That's how I learned to cook. My two older brothers, Edward and Johnny, were saved during VBS, I think in my mother's class.

I don't remember just when I was saved. I was very shy and backward and hated saying or doing anything where others would look at me. I was a "Mama's girl," always staying around her and listening in on her conversations with other people.

But one Sunday evening, we saw a film in church about the rapture. This instilled fear in me because I knew Mother and Daddy would go to meet the Lord in the air when He returned, but I wasn't sure about me. I didn't want to be left behind. So that night after church, before I got in bed, I asked the Lord to save me. I think I was about eight years old.

But it wasn't until I was eleven years old that I was baptized with some of my friends. Even then, our pastor's wife, Mrs. Eilene Troester, was the one who urged me and gave me the courage to do it. I was so short, that I had to stand on a chair in the baptistry so people could see me. At that age, it was difficult for me to see just what difference salvation made in my life. The biggest change was an inner one, in that I was a lot less fearful. I used to have nightmares, but the Lord gave me new confidence. I don't remember ever having nightmares again.

It was when I was still eleven years old, that the young people of my church were going to have a retreat. I wasn't supposed to go because I wasn't old enough yet. But one of my older friends invited me, and I was given special permission to attend. The Lord had been working in my heart about surrendering my will to His, but I was afraid. I feared that if I gave in to God's will, He would send me to Africa or some other horrible place. But I knew that was foolish thinking, and I really should trust the Lord. During that retreat, I submitted to serve Him however He led, even if it meant going to Africa!

God used all these events and people in my life to mold me and draw me to Himself. Mother's faithfulness in teaching was perhaps the overwhelming influence that led me to Him. But God also uses many situations and things that are not pleasant to form our character and "polish" His vessel. Although I can look back on my childhood as a very positive and pleasant experience, there were some difficulties that the Lord used.

When I was a teenager, I heard the terrible news that my favorite uncle had separated from my Aunt Miriam (yes, we shared a name!). He was unfaithful to her and wanted to marry a dear friend of hers. Aunt Miriam was ill at the time with tuberculosis, and her friend from church offered to stay with her and help nurse her through the illness. During that time, my uncle was taken with this lady and wanted to divorce Aunt Miriam. She refused, saying she didn't want to make his sin "legal." They had no children, so she saw no need to give in to his request. She was devastated, as was her sister, my mother. We all grieved over this. I personally implored the Lord to bring him back and make everything right again. For some time, Uncle Frank kept up his request for a divorce. He moved in with his sister in the meantime. Finally, when he realized that Aunt Miriam was not going to relent and grant the divorce, he decided to just move in with his girlfriend and live with her, married or not. So he packed up his belongings in his station wagon and drove to her house. It had snowed that day, and her driveway was blocked. He got out and began to shovel the driveway when suddenly, he had a massive heart attack and died. The Lord taught me that we are accountable to Him. He tells us that we are the temple of God and that "If anyone defiles the temple of God, God will destroy him. For the temple of God is holy, which temple you are" (I Cor. 3:17). This was a vivid illustration to me of the consequences of our actions.

Not only did I learn this lesson, but I also saw what God did in Aunt Miriam's life. The heartbreaking event drew her closer to the Lord. It strengthened her faith, as she had no one to lean on but Him. She had no other source of support but Him. So I watched through the years of my schooling how the Lord met her needs. I saw her faith grow as she trusted Him by giving of her meager finances. When she realized her utter dependence upon the Lord, she promised that she would give Him fifty percent of everything He gave her. Time after time, when she would be down to her last nickel, the Lord would send her just what she needed. A friend paid off the mortgage on her home, she received checks in the mail from strangers, and church friends rallied around to see that her needs were met. And she faithfully remembered her promise to the Lord and gave back generously.

One Sunday, she went up to an orphan boy in her church and said to him, "I notice that you need a new pair of shoes." He was embarrassed and admitted that he did need new shoes, but he had no way to get them. She said, "I'm going to pray this week that God would send me some money so that you can get new shoes." I wish I could have been there the next week when she handed him a check and said, "See, God does answer prayer!" I don't know if that strengthened his faith or not, but I know it did mine!

Upon Aunt Miriam's death, Mother discovered her old check stubs and learned just how much she had given to missionaries, her church, and other Christian organizations. What a legacy!

God was in control of Aunt Miriam's life, and I saw Him at work in her daily experiences. God certainly is trustworthy, and I knew I needed to believe that every day. I had given my life to Him. I wanted to trust Him for all I needed, too. But He had to test my faith, as well.

Shortly after Nancy was born, Daddy and Mother experienced serious marriage problems of their own. Daddy was attracted to another woman in our church, my Sunday school teacher. It caused heartbreaking events in our family. It was never talked about to us children, but we saw and heard things at home and outside our home. Daddy ceased going to church on a regular basis; he was "gone" most weekends. Mother tried to put on a good front for a long time.

I remember Aunt Miriam telling me one time that I had put Daddy on a pedestal and felt he could do no wrong. How torn I was over the upheaval in our home! I felt wronged, like I had to choose between my two parents. Being of a stubborn nature, I rebelled at that and refused to take sides. Later on, I regretted this decision and felt guilty as I realized Mother had needed my support. The anguish and turmoil she went through was tremendous. It could have been made a bit easier had communication been open among all of us. However, that was not done in our family. We didn't talk on a deep level, sharing our feelings or problems. Most were borne silently. At least, this was my view on the situation. As a result, I tended to distance myself from parents and home.

I left home to go into nurse's training at the West Jersey Hospital School of Nursing in Camden, New Jersey. I studied there from 1960 to 1963. While there, the Lord met my needs by giving me a close friend and her family. I knew no one at the school which the Lord had chosen for me. On the door of the dorm room next to mine, I saw a little sign: "Watch God Work!" This was a challenge for me! Ruth Sharp lived in that room, and I was excited to meet a Christian student. It didn't take long for our friendship to develop (due to her skills and not mine).

The Sharp family lived in Woodbury, New Jersey, and it wasn't too far from the hospital where I trained. The Lord gave me this family; they included me as one of their own. I spent my days off there with Ruth. Even when we had different schedules, Mr. Sharp would come and get me at the hospital and take me to their home. As I look back, I can see how faithful the Lord was in providing the home and the acceptance of a Christian family, just at the time I needed it. He knew what I needed. I was still quite shy and found it difficult to make friends, but God gave me the best friend-maker in the whole world! Ruth doesn't know a stranger. She has a real gift of showing friendship to all she meets. I learned a lot from her, and again, I saw how God uses His children in each other's lives.

A note from Ruth Sharp Cochrane, Miriam's nursing school friend:

Miriam and I, of course, went to nursing school together. I met her family and she mine. Miriam had better grades, but I had more dates. I followed her to Glen Cove Bible

School. We connected first because we were Christians. We had adjoining rooms, and we spoke the same language, as far as wanting to do God's will. It was a wonderful experience for both of us. I met my husband Paul at a camp for handicapped children where I was working for the summer. I had to choose to wait for Paul who is three years younger than me or to apply right away to a mission board. I really had to pray through that decision. I chose to wait for Paul.

But Miriam knew she wanted to go on to the mission field right away. Originally, I wanted to go to South America (Ecuador) due to the Aucas and the Jim Elliot incident. Miriam wanted to go to Africa. But it ended up that Miriam went to Brazil, and I went to Chad, Africa for 18 years. We had 3 children, and I named my daughter after Miriam.

Miriam was known for being deeply spiritual, diligent, and for her faithful walk with the Lord. She was disciplined and faithful to do what God wanted her to do, even in relationships. She lived her life in a self-sacrificing manner. Miriam possessed a great knowledge of the Word. You can't handle the Word as much as she did and not have it affect your life. And she dealt with disappointments in the power of the Spirit. Of course, she had a tremendous sense of humor.

While Miriam was in nursing school, she continued to live a life of service and dedication to the Lord. She did not participate in the "fun" that the other students were having, like drinking, dancing, or going to movies. Her classmates often pitied her, because they thought she was not enjoying her life.

Miriam knew that she should influence those young people for the Lord, but she was unsure of how to do that. As she finished up Nursing School, Miriam struggled with a question in her heart: "Why does the Lord want me to be a missionary, when I have no influence among my classmates in Nurses Training? How can I do any good at all?"

Her mother had wisely taught her that all the answers to our questions lie in God's Word. So, from 1963 to 1966, Miriam attended the Glen Cove Bible School in Rockland, Maine, where Pastor Al Troester served as the dean. As she studied and worked, Miriam told the Lord she could never make a good missionary. He responded with, "Yes, you are right. You can't do it. . .on your own!" John 15:5 reminded her of that truth: "I am the vine, you are the branches. He who abides in Me, and I in him, bears much fruit; for without Me you can do nothing."

But then He graciously showed her Philippians 4:13: "I can do all things through Christ who strengthens me." She had her answer directly from God.

He wanted her on the mission field.

Chapter Two

God Chooses

*Because God chose ignorant ones in order to shame those
who've made themselves knowing, and He chose weak ones
in order to shame those who are strong. . .*
— I Corinthians 1:27, Macushi Back Translation

*But God has chosen the foolish things of the world to put to
shame the wise, and God has chosen the weak things of the
world to put to shame the things which are mighty.*
— I Corinthians 1:27

One of Miriam's assignments while at Glen Cove Bible College
was to write to several mission boards, asking for their doctrinal
statements, policies, and other general information. Of her 25
inquiries, she received only a few responses. Unevangelized Fields
Mission (UFM, now Crossworld) impressed her most. Their
answers came from a man whom Miriam had met previously. As
he traveled in his ministry, he had spoken at her church and even
visited in her home. That UFM was located in Philadelphia, not
far from her home, was another plus. She wrote to UFM's board,
inquiring about available fields and whether they might accept her

as a missionary. Their response was an invitation to their candidate school, which Miriam happily accepted.

There, she learned UFM's policies and procedures, as well as valuable information to help her begin an effective, fruitful ministry in God's chosen place for her. She was primarily interested in two fields that were open at the time: Indonesia and Guyana. God used a handful of His servants at the candidate school to help Miriam choose her place of service.

First, she met missionaries already serving in Guyana, Bob and Florene Hawkins, who told her of the great needs and opportunities in their field. Then Miriam met a fellow student, a doctor who was very interested in Guyana. He thought that with Miriam as his nurse, they could set up a clinic or hospital. Finally, there was a Bible teacher Miriam already knew from Nurses' Christian Fellowship, Mrs. Burrowes. She and her husband had supported the Hawkinses for years, and they encouraged Miriam to join them in Guyana.

Upon completion of candidate school in 1966, Miriam went to Michigan to Missionary Internship. They placed her with Juniata Baptist Church in Vassar. The missionary internship lasted for about eight months, during which time Miriam took classes once a month. She lived with three different families during her stay in Michigan. Her ministries focused on visitation and teaching in three different towns. She also taught two Good News Clubs each week and started a Wednesday evening program called Whirly Birds for primary-aged children.

During this time, the pastor and the director at the training center in Farmington provided counseling to the interns about the responsibilities and difficulties involved in missionary work. Ironically, the director told Miriam she would never make a successful missionary on a foreign field because she was shy. Miriam decided that by God's grace, she would try anyway.

Throughout her time at Candidate School and her ministry in Michigan, Miriam had visited a number of churches to share her burden for evangelizing the lost on a foreign field. Thus, by the time her internship was completed, her full support of $150.00 per month had already been raised. Lessons in faith and trusting the Lord from earlier in her life now came into use, as Miriam saw God providing for her needs daily.

But Miriam wasn't the only one who had been preparing for this big event. Miriam's mother, Mrs. Maude Abbott, also needed to settle this matter with the Lord. She journaled about her initial struggle and subsequent peace from God.

"How does Africa sound to you, Mother?" Startled momentarily, I looked up from the letter I had just opened. How DID Africa sound to me? I honestly tried to face the question put to me by my own 'little girl.' What a different question it seemed from THIS viewpoint.

How many times had I sat in services and listened to missionary speakers, thrilling to their experiences, my heart humbled at the realization of their sacrifices made in order to carry the gospel to "those who have never heard." But now!

Face to face with the issue brought so close to me, I realized that I MUST be honest with her, with myself, and with God!

Just how did Africa sound to me? The Holy Spirit, probing, brought to mind a prayer on my lips almost immediately after hearing the doctor's words, "You have a baby daughter!" With a grateful heart the prayer welled up, "She's Yours, Lord! Thank You for giving her into my keeping. Whatever You have in mind for her, dear Lord, just lead me that I may train her for it." I meant it then; I mean it now, Lord.

"How does Africa sound to you, Mother?" It seemed ALWAYS that she wanted to be a nurse. Dolls, the cat, little brother...the patients were endless. Her goal seemed reached when, after high school graduation, I accompanied her to the hospital where she chose to train.

From this vantage point, I know now it was not HER choosing, but HIS leading.

In filling out her application, she was prompted to include this as her goal: a missionary nurse.

The busy years that followed, the friendships, the various opportunities that beckoned after she earned that coveted RN somewhat dimmed this earlier vision at times, but the Lord in His infinite wisdom allowed a tragic occurrence during training to bring her up short. . .turning her thoughts God-ward once more. (Two of her nurse-friends were killed in an automobile accident while on their way to the nurse's graduation ceremony.)

Enrollment in Bible school the following year came about by the deep realization of a real need to know, really know, God's Word, in order to follow His will. I was often stirred in the reading of her letters. . .amid the humorous anecdotes of life in the dorm, plus the interesting cases in the hospital where she nursed in order to pay her way through school, to find allusions to the Lord's leading her into deeper spiritual experiences through study of the Word.

Nursing at Christian Camps during her summers in Maine (where she attended school), brought new experiences in her dealing with boys and girls, leading them to know Christ even while bandaging scraped knees, administering aspirin for fever and colds, and soothing homesickness. The Lord brought out in her a concern and tenderness, missing at times in hospital routine. In these and many, many incidents and experiences, I had followed in her letters the leading of the Lord throughout those years.

Yet, here I sat, stunned by those words, "How does Africa sound to you, Mother?" Yes, I needed to settle then and there how Africa. . .or India, or Asia, or South America, or the Islands of the Sea...sounded to me as a place of service for my girl. And then the Lord brought to mind the years of separation...nurses' training, schools, camps—just short intervals of seeing her, just letters for communication—with little REAL fellowship that the closeness of having her nearby would bring.

"I love her so, Lord! Sometimes I've thought how nice it would be should she settle down somewhere in visiting distance and raise a family for me to see. But, what do I know about love,

compared to YOURS for her? But I am her mother, Lord; I folded that little one to my breast and watched her grow, tenderly watching over her, nursing her through childish illnesses, soothing bumps and bruises, helping her weather the storms of adolescence, and now that she is just blossoming into beautiful young womanhood."

"But I died for her!" He softly answered. "AND for thee," He reminded gently. "Would I ask for her life to serve ME anywhere without protection, provision, and strength, for one I love that much? Could she be happier anywhere other than in the place of MY CHOICE?" These questions and many more reminders raced through my mind and into my heart as the Spirit of God, ever so tenderly, dealt with an understandably human mother's heart. I was humbled by such love as He unfolded before me. "But Lord, how do I know that she will not face grave danger, even death? Some have had to pay such a price!"

"You don't know. . .you must TRUST!" was the piercing answer. "Never one of My own laid down his life for MY sake in vain. . .was it in vain that I laid down MY life for thee?"

My heart broke. I wept! He had won! Could I dare to think of withholding ANYTHING or ANYONE, regardless of how dear, from my Savior, Who so willingly shed His own blood that I might live?

My daughter! God's Son! Yes, my daughter, but His child... loaned to me by His grace, to teach small hands to serve Him, small heart to love Him and worship Him, that He *might one day speak through her lips, work through her hands, love through her heart, to make His love known to "those other sheep, not of this fold."*

And then. . .He graciously drew back the veil from my eyes. And lo! I wasn't giving Him my daughter; I wasn't sacrificing anything that He might use her. No! He, the Infinite God, was bestowing on me His wondrous grace, in bestowing upon her—His child! My daughter! The life I helped to form—the crown of rejoicing for bearing the precious seed!

The pieces were finally all in place! Miriam had completed Nursing School and earned her RN license. She had completed Bible school and received God's confirmation to be a missionary. She had completed the candidate school requirements, and now she had her parents' blessing. Miriam was ready to begin her ministry in Guyana!

Chapter Three

God Sends

*They put their hands on their heads in order to send them
like that. After that, they said goodbye. The Holy Spirit sent
them out.*
—Acts 13:3–4a, Macushi Back Translation

*Then, having fasted and prayed, and laid hands on them,
they sent them away. So, being sent out by the Holy Spirit. . .*
—Acts 13:3–4a

Miriam traveled from Michigan back home to Delaware to prepare
for her move to Guyana. She packed barrels full of the necessary
supplies with the help of her brother, Edward. These were sent by
boat to the mission headquarters in Guyana, where she would pick
them up later. With a one-way ticket in hand, it was soon time to
leave.

On November 4, 1967, at the age of 24, Miriam left home. A
crowd of family and church friends saw her off to Guyana via
Philadelphia and New York. Immediately, she began writing letters
to her mother, a practice that she would continue for the duration
of their lives.

Guess I must write right away and let you know I arrived safely and am fine. I had a little trouble in New York with my ticket, but they finally decided to let me come. (The airline does not typically allow anyone to travel to South America with just a one-way ticket.) The trip was very uneventful, and I arrived here a little behind schedule since we were an hour late leaving New York. We are an hour and fifteen minutes ahead of you. It's now 8:50 here and only 7:35 where you are. Don't ask me to explain that 15 minutes. This is the only country that's like that.

Must tell you that the folk here didn't get the message that I was coming, so no one met me at the airport. But there just "happened" to be a couple on the same flight as I who knew the missionaries very well. So when I had Russ Sasscer (the missionary who was to meet me) paged, they looked me up because they knew he wasn't there. Then they brought me into town. I was too confused to be scared or worried. At customs, everyone was so busy, I had a full-time job to figure out what I was to do. I was a little tired that night and was glad to crawl into my mosquito net and sleep.

Miriam spent her first week as a missionary tackling the many necessary details of overseas living. When asked if the reality of Guyana was different from her expectations, Miriam answered, "Yes! It isn't nearly as bad as others make it out to be!" Her first impression was recorded in a letter.

The traffic here is terrible. Sounds like New York. Everyone drives with their horns. Small cars, but fast for these narrow streets. Bicycles, pedestrians, and animals make the roads a regular obstacle course. They drive British style, on the left, so it is quite confusing to me, to say the least.

I had chicken curry yesterday and nearly burned my insides out. They do like their food hot here! The weather has been hot but have had a delightful breeze the whole time, and it cools off at night, so it's great for sleeping.

Will be here for a week before going interior, to get registered with the government, get a nursing license, driver's license, open a bank account and a charge account with the local grocery store. I will be going interior to Lethem, Parishara, and then Kanashen until Christmas. I will be coming back to Georgetown for the field conference and will get supplies in then to go to Parishara to settle down.

The bugs here are not as bad as I thought. The first night I didn't know why I had to sleep under the mosquito net. But there are a few mosquitoes, and it's better to be safe than sorry.

I have been very impressed with the missionaries and really appreciate the work they are doing. The people here are very friendly, and I met several last night at church who really love the Lord. I sure will be glad to learn something so I won't feel like a fifth wheel around these missionaries.

Thanks for coming to the airport to see me off. I sure was glad so many came. Some of you should have been on this end though. Ha! I'm just so glad that I am well and like it so much still. The Lord certainly has been good to me, and I know He will continue to care for me.

Within two weeks, Miriam was on her way to live in the interior among the Indians. Her itinerary included a commercial flight from Georgetown to Lethem, followed by a Missionary Aviation Fellowship (MAF) flight to the village of Kanashen.

Right now I can't hear myself think because I'm flying to Lethem in a DC-3. I'm sure glad I don't know much about planes 'cause I'd swear this one is going to fall apart any minute. Wish I had some milk—I could make a real good milkshake! Everything is rattling and shaking—including me! It's impossible to talk to anyone, so thought I'd write to you. I'm sitting right behind the pilot and can see all the buttons and gadgets he's playing with. I don't think the MAF plane will be as bad as this, even though it's smaller. All I see below is jungle! There's nothing else there!

Miriam continued her letter after arriving at the village.

Well, now I'm at Parishara! The MAF pilot met me at Lethem and whisked me right off before I could even smell the place! It's wide open spaces here in the savannah, like Arizona. We were at Parishara in seven minutes. It's the dry season now, and they don't expect rain until April. There's the same cool breeze here as is in Georgetown, which makes the heat bearable. The house I'm sharing with Lib Weeks is mud brick (which looks like regular brick) and thatched roof. It's a lot bigger than I expected. It's real tall up to the middle, and the sides of the roof are still taller than me.

Today I visited the school for a little while. The kids are so cute and most of them look neat and clean. I was very surprised to find this place as clean as it is. They don't have any concept of sanitation, however, as far as their water is concerned. So it's not safe to ask for a drink of water while visiting.

Miriam's final destination was Kanashen, a Wai Wai Indian village, where the Hawkins family lived. Bob Hawkins was the current field leader for her mission board, and he wanted her to have field orientation with them. She acclimated to the Indians' lifestyle and customs while making copies of books and stencils, which Irene Benson used to teach the Indian children.

We went to Yaka Yaka, the next village from here, and they had a work party. They were building two houses, and the women served smoked fish and cassava and palm drink. That drink is about 100% pure oil from the palm. They put starch with it, and it is so very bitter. It looks like chocolate, but it sure doesn't taste like it! Sitting there today in the work house, I thought it was just like the movie I showed at home; those big bowls of drink went round and round, and everyone drank from the same bowl. The cassava doesn't have any taste. At home, we put butter and jam on it or eat it with meat and gravy and it tastes good then, but just plain it is just flat tasting. Grandmom would like the palm drink 'cause it just gives the ol' gallbladder a real treat! I don't think it could be any richer.

Here at Kanashen the houses are pole and thatch construction. The floors and walls are palm slats that are quite flimsy, and there are wide cracks between the slats. You can see through them quite well. However, it makes house cleaning quite easy. You just sweep the floor and shove the dirt thru the slats.

The garbage gets tossed out the windows for the chickens and cows to eat. If you would see them, they look like they need a lot to eat. Another amazing thing about this house, at night when I'm just about asleep, I feel the whole house shake like there's an earthquake. I found out it's only the cows rubbing against the poles under the house. It's a weird feeling! I'm always glad to crawl inside my mosquito netting, not because of the mosquitoes but because of the bats. They play on top of my netting each night. Just so they don't get inside! The net really makes you feel secure from all the company you might have.

When I arrived in Kanashen, a lot of the Wai Wais had gone down river to poison fish (that's one of the ways they catch them). Anyway, a few of us "brave" missionaries went a couple days later with an outboard motor on our canoe to join them. Sunday night, just as we got into our hammocks to sleep, it started to rain (very unusual for dry season), and we got exceptionally wet! Well, it poured all night! About 2 a.m., I was feeling like a wet sponge that just couldn't get wrung out! Talk about disillusionment! I thought I was coming to the tropics, but it felt more like the arctic! Daylight finally came, and we went fish poisoning (in the rain). It never stopped all day. We did go back up river to some shelters for Monday night, but of course, everything we slept on and in was wet! It was still a relief not to have it pouring in your face! I sure was glad to get back to Kanashen and my nice, hard, dry bed!

God Sends

Most importantly, Miriam learned of the faith of the Wai Wai, a testament to the power of the gospel in any language or culture.

Elka's (the Wai Wai chief and spiritual leader) faith has grown strong. There are many men here who are really strong in the Lord, and it is refreshing to see that Christianity here is a man's religion. They are the ones leading their wives and families. [A book has been written about Chief Elka and his faith entitled Christ's Witch Doctor, *by Homer Dowdy.]*

Bob Hawkins said since he's been here (17 years) the Wai Wai have taken about twenty missionary trips. This next one to the Atrois, I believe, will be the longest and most dangerous for them. I've never seen such dedication and spiritual understanding as these Wai Wai elders have! It's amazing!

For as many Christians as were found in Kanashen, there were just as many Indians still steeped in their tribal traditions.

The new ones who have just come to Kanashen are still in witchcraft and superstition. They don't wear any clothes yet and are like the Wai Wai used to be. One little girl died the other night from pneumonia. Flo said she had given her everything she knew about, but the girl didn't respond. After she died, the mother showed no emotion at all. When we told Elka, he shook his head and said, "She still believes the spirits."

In passing, Miriam mentioned to her mother a conversation she had with Bob Hawkins. At the time, she had no idea of the vast scope and influence this would have on her ministry to the Macushi.

One special request that I can think of now. Bob Hawkins mentioned yesterday about possibly working in linguistics. He said he thought I had the mind for it! This summer at S.I.L. (Summer Institute of Linguistics) I kept thanking the Lord daily that I didn't have to spend my lifetime doing that!!! Now...I don't know what to say. I certainly know the need, but I don't know that I can do it or if that's what the Lord wants. So pray that as I begin learning the language, the Lord may show me what He wants me to do.

Miriam experienced all of these things and more during her first months in Guyana. She told of helping a visiting dentist pull 65 teeth on Christmas Day. She told of chigger bites, lice, exhaustion, and hard work, as well as the thrill of seeing Indian faces light up with joy at the Christmas story. Young, single, and away from loved ones, she harbored no homesickness or regrets about serving the Lord in South America. God's grace was truly evident in her life!

Chapter Four

God Provides

But I say to you all, Keep on asking without getting fed up,
and you all will receive it.
>   —Matthew 7:7, Macushi Back Translation

Ask, and it will be given you; seek, and you will find; knock,
and it will be opened to you.
>   —Matthew 7:7

After the whirlwind of deputation, Summer Institute of Linguistics, internship, packing, moving overseas, and becoming acquainted with UFM's work in Guyana, Miriam was finally ready to settle down to her new assignment among the Macushi at Parishara. Eager to learn the ways of the Macushi and to get involved in ministry, she wrote a special letter to the young people that had promised to pray for her.

The beginning of this New Year (1968) was full of new beginnings for me, and this letter is one of them. I have wanted to write to each of you, but I realized there are about

100 of you who are praying for me, and that I just can't write 100 letters all the time. So I thought you would understand, and I could write this one letter to each of you.

First, I would like to thank you for your prayers and tell you that God has heard you and answered you. You prayed that I would get to Guyana. I am here! You prayed that the Lord would give me enough money to take care of me and buy the things I need for my work. The Lord has given me enough. I was able to buy the things I needed for my house while in Georgetown and enough food to eat well. I have even gained weight! So you see that the Lord has answered your prayers, and I am well and safe in the work He has given me to do.

Let me tell you about Parishara, where I am living. The people around us are Macushi Indians. They have been with outsiders before and have learned some civilized ways. They like clothes and nice things but are very poor. They live in mud houses like mine but only have a small table, chair, hammock, and clay pots in their houses. They eat meat, fish that they catch, and farine. (It's like a coarse grain meal that is used like rice or potatoes. I eat it with eggs, in soup, with milk and sugar for cereal, with fish, or just about any way.)

I arrived at Parishara yesterday. We landed at Lethem to an hour's Jeep ride over the roughest, dustiest roads I have ever seen. I was sitting in the back with my luggage. (I should have soft, padded suitcases.) We never met a car the whole way. It's just wide open spaces filled with nothing. Every now and then you see a thatched roof off in the distance.

God Provides

I found out that the Macushi have nothing written in their language. Lib Weeks has made a couple of primers to teach them to read, but that is it. Pat Foster is working on translating Mark, but he doesn't have much time to spend on it, and it's going slow. This is the most desperate need right now. How can Christians grow without the Word?

Yesterday I started language study. I learned John 1:11. It sure doesn't mean anything to me, but at least I can do as well as a parrot. I was glad that the believers are learning a short verse this week!

Miriam described the details of her living situation.

Tonight it's cold here! I have my flannel PJ's on! Know why it's cold? Well, I've been waiting all this time for my refrigerator and connections, and they came yesterday. Pat hooked it up. Lib and I have had our tongues hanging out for ice cream, so we made some right away. Well, today we had a big rain, and it's been so cold, we didn't even want ice water. But at least we don't have to cook our meat every day to keep it. Meat that's been cooked for three or four days straight gets kinda blah!!!

I wrote a letter to Mrs. Troester. She was always telling us in Bible school what good missionary training we were getting by having to keep our rooms and bathroom clean. Well, of course, no one wanted to clean the bathroom, so it seemed it was always a fight. I just wrote her and told her she was full of hot air and that wasn't good missionary training at all because I haven't even seen a bathroom since I've been here! Our bathroom is used as little as possible 'cause it's such a

47

horrible place. When I go out there, I kick stones and rocks and bang on the door real loud so that I scare out all the little inhabitants before I go in. (Things like roaches, lizards, etc.) I'm glad I was never the type to sit and read!!! Mother, I've never seen such big roaches! I'd send one enclosed, but it would make the letter too heavy, and I'd have to pay more postage! Ha!

My kitchen is my study room—has all my language papers, books, writing paper, files, tape recorder, all on the table I use for my desk. Then my "living room" has two chairs and the medicine closet.

The fridge and stove I have are real nice. Probably nicer than what I would have in the States. Oh Mother, the Lord meets each need in ways we couldn't possibly do ourselves with all our struggling and trying ourselves to get the things we need. All the things I have are just so much more than these poor people around me. I am rich in their eyes. Pray that this won't be a barrier to establishing friendships. As soon as I can speak some, I want to get out and spend time with them, staying in their homes, going to their fields, fishing, etc. This, I feel, helps you to get to know them as you share their experiences. Pray that this might be soon.

In order to learn a foreign language, especially one that has not been written down, linguists often use native speakers to help them learn.

I must tell you about my first Macushi helper. She seemed like a very nice girl and was doing fine. When the study hour was over, I stepped into my bedroom to get her some money for helping me, and when I came out, she had stolen the candy bar that was on the table. I told Lib about it and so faced the girl with it. She told lies, one right after another, and it was so easy to see that she was lying. She finally admitted it and gave me back the money I had paid her. Mother, this is so common here. Lying and stealing are just a natural part of their life. I'm afraid I'm not so very used to it. One encouraging thing is that they say the Wai Wais were like that before they were saved. Now no one ever takes anything, except "borrowing" canoes or canoe paddles to use for a while.

Up to this point, very few Macushi had become believers. Miriam wrote about the ever-present spiritual and physical battles. One such occasion was a Macushi wedding. Typically, weddings were preceded by drunken parties that lasted for days, so the missionaries wanted to give the Christian young people an alternative. They held a party, complete with popcorn and games.

It's hard for these young people to say no to the crowd. You know at home how hard it is for them, and yet there's plenty of things for them to do. But here, there's nothing! So we had a good time with them. Pray for them.

These young people sure have a hard time of it, and the situation is practically impossible for them to find a Christian mate. The racial prejudice is so great that those with lighter skin have to marry light skin. The poor Macushis are looked down upon so much that even in the Christian families it's seen in this question of marriage.

Miriam discovered that some of the Macushi's largest obstacles involved their language. She was eager to be part of the solution, rather than adding to the problems.

The Macushi are people that want to be like other Guyanese people, but the town people won't accept them and look down on them. This has made many problems. One is the language. Some have learned English. Some have learned Portuguese. But most know only Macushi. Those who know other languages look down on those who only know Macushi. Some don't want anyone in their family to speak Macushi. So you see, if I learn Macushi, it may help them to understand that their language is good, and being Macushi is good because that is the way God has made them, but it will also help me to gain their acceptance and tell them of Christ. These people need the Lord as their Savior, but right now they don't have any of the Bible in their language.

For the second time since arriving in Guyana, Miriam was approached about tackling the language of the Macushi. Bob Hawkins, Miriam's field leader with UFM, spoke to her about her gift for language. She was still a rookie by anyone's estimation, but Mr. Hawkins believed Miriam was the right person for the job.

Bob Hawkins wants me to do a language course for Macushi, and he wants me to start now. He said to do it as I go along learning Macushi. This will really give me something to work toward that will help others learning the language and not just plunge blindly into it for my own benefit in learning Macushi.

God Provides

Despite her newness to the field, Miriam took this responsibility seriously. Pat Foster, a veteran missionary among the Macushi, knew their language well and had created a way to write it; however, he was the only one ministering in the Macushi language. Miriam was determined to learn Macushi in order to improve their ministry among them. Thankfully, Miriam's coworkers were eager to help her with this huge undertaking.

> *I'm staying with Fran Tracy for a few days because she's a linguist and is helping me to get organized in Macushi. She's showing me what material to get from informants and ideas on how to get what I want. Bob Hawkins is working on a language learning course for new missionaries, which is badly needed! Too bad he didn't do it just a little sooner so I could benefit from it!*

Miriam got right to work and by March 1st had written ten lessons. Pat Foster checked the lessons for her. He revised, eliminated, and occasionally approved them for further use. Within another week, she had completed 20 lessons, although, after review, only three were usable. She was going too fast for others to learn and keep up with the pace.

> *I not only have to learn the Macushi language myself but write a course to teach others! A big job! Am sure I can't do it! But if the Lord wants it done, He'll give the wisdom, I'm sure. So pray concerning this long-range project.*

Just a short time later, Miriam wrote again.

> *This language course is getting harder all the time. Bob wrote me a note today and said he had thought it would take me*

a year to get any lessons ready to teach somebody, but Lib wants to start after Easter (just a few weeks away). He said it looks like an impossible thing for me to do, but sometimes God wants us to do impossible things. So pray for me, that I may be able to get something for her to learn. I won't have the final polished course for her, but whatever I have will be a help. Having her learn, too, will keep me pushing and busy learning myself. So maybe this is the way the Lord is teaching me. He knows how much trouble I have to push myself! I'm the lazy type!

Miriam was not content with "just" writing a language course for Macushi, however. She already had bigger plans and goals in mind. First, she wanted to move to another Macushi village, one where the people did not speak any English. This would force her to communicate in Macushi, and she believed she would learn faster. Then she had yet another plan.

When I learn the language, I do have an idea in my head of traveling from village to village holding Bible classes, literacy classes, and clinic. Don't tell anyone yet, because I get the impression that it may not be possible to travel alone. I do find it a handicap being single and not being able to go into different homes at will. But pray concerning this.

She already sensed the problem that would plague her ministry for years. Not having a partner severely limited her ability to travel and work as she desired. This became the topic of many letters to her mother and many prayers to her heavenly Father. But for the time being, she threw her energy into the language course. By March 30th, just a month after being approached about the idea of creating the Macushi course, her thoughts about her ministry had changed drastically.

> *My work is now language learning, not medicine. Please pray for the Lord's leading in these things and during this time of learning, observing, and waiting, that the Lord may teach me principles to work with to prepare me for future years.*

With abundant distractions and interruptions, Miriam found it necessary to establish a schedule for herself.

> *Each morning I spend studying Macushi. Sometimes I have Macushi speakers come to my house, sometimes I visit them, usually two or three times a week. I memorize words, phrases, Scripture verses, and songs in Macushi by listening to them over and over again on the tape recorder. Monday afternoons I like to get out and visit a Macushi family and hear them speak. Tuesday afternoons we have a station prayer meeting, and all the missionaries meet at the Fosters for prayer and bring requests usually concerning our work right here at Parishara. (Once a month we have a day of prayer for all the stations in Guyana.) Wednesday afternoons we have literacy and Bible class for the ladies. I've been attending and helping the ladies read Macushi. After this, the believers meet for prayer. This is strictly a prayer service. We sing one song and then each one prays. Thursdays the young people meet for their Bible class and then play volleyball. I have not been attending this regularly, but occasionally play volleyball. Friday afternoons are usually free, except I have taken the young people into Lethem for the youth meeting. Saturdays are free, too, to prepare for Sunday. 8:30 a.m. is*

our first service on Sunday. Sunday school for the children, believers class for the adults, followed by a morning service for everyone. Then the ladies have a literacy class after that. In the afternoons, we have a service in the village one Sunday and the next on Clement's Hill, which is further away than the village. Just before dark, the believers meet at someone's house for a hymn sing. This gives us most of our evenings for letter writing, study, cleaning, etc. As I said, this is an average normal week, but that rarely happens. There are always interruptions.

Even as Miriam immersed herself for months into the Macushi language and culture, she never lost her sense of humor. She shared dozens of unique incidents with her family: dusting with a monkey tail; enduring her first rainy season; riding a bike 25 miles over a hilly, muddy road; finding two alligators in the waist-high water where she had bathed just the day before; assuming the entire responsibility of clinic trips upon Dr. Davis's departure; and longing for a home of her own. Above all, though, Miriam never lost sight of her heavenly Father's goodness to her.

Sometimes in our prayer lives, we begin to wonder if and how the Lord is answering our prayers. It seems there are many times when the Lord calls on us just to be faithful in praying and doesn't allow us to see answers, but then He also knows when we need encouragement and in His grace, gives us a glimpse of what He is doing. Oh, the joy of seeing God's work in our lives!

I want to share with you some of these things that the Lord has allowed me to see recently and because you have had a personal interest in praying for me, I feel I must share personal answers to your prayers.

Perhaps the Lord has burdened you most to pray for language learning because this is an area where I see Him working most recently. Back in February, I asked the Lord for a real breakthrough in language. The Lord has wondrously answered. My main concern was speaking Macushi in conversation. Just this week I have been able to put pieces together and speak in whole sentences. This is a real encouragement to me. And then another blessing is that also this week I've started to pray in Macushi! This is a real encouragement to the believers as well as to me. I've been studying now for four months, and the Lord has given real discipline, strength, and wisdom in it, and now He has given real encouragement.

Another item you've been praying about is my adjustment to this new area. Praise the Lord for answers to this also! I've been well and healthy physically and have enjoyed the climate and physical surroundings. One of the hard things for me to cope with was loneliness. During those times, however, it brought me closer to the Lord, and I experienced His friendship and fellowship.

The Lord has also answered your prayers concerning financial needs! The only thing I can think of that I need is a good can opener. The one I have works slightly better than my teeth! But I'm getting one soon. I've learned some lessons from the Lord concerning finances. One thing—you can't out-give the Lord. Missionaries need to give too. Just recently a need presented itself, and the Lord burdened my heart to give. Right afterwards I received the exact same amount in the mail from the US. But I figured it closely, and I had given in Guyanese money, and the Lord gave in US money, so His was twice as much! Isn't that just like everything we do? We give according to our resources, and the Lord gives according to His riches, which are always more valuable!

By God's grace, Miriam had eagerly adapted herself to the people, language, and customs of Guyana. She was at home among her new Macushi family.

Chapter Five

Revolt!

What God has made for those who love Him.
  —1 Corinthians 2:9, Macushi Back Translation

But as it is written: "Eye has not seen, nor ear heard, nor have entered into the heart of man the things which God has prepared for those who love Him."
  —1 Corinthians 2:9

Miriam enjoyed her first year in Guyana, working among the Macushi people alongside the Unevangelized Fields Mission (UFM) team, specifically with Pat and June Foster. She spent most of her time learning the language and culture of the Macushi, but she also served as nurse, secretary, teacher, and linguist. With Christmas quickly approaching, Miriam looked forward to a short visit with a friend and then the UFM yearly conference.

We're trying to have a get-together at the hangar on Christmas. Then I'll come back to Nappi Wednesday night, pack on Thursday, and go to Georgetown Friday so I can do some shopping before conference. I'm going to make an overnight trip next Monday and Tuesday to visit Doris

Wall. I've volunteered to have the children's program during conference, so I have been busy making up a VBS program for four days.

However, none of her experiences or plans could have prepared her for the uncertainty and turmoil of the next days and weeks.

Here it is five days into the New Year, and I still am at Doris's and don't know what's going on in Lethem. Haven't heard at all from Fran or the Fosters—the others are all in Georgetown. Two planes have come for me here, but the first one, a small aircraft, flew around and looked the situation over here and was afraid to land. Jim called to him on the radio and told him to land here, that everything was fine, but he flew away and told Georgetown he thought this was a trap. That was Friday. Yesterday, the twin otter came in, but the fog was so low he couldn't land. So he flew on too, and I'm still here.

I'm standing by the radio now while the others are in church. This is the 4th day that we've had to stand by all day just fighting for a little bit of news. This silence and waiting are almost unbearable.

I don't ever remember being so homesick before this. And I'm mostly homesick for Nappi. It's hard to be out of the area knowing so many of your friends are having trouble.

Don't ask me what the trouble is in Lethem. We've heard all kinds of rumors. Some say it's an Amerindian uprising, some say it's Brazilian, and some (we) feel it's communist inspired right in this country. If that's what it is, we'll probably never hear the truth of the matter.

What Miriam did not yet know was that there had been an attempted coup in Georgetown. History records this event as a small uprising, instigated by cattle ranchers who were afraid the new government would not renew their land leases. An American rancher had stirred up several of the other influential ranchers in the area and had even contracted guerrillas from Venezuela to help overthrow the Guyanese government. Because an American had instigated the revolt, and because several Macushi had participated in it, all Americans and Macushi were held in suspicion. Of course, this doubly impacted Miriam and her ministry.

> *I talked with Pat last night, and we are all at a loss as to what to do. The word seems to be—WAIT! There are rumors of an anti-white demonstration here in town. Yesterday the paper's headlines were Send the Foreign Missionaries Home! But these are radical groups from what we can determine. The unfortunate thing is that the man who led this revolt is an American citizen! Because our plane was flying interior at the time, MAF is closed down indefinitely.*

The revolt was squelched in one day according to newspaper articles; however, for those in outlying villages, the fear and uncertainty persisted much longer. Criminals took advantage of downed communication lines and a lack of policemen to patrol neighborhoods. As time passed, information slowly became available to Miriam.

> *Every day I hear a little more of the story and try to piece things together. It makes me sick to hear of friends who are now murderers. Families scattered. Only one shopkeeper in Lethem is going to continue his business. Castro is being held*

for carrying a gun. Tarscilla and her family are in Boa Vista and will probably stay. Papa Marco is in Boa Vista; his wife is here in the Georgetown hospital with diabetes. Norman, the man who put in our cement floor, is in jail. These are just a few of the people. The main ringleaders, who are Guyanese ranchers, have escaped to Venezuela.

Things are very uncertain now, and I don't know when we can go back in. Oh, every one of us is here in Georgetown now, but all got here a different way. Some of their stories are hair-raising! Camping overnight in rebel camps. Fran (another single UFM missionary) went to Nappi to investigate and try to find Fosters. She saw that our house was broken into and plenty of things were stolen. She found my passport lying on the ground outside the house! Don't know just what else, but she said all the drawers were just plain empty! Fosters had gone to Boa Vista. It took them two days, over $200.00, and lots of hair-raising experiences. But I guess the Butlers had the greatest scare when it first broke out. Joe was held at gunpoint; he had to wave planes down so they could be captured. Well, I could go on and on with gory details.

As news continued to trickle in, it became apparent that the revolt would severely hamper UFM's ministries in Guyana. The government put dozens of restrictions on anything that had to do with foreigners and refused to grant permission for anyone to travel to the interior villages. The situation was precarious and dangerous for the Americans, even a young, single missionary named Miriam.

Chapter Six

God Proves

Many times while hard testings arrived upon us, it did not make us fall. . .
—2 Corinthians 4:8a Macushi Back Translation

We are hard-pressed on every side, yet not crushed; we are perplexed, but not in despair.
—2 Corinthians 4:8

The revolt occurred after Miriam had been on the field for just one year. Because the Guyanese government suspected that Americans were to blame for the unrest, they immediately became suspicious of all foreigners. Freedom for the missionaries was limited, especially to travel to the interior villages. While some of Miriam's coworkers found alternate places to serve, others took their furloughs, which were either overdue or due soon anyway. But since Miriam had no desire to leave her Macushi friends, she considered moving to Brazil, either to attend language school, work as a nurse, or serve the Macushi there.

Pray that I may know what the Lord wants me to do. I really feel bad about Parishara. Never thought I could love anyone so much in just a year as I do the Macushi. Guess when they are taken away from you, you realize how much they mean to you. Regardless of whether or not we can return, things will never be the same there.

Even through the danger and uncertainty, God continued to teach Miriam about Himself.

It seems like the Lord's return is very soon. With things so unsettled in governments, and the devil on the rampage to keep people from hearing the gospel, I don't see how it can be very long before the Lord does come. One thing this rebellion has taught me is that my home is not in this world. Things aren't important! Only what's done for Christ will endure.

Having established in her mind that God's purposes would be accomplished, Miriam was thrilled to learn on February 7, 1969, that the Guyanese government had given her permission to travel back to Parishara for two weeks!

As you can imagine, I've been busier than a one-armed paper hanger with fleas! And to top it all off, the Sunday before I left Georgetown, I burned my leg with hot grease! Can't even cook an egg and do it right! Since then I've been hobbling around. The burn is healing nicely, but every day my ankle is swollen bigger. Today it's a dilly! But I guess I can't expect it to go down when I can't stay off of it! Another delight since I came is that the water pump busted. So I have been hauling water. Then today the battery ran down on the radio, so since I didn't know how to recharge it, I had Ronald, the village school teacher, switch it with the one in the Jeep. The radio works fine now—but the Jeep won't start!

It took me a long time to clean up here. The place was a mess. But I finally got unpacked and straightened around, and now it's time I started to pack again. There were a lot of things taken—all our food (not a scrap to be found), sheets, towels, silverware, blanket, mirrors, clock, camera, hammock, flashlight, batteries, pillows, and other odds and ends. But the Lord has graciously supplied enough Christmas money so I can replace everything I need—if we can come back.

I have been quite busy treating the ill, holding services, plus just trying to live. The Lord has been granting strength for each day. Pray that the Lord would continue to lead in our work here. Many families have left for Brazil, and more are threatening to leave. So with no people around, there's not much for us to do!

I am not discouraged, praise the Lord, although sorrowful about the situation. But it's all in the Lord's plans!

Miriam's 17-day visit convinced her that she could not stay alone at Parishara indefinitely. She prayerfully considered other opportunities while waiting for the government's approval or denial of her request to remain in Guyana.

A possibility that has been presented this week is going to SIL (Summer Institute of Linguistics) this summer and taking their course in literacy. After talking with one of the government officials, Pat and Rod thought this may be the key in returning interior—linguistics. I've only had one summer at SIL, and so I would need more training if I were to go from village to village to teach literacy and make primers. Another advantage is that I'd only be away from the Macushi language for three to four months instead of nine months. At the end of the summer, if I couldn't get into Guyana, I could then go to Belém, as the language school has a term starting in the fall also. If I were to go to Brazil to work, the literacy training would also be handy.

It's so hard to decide. Have been praying about it and really don't know what the Lord would have me do. I really kinda dread going back to school—any school—but if it is what the Lord wants—O.K. I'm sure the Lord will take care of my feelings towards it.

Whether she understood it or not, God soon revealed His plan to Miriam. She trusted His wisdom and obeyed joyfully.

Little did we realize as 1969 came, how many changes there would be in our work at Parishara, due to the revolt against the government on January 2nd. But the Lord knew all about it and is still in control. We have not yet been allowed to return to the interior to resume our work. Because of this, we felt it would be most profitable for the Macushi work that I come home and study this summer in Oklahoma at the Summer Institute of Linguistics. This training enables me to have a part in our goal of teaching the Macushi to read the Word of God in their own language.

My courses are hard this summer. I'm taking advanced grammar, as well as literacy, ten credit hours in all. I think it's a little more than I bargained for. Learning Kiowa is part of the grammar assignment. We had a test yesterday, orally saying 25 expressions in Kiowa! Of course, we only learned them in one week, along with everything else! My literacy course is really profitable. I hope I'll have the time I want to spend in the library studying. We have a research paper to do, and I will have about four weeks to spend on it.

Did I tell you that the Lord met all my expenses? The scholarship I got from SIL was $135.00 instead of the $30.00 I thought at first!

When the summer classes ended, Miriam made a short visit home and then returned to Guyana.

Just a quick first note to say I arrived safely with few complications (baggage got left in New York, but arrived later). I have gotten things taken care of in Georgetown. I got a driver's license and chest x-ray; went to the post office for stamps, etc.; shopped for groceries, mosquito netting, etc.; went to the hospital to visit Doris Wall, the Pilgrim Holiness nurse I know.

Will be going to Lethem Monday at 6:30 a.m. on the freight flight if our permission comes through. Bob is going also to visit all the stations. Sure hope we hear from the prime minister's office that we have permission soon!

But she did not hear soon, and Miriam's and UFM's future in Guyana did not look good.

Delayed in Georgetown due to lack of government permission to travel to the interior. Refused permission for September; pray concerning application for October. Pray also for those missionaries already in the interior, that they may be able to stay. The way things are going, we may get kicked out. No, it won't be any big deal—they'll squeeze us out one by one so no one hears much about it. Already they're clamping down on new missionaries getting into the country.

We are thinking quite seriously of my going to Brazil, though there are a lot of problems to be worked out. Mainly, Bob is hesitant to send me alone. My opinion is—if they can't send me anywhere alone, they'd better send me home. Because the fact of the matter is, I'm single! I feel it would be more profitable to go over there than to sit here and try to find a Macushi in town to work with on language. Well, nothing is definite yet. We're writing to the Brazil side, but it will take a long time for that correspondence to get back and forth. So pray about this.

Time slowly marched on, as Miriam waited and prayed for the Lord to direct her path. Finally, in early November, she received good news.

As we have been praying together, let us rejoice together in what the Lord has done! It is with real joy and thanksgiving to the Lord that I write this letter. I shall be leaving Monday (November 3rd) for the interior of Guyana. Permission has been granted for me to return to Parishara for the month of November. The government seems very interested in the medical assistance we can offer, but we are still in a very precarious position as a mission.

It has been only the Lord who has gotten this victory for us, and it will be only through prayer that we shall be able to remain in the interior month by month.

Now, what will I do? It has been impressed upon me the shortness of my time at Parishara, and so I feel a real burden to leave something permanent behind. Most of my time will be used in language work and the production of literature in the Macushi language. Of course, this will be very limited and elementary at first, but I want to stimulate motivation for reading among the Macushi.

During November, Irene Benson will be coming out from Kanashen to stay with me for a couple of weeks, and then I shall be with Fran Tracy for a couple weeks. It will be rather difficult to stay in one spot very much as I can't stay alone. Pray that this situation may not hinder us from accomplishing our jobs during this year.

Nearly a year after the uprising, Miriam held only a sliver of hope for her future in Guyana. She trusted God to do what was best for her and for the Macushi, and in that confidence, she pressed on. But God had other plans.

Chapter Seven

God Tests

*Don't do according to what I want; but only do according to
what You want.*
> —Mark 14:36b, Macushi Back Translation

Nevertheless, not what I will, but what You will.
> —Mark 14:36b

Every year at Christmas, the Macushi believers in Brazil gathered
for a time of teaching, worship, and fellowship. Miriam desperately
wanted to take the Guyanese Christians to the Brazilian Christmas
conference of 1969, both for their encouragement and her own.
But her mission board did not allow her to go because they felt the
border crossing would be too dangerous.

> *It seems it just wasn't the Lord's will for us to go to the
> Brazilian Macushi Christmas conference. As a result of the
> conference, there were four Macushi churches organized on
> the Brazil side. The pastor is the Brazilian evangelist, João
> Batista, who has been working with our mission since 1967,
> and of course, it's all Portuguese work. So it seems more*

urgent than ever now to get some Macushi literature and also to start a literacy program. Most of the leaders in these new churches are illiterate! How can a Christian grow without the Word?

Well, we finished our UFM conference, and it was a real rough time for me as we considered the insurmountable problems confronting Parishara at this time. We had special prayer concerning the many problems and decided on some of the issues.

We just had a two-day conference with Dr. Alan Redpath, who came to us from England. He has been associated with UFM in England for many years. He spoke to us on the temptation of Christ in Matthew 4. What a teacher! We all received a real blessing from it and from him and his wife personally. At the beginning of our field conference, Dr. Gannett from our home office was here for our council meetings and gave of his time to each of us personally. He is our "pastor" on the home staff of UFM. . .What wisdom he has when it comes to mission principles.

So now I'm ready to go back to Parishara and face the battle again. The government is still unfriendly but has given permission for this month. I had to have another interview with that same official as I did before, and he put me through the third degree. He kept trying to pry information out of me concerning any rumors I've heard or negative attitudes against the government while at Parishara. He refused to believe me when I said I knew nothing. I felt like he wanted me to be a spy or something! What a hard time he gave me!

I was a nervous wreck when I got out of the office. "Why?"
you ask. I think he enjoyed seeing me squirm and exerting
his authority!

Living at Parishara was a blessing in many ways for Miriam, as she
was near to the Macushi and working on their language. It was also
a trial, as it took a lot of work just to survive. The radio, Jeep, and
kitchen appliances were constantly breaking down and requiring
attention. Often, she did not know how to fix them, so she had to
wait until someone could come out from Lethem to make repairs.
But she kept plugging away. The lack of a partner also slowed down
her ministry efforts.

Irene Benson, the teacher at Kanashen, is with me now. She'll
be here another week I guess, then go back to Kanashen. I will
probably go with her, as I can do quite a bit of language work
in there. The situation is likely to be the same until August,
as far as my moving about is concerned.

In February, the Lord opened an unexpected door for ministry.

I went to Yupakari yesterday and had a friendly chat with
the Anglican priest. He invited me to speak in his church
next Wednesday morning for their Ash Wednesday service.
He wants me to speak in Macushi. Well, I told him I didn't
know much but at least could read some Scripture and pray.
Afterward, I'll hold clinic. I'm scared to death! But maybe
this is what I need to get me going. I will be reading Mark
5 about Jairus' daughter. My Macushi helper gave me that
story as well in her own words, so I can get familiar with
it and maybe tell it. I will work on memorizing some more

parts to my prayer so I can pray, as well. How do you like this for being ecumenical? It probably is to the priest, but the Macushi people don't know anything about it. In fact, very few even know what the Anglicans teach. All they've learned about religion has been in English, and they have never associated it with their everyday Macushi lives. Just like Christendom at home really. It's a coat you wear on Sunday and most never associate it with their everyday lives. It may as well be in a foreign language, as much as they understand.

Sometimes, the Lord even used conflict and opposition to advance His work through Miriam to the Macushi.

Ever since the mission has been here at Parishara, one man has especially opposed the work. He's a hardened ol' sinner who knows the Bible fairly well but in a distorted way. Anyway, he's been the worst hindrance to the Christians and every time someone makes a decision, he does his best to get that one drunk. He's always speaking blasphemies about the missionaries (behind our backs, of course) and makes a general nuisance of himself. He has been very nice to our faces, but from time to time goes on the "warpath."

Well, this time he has stirred up various parents of the school kids and many were angry at the head teacher. The teacher took away the books of the children who have not as yet paid for them, nor made any attempt to do so. Well, this guy, Malcolm McDonald, called the counselors and chief together to hold a village meeting and requested the teachers' and my presence. Being the manager of the school, I had to speak, and it was a general gripe session. They threatened to take the matter to the prime minister himself and lots of other wild things. As it was getting late, the chief just left—bored with the whole thing! Not many parents were really involved; only a few who always side with Malcolm (one a backslidden Christian) really got angry. They stayed late and got drunk last night after the rest of us left. It was a terrific mess, and I know if Pat Foster had been here, Malcolm would never have done such a thing. I really felt his absence yesterday! Anyway, I'm thankful for the friends I do have. One old lady was so upset, she cried last night. She's a real believer and the backslidden Christian is her son. None of the Christians had any part in it, and Papa Marco—our only man Christian— was sick in his hammock and didn't come. It's been the first time that I've been in the position to receive comfort from the Macushi themselves. Most of the hard times and trials that come my way, they can't understand. This one they could, so I praise the Lord for the new relationship it's given me with some of them.

As time passed, it seemed that more and more problems came up for Miriam. The battery for the radio would not hold a charge, and the generator quit working. If she wanted contact with the outside world, she had to connect the radio to the Jeep battery. That was all right because the Jeep didn't run anyway. Her typewriter broke, as well as her clothesline. The roof blew off the outhouse. Rainy season came, bringing with it plenty of mosquitoes. In spite of all these obstacles, Miriam progressed with the Macushi language and literacy.

During March, I was able to finish a reading booklet designed to teach English readers to read Macushi. I've begun to test it somewhat with various individuals and am finding out the trouble spots. You may wonder why we want to teach people to read Macushi if they can already read English. Most of the English readers do not understand the language very well at all. And then too, I feel that these are the key people to get involved in teaching adult literacy in the future.

My own language learning is progressing, but slowly. I've been trying to learn some Bible stories to give in various places. Last Sunday I told about Adam and Eve when I went to Ayawa for a service. They seemed to be able to understand me, so I praise the Lord for this little progress. I always enjoy visiting that village. The people are so friendly, and I feel right at home there.

Along with the difficulties, Miriam also saw answered prayers.

For several months now I have been requesting prayer concerning two big needs: that of transportation and of a partner. It seems that our prayers have been answered. The new Mini-moke we ordered arrived in Georgetown, and it has been paid for. I think there is even enough left over to pay for freighting it into Lethem.

When I returned from picking up the vehicle in Georgetown on July 3rd, Edna Roseberry accompanied me to Parishara to spend the month of July with me. And then the Foster family will be returning in August, so it seems my days of solitary confinement are over. I do praise the Lord for His faithfulness to me during this past year and for all He has taught me. At times I feel as if I haven't gotten much accomplished; it is such slow work. But I trust that soon there will be something tangible to show for the months of tedious study.

The trip to Georgetown proved to be a much-needed time of refreshment and fellowship for the lonely missionary.

To make a long story short, Carol James came to Georgetown, and one morning on the radio, they told me she was in town and couldn't come interior. So I packed up the next day and left to see her. I just spent two glorious weeks in Georgetown. We stayed with Sandy at the Southern Baptist house—those who usually live there are on furlough now. So the four of us stayed there—Sandy, Edna, Carol, and I. What a ball! It's a big, spacious, beautiful home with plenty of hot water and a real bathtub. Edna said after we took our first baths that half our tans came off! I tell you, it sure was nice to sit and soak in a nice, hot bath. Then we drank Pepsis like crazy. But we were busier than a paper hanger with fleas. I had a shopping list longer than my arm, and Carol did, too. I spent half my time in the Ministry of Education getting papers and forms and information for our teachers. Then I spent a lot of time in the garage getting the kinks out of my new Mini-moke.

Well, we were going from morn till night—out to dinner and churches a lot. Sandy made me five dresses. I paid $21.00 for material (that's $10.50 US) so that's pretty cheap, I guess! So now I have some decent clothes.

It sure was good to see Carol again. Seemed funny to notice that we've both changed in the same ways. Guess 'cause we have similar situations. It was really wonderful to pray with her. I hadn't realized how much I missed praying with people. I hated to say goodbye to her yesterday when we left, she for Boa Vista and me for Lethem.

Guess what, Mother? Edna came back with me! She's going to stay for a month. I could hardly believe it when she said she would come.

Miriam found a poem that clearly described her feelings on the upheaval of the past 18 months.

Between the exhilaration of beginning...
And the satisfaction of concluding,
Is the Middle Time of enduring, changing, trying,
Despairing, continuing, becoming.
Jesus Christ was the Man of God's Middle Time,
Between Creation and Accomplishment.
Through Him God said of Creation, "Without Mistakes,"
And of Accomplishment, "Without Doubt."
And we, in our Middle Times of wondering and waiting,
Hurrying and hesitation, regretting and revising—
We who have begun many things and seen but few completed—
We who are becoming more...and less—
Through the evidence of God's Middle Time
Have a stabilizing hint that we are not mistaken.
That our Being is of interest and our Doing of purpose,
That our being and doing are surrounded by Amen.
Jesus Christ is the Completer of unfinished people...
With unfinished work...in unfinished times.
May He keep us from sinking, from ceasing, from wasting,

From solidifying, that we may be for Him
Experimenters, Enablers, Encouragers
And Associates in Accomplishments.
> —Author Unknown

Dear Mother, don't ever say that every avenue of Christian service is closed to you when you can pray like you do. I know I would never have come here nor stayed here this long, without your work in prayer. Of course, I realize prayer is a work that we seldom realize just its effectiveness and power, but we must obey and trust the Lord for the results.

Just when the doors of opportunity seemed to be opening again, Miriam and her coworkers received some devastating news.

Things have been happening—will try to tell you all. Edna was planning to stay with me all month; however, she's leaving today. We got word that the government said she could leave the country and get back in for school in the fall. So she's going home. She'll probably call you when she gets to the States. We also heard that the government will let Lib come back in to teach school in Georgetown. We also heard that they will not let the Fosters into the country! Guess you know what a bombshell this was. So now everything is just plain up-in-the-air, and no one knows what we will do. If this word is definitely final, I suppose Fosters will plan on getting into Brazil, and we'll see about moving our Macushi work over there.

I've decided if Pat can't come back here, I can't keep it going alone. It's been hard enough temporarily, but it would be impossible to do it indefinitely. So pray about what I should do—where I should go. Brazil is in the picture still, but only if Pat and June would go there. Again, I couldn't go and open up a new station by myself! So a lot depends on what they do. Of course, I would vote for working with Macushi anywhere before doing something else, but we just don't know what is going to happen. There are drawbacks to Brazil, you know, the main one being that I'd have to go to language school and learn Portuguese. So it may be that I'll finish up my term the way I started it—adjusting to a new culture and language!

Despite this unexpected setback, Miriam continued to trust the Lord and wait for Him to lead. Promptly, He directed Miriam's future plans.

Well, I guess I am going to Brazil. We decided it in Council this week. So I'm planning on going to Belém to language school. It's not like I'm leaving tomorrow though because we have to hear from Boa Vista, home office, and Belém about whether they want me there and about visa procedures.

I don't know the future of the ministry right here at Parishara. Since I've told the people that Fosters will not be coming back, just about all are talking of leaving.

You see, when it was first started here, back about 12 years ago, this is the only place the government would give us and there were no people here. But when the missionaries started here with a school and medical help, it attracted the people, and several began to settle around here. A lot of those who settled, however, are the misfits that couldn't get along in other villages, and also the mixed nationalities and mixed languages, which has given rise to some of our greatest problems. So it has seemed all along that Parishara has been a problem center in many ways. There have been ten missionaries who started out here, and only Pat Foster has been able to learn the language enough to minister in it. Yet we can't say it's all been a waste—there are some Christians, but we can't expect to have a strong, thriving church without the Word. So we can see many reasons for leaving and going to Brazil.

But where I'll be for the next few months, I have no idea! I decided though, I'm taking my language work with me wherever I go, no matter what the overweight costs, so I don't get put somewhere with nothing to do! I'm working in earnest now on my primer and getting pretty excited about it. Of course, there's no one to check it and tell me it's all wrong, so I think it's great! Ha. Just pray that they'll put me somewhere (anywhere) with someone (anyone) and let me work!

The Guyanese government continued to restrict the missionaries' activities. Some were deported; others were arrested or summoned to court for "failing to register as an alien." Many were prohibited from entering the country, no matter their previous record in Guyana. However, the Lord kept Miriam from any trouble. She stayed in Georgetown and began Portuguese lessons as she waited on the necessary permissions to move to Brazil and begin work there.

Boa Vista is our main base for the North Amazon work. At present, there are no missionaries among Macushi on the savannah. However, a Brazilian evangelist, João Batista (with our mission) has been visiting many Macushi villages once a month for a couple of years now, ministering in Portuguese. He and the MAF doctor over there (who is now on furlough) have been carrying on these medical-evangelistic flights. Each year at Christmas, they have a Macushi conference in Napoleão (a Macushi village), and Macushi gather for four days of Bible study and fellowship from many villages.

Right now there's a Brazilian girl living at Napoleão who is interested in literacy and has been teaching Macushi to read and write in Portuguese. There's a possibility that I may go there, and we could work together in Macushi literacy. (This is after I learn Portuguese.) The Fosters have thought of us locating in a Macushi village in the mountains called Macedonia. They have been asking for years for a missionary. It's a fairly large village, and people are very receptive. They have a small church but no trained leadership. However, this village is only about ten miles from the Guyana border, and it's doubtful whether the mission would agree to open a station that close to the border. Our Brazilian missionaries are very cautious not to raise any question from Brazilian authorities of any contraband practices, etc. And one rule is, not to live very near or on the border, and never cross the border except via large cities. So we don't know just where we'll locate.

The language school is at Belém, right on the east coast of Brazil at the mouth of the Amazon—not near Boa Vista at all. That is the base for our work in northeastern Brazil and where the language school is. Probably I will go to Belém in January and stay 'til September, the length of the course. Then I will go back to Boa Vista.

After several more weeks of waiting for paperwork to be completed and approved, Miriam finally received permission to travel out of Guyana and into Brazil.

Well, I'm leaving tomorrow, Thanksgiving Day, for Brazil, so wanted to write you a note before I left. Got my visa completed today, so I am all ready to go. Doesn't really seem like I'm going, but I think when I land there and can't understand a word anyone says, I'll believe it.

Looking back on this time of uncertainty, Miriam recognized how God had led and provided for her through it all.

I'd been invited to attend the 1969 Christmas conference on the Brazil side. I was so excited about it, and I thought, "The Lord's opening up the way!" So, I was working hard to take some people from Parishara over there. We were all thrilled getting ready for it.

And then the news came that I couldn't go because the mission didn't want an American crossing the border that way. I would have had to go all the way to Georgetown with a passport and back again. So, there was no way that I could take Macushi people over to it. It was such a huge disappointment to me because it seemed like everything was going wrong.

I couldn't get permission to stay interior. I couldn't keep the station open by myself; things were just too hard. And then this one bright spot was just shattered. I had been praying about it, and it just seemed like the Lord wasn't answering anything. I couldn't penetrate, and God wasn't hearing me. It was such a deep disappointment. I didn't know what to do. During that dark time, the letters that I got from home were very sad, and Mother would write and tell me things that were going on. They were really difficult and upsetting. Nothing seemed bright at that point.

Then afterward, when plans started to work out so that I could go across to Brazil and get a visa and work on that side, things were opening up again. Just before leaving for Brazil, I remember getting my mail, and there was a letter from Mother. It was at that point that things started to turn around for her, too. Things were being made right at home. It seemed like the Lord was working and showing His power.

With God's help and leading, a new chapter in Miriam's life had begun.

Chapter Eight

God Directs

Don't be afraid, but keep on telling the news to people because there are many of My people here in this city.
　　　　　—Acts 18:9b–10, Macushi Back Translation

Do not be afraid, but speak, and do not keep silent. . .for I have many people in this city.
　　　　　　　　　　　　　—Acts 18:9b–10

Miriam immediately began learning Brazil's currency, language, culture, and government. Although her time in Boa Vista was short, it was necessary to secure all of her papers. She enjoyed her first Brazilian Christmas and New Year before heading to Belém to begin Portuguese language school.

Things here are in a state of confusion. They've just had their field conference and the Belém field is so large. 115 were at the conference, about 85 missionaries and their children! But they found a temporary corner for me last night. Don't know whether it will be the same corner tonight or not! I'm beginning to realize though that there aren't any missionaries who have a "normal" routine to their lives! Ha. Everywhere I go, they say, "Oh, this isn't normal!" Most of the missionaries I've met are English, Swiss, Scotch, and German. Two girls who will be studying with me in Portuguese language school say they have to learn English, as well. So we're a weird bunch here!

I want to take this nine-month course in six months. I'm praying that I'll get back to Boa Vista by July. Isabel, the Brazilian missionary with whom I've been living in Boa Vista, will be starting her second school in Napoleão in August (teaching Macushi to read Portuguese). I'd like to get back before she starts and take her with me to do a survey of the Macushi villages to find out how much bilingualism there is and to test for degrees of comprehension in Portuguese. If she goes with me and sees the need for Macushi literacy, I may have some help! She's a terrific teacher and has the patience of Job (she was teaching me Portuguese) and just loves the Macushi people. So all I have to do is convince the people here that I have to get back. I don't know if I know enough Portuguese to start the second term now, but I'd like to try and work extra to catch up and fill in what I don't know.

The days and weeks of language school passed quickly, and Miriam found that she was able to catch up with the class ahead of her.

Portuguese learning is going fast. I understand now why it didn't take Edward so long to learn Spanish! (And all along I thought it was because he was smart!) I'm enjoying it, as the rules are all written out for you, and it's so much like English! It is from my perspective anyway, after studying Macushi for three years! But Portuguese study can't go too fast for me because I'm anxious to get back to Boa Vista and work with Isabel in the Macushi villages.

Miriam made plans to take a vacation during Easter break. But her plans were changed, which led to a providential meeting.

I'm in the hospital! No, not as a patient. I'm a nurse, remember? I think I've forgotten! Anyway, let me tell you the story.

I think I had written you about our plans to go to Portel by boat. Well, we went to see about tickets and found out there would be no boats, as it was Easter week. So we decided to try planes, as we didn't want to disappoint the girls in Portel and thought the extra money would be worth it. We checked several small planes and none had any room. Finally, we found one with only one seat. So we felt it must be of the Lord not to go, though we didn't know why. I was disappointed for their sakes more than mine, as I know what a visit means when you're way out in the boon docks. Anyway, I'm getting kinda used to changes.

When we arrived back at the mission, we learned that a terrible thing had happened in Portel. A gas bottle had blown up in the missionaries' kitchen, and the girls were burned. It took several hours to get a plane up there and bring them to the hospital. One of them, Phyllis, was quite bad. She has slight burns of face and hair singed, one arm has a first-degree burn (like a bad sunburn), the other arm has bad second-degree burns, and both legs from the knees down are second and third-degree burns. When it happened, she jumped through the kitchen window and landed in a pile of mud and banged her head on something, so she also had a big knot and bruise on her head and was full of mud! Jane had her hair singed quite badly—in fact, a lot of the top of her hair is only a half-inch long now! But her face only looks sunburned and that's all. The other girl, who was in another room at the time, only got her hair slightly singed. It's really a miracle they all weren't burned to death. And only one kitchen wall burned out.

So you see, the Lord kept Marilyn and me from going into a situation like that. And now I'm helping Jane with nursing Phyllis. Jane has been pretty shook up—hasn't been able to sleep, etc. So I am staying nights at the hospital with Phyllis.

I have really been enjoying Jane. She's a good nurse and has been fun to work with. She has had a very rough time since she's been here, and the Lord has done so much for her that she's a real gem to be around. The Lord can keep people in times of real trial from bitterness and despair, and those kinds of people are usually such a blessing to everyone else.

So, Mother, that's how I am spending my "vacation."

And so, in many ways that Miriam could see and in some ways that she could not, God had begun working for her future.

Chapter Nine

God Instructs

*God is very great, more than we can know. And how He is
very knowing, more than we can tell.*
> —Romans 11:33, Macushi Back Translation

*Oh, the depth of the riches both of the wisdom and knowledge
of God! How unsearchable are His judgments and His ways
past finding out!*
> —Romans 11:33

Upon completion of Portuguese language school, Miriam traveled
back to Boa Vista, visiting several missionaries along the way.

*I arrived back here at Boa Vista last Saturday (July 10, 1971).
This week has been one of sorting, shifting, and getting back
in the swing of things.*

*Also this week, I've been studying with Pat some of the
problems we have in Macushi. I'm trying to line up my work
to do in the villages when I go. I'm also waiting for Isabel, who
has been taking her vacation at home in Rio de Janeiro. She
is expected back any day now. I will be leaving with her for*

Napoleão around the second week in August. Her school will be starting then, and so I'll go with her to live in a Macushi village and get started back to work. I feel as though I have some direction in which to start now. First thing, I'm going to start on a transition booklet to teach the young people who already know Portuguese to read Macushi. If we do that, we'll have a reader in almost every family right away. Also as we hear them read, we can check our orthography, or alphabet, and see if they have problems reading it. If they do, we can change it to make it easier for the older people to learn to read.

Right now it's somewhat of a mess as far as the languages in my head! I visited a Macushi lady in the hospital the other day and started to pray with her in Macushi. Before I knew it, I was praying in Portuguese. I've been mixing them up something awful and sometimes even English gets in there, too.

One consolation, Isabel is a good teacher. So, she'll correct my Portuguese and help me weed out the Macushi. I just hope I can continue learning Macushi at the same time.

One other news item: the mission bought a house for the single girls on this field. There are 10 of us. It needs a lot of fixing up, and we're going to start on it tomorrow. I'm taking a couple of Macushi girls over, and we're going to clean it first from top to bottom. It's a good house and has lots of possibilities, but will take some work. It'll be nice to move in it. I'll be using it as my base and then visiting the villages, living much like the Indians there, though I did buy a folding cot to take around with me. I can sleep in a hammock, but for more than a week at a time, it gets pretty tiring.

With plans settled, Miriam moved forward to do the Lord's work.

We are in Napoleão now. Isabel and I arrived Thursday afternoon. School for her starts on Monday. She has about seven students whom she is training to be teachers of their own people (in Portuguese), so I think seven is a good number. I also will use them some to help me write Macushi stories and teach me the language.

Our house is a Macushi one—mud walls and floor with a grass roof. It hasn't rained much yet, so we don't know if it leaks or not.

We visited the chief yesterday, and he gave us some corn and watermelons. That's our chief diet these days, as it's in season now. We had fish yesterday but no meat today. I think this is a good time to go on a diet, eh? We're taking vitamins to supplement our diet and a malaria preventative, and also boiling our water. So we should keep healthy. However, yesterday and today I've had a pain in my stomach, which is probably from worms.

Isabel is a fine girl to work with. She has done a terrific job of teaching me Portuguese and will help me in the Portuguese part of my books that I make. She's a very enthusiastic person and really loves the Macushi. She's a worker too, so will keep me on my toes, I know.

Although Miriam made learning the Macushi language her primary goal, she never lost sight of the true reason she was in Brazil: the people.

Got a lot done this week. I think the time here will be very profitable. I even took the day off yesterday to go to the field with a lady. It was the first time I attempted it in bare feet, and coming back I carried a one-year-old baby. Today I'm quite sore, and I have a blister on my foot, but I'm still alive. The lady I went with carried back a basket I couldn't even begin to lift! She'd stoop down, and I'd try to help her get it on her back, but I couldn't budge the basket. As we came back— two hours walk (fast walk), I'd get tired carrying the baby. She'd tell me to put him on top of the basket she was carrying for a while. I did, and we'd go on, and a little while later, she'd ask me to take the baby again. Well, it was interesting, to say the least, and I think I got to know some of the people a little better, and they me.

Miriam outlined details for the literacy work as she continued to learn.

Isabel will be leaving September 4th for Surucucu to attend the Field Council meetings. She's on the council so will be gone until September 13th. I'll stay on here and teach her students to read and write Macushi. It will be easy for them to learn, as they know Portuguese. But I want to encourage them in their writing, so they can write some stories for me that I may be able to use in my primers. I also will test the students (there are 12 of them now) in Portuguese-reading comprehension. Isabel has made up some different easy texts for them to read and questions about the reading. This will be my start in a bilingual survey of the Macushi. I want to find out how much they understand in Portuguese and how many understand. They are excited about reading Macushi, too. I'll have them read all the stories I have and also get their opinions of the content matter (which stories they enjoy more, etc.). This too will help.

This week I've outlined my primer construction. The first stories (using the letters I want to teach first) are about Big Sister weeding the grass and digging a hole in the wood for a mortar to grind corn. However, I found out the word I used for grass, they don't use much here in Brazil. They use the word for weeds! Why? I don't know, but it sure messes me up if I can't use the word for grass! So you see why it's slow going in making primers! But I feel I'm getting lots done.

Miriam continued to employ her good sense of humor.

One funny thing I thought you might enjoy: A lady and I were walking together, going over to a sick person's house, when suddenly she started laughing. "Boy, are you <u>really</u> white! Look at those arms, so pale!" And she laughed and laughed. Guess this is a part of getting used to me.

It rained so hard last night, and the wind blew so much, that my room was a pool of water, even the end of my bed. I was thankful that I was short and could sleep comfortably without using the end of the bed! Our house is fairly leak-proof when it doesn't blow at the same time it rains!

And she loved to review the good things that God had accomplished.

Have been in this village now since October 9th, after spending two weeks in Boa Vista. This time I'm working on primers (still). I have two completed in rough form that I want to try out. I have started teaching one lady to read, and we're halfway through the first booklet. She seems to be catching on well. I'm encouraged with her because she's proving that my primers must be good (I'm a lousy teacher, so the books must be good, eh?). Also, I'm helping a couple others who read some Portuguese to read Macushi. They do well but are just slow.

Yesterday was a first for me to "preach" in Macushi. It was a very short sermon, to say the least, and memorized! But it's a start. I want to memorize something each week now for the ladies' classes. I have been just reading to them.

This week will mark four years since I first left the States, November 4th. You would think after four years I'd be able to speak Macushi rather well, but considering that I've only spent about half that time with the Macushi, I don't know too much! But it's encouraging to see some progress.

I have been teaching a "first-aid" course in the school. It's quite a challenge because I teach it in Portuguese and have to learn all the names for things all over again. I feel it may do the students some good, too, as I'm stressing soap and water as a cure for most things. And around here it really is! Another thing I'm stressing is "Don't use any medicine in the house for just any sickness!" It's quite a modified first-aid course, as you can see.

Progress is slow, but I feel we can see some things. When we first arrived, no one knew any Bible verses by heart. I started teaching the women in Macushi, and now they know seven. And the men started memorizing in Portuguese, as well as the children. Isabel is training two girls to teach Sunday school, and they are really doing well. One of the church leaders, Domingos, is teaching the men's class. He prepares his lesson each week, and Isabel checks it. She gave him an easy-to-read Portuguese lesson book. When we leave, I have an idea it will continue. His wife I'm training to take over the women's class. It's harder, as she can't read Portuguese very well, and we don't have the Bible in Macushi yet.

Although things seemed to be going very well, another blow struck Miriam: Isabel was leaving. Yet God continued to instruct Miriam of Himself, His ways, and His purposes for her ministry.

I'm praying for a coworker. Sometimes I wonder why the Lord has me move around so much and live with so many different people, and sometimes I think maybe it is because no one could stand me permanently. But then I don't really have much trouble getting along with others, and my list of friends keeps growing rather than diminishing, so why?

Well, Mother, don't tell this to anyone else, as people would think I'm bragging or proud or something, but more and more the Lord has shown me how He can use me. As you know very well, I'm not one much for talking—in any language— but I'm great at listening, and I'm convinced that people all over the world need listeners—including lonely missionaries. It's not a very glamorous job, and nobody realizes what a "listener" is doing—not even the person doing the talking. But it seems that in all my moves, there have been people that needed someone to talk to. Missionaries are very lonely sometimes because they can't talk to their coworkers, as they are too close or not close enough. And so I feel the Lord has called me to this task as well. It's nothing I can put down in my job description or even tell any fellow missionaries about, but I feel the Lord has given me a personality that is comparatively stable, and because there are so many unstable people and things in this world today, I want the Lord to use this for His glory.

I don't know if you understand what I mean, but I can see how the Lord has been working in my life, even using loud-mouthed brothers in helping me to watch and listen rather than speak (Ha!), and then nurses' training, and psychology courses, then circumstances and problems in Bible school in learning what the Lord can do.

A long time ago, in one of my first deputation travels in a church in Flint, Michigan, I had a women's meeting at a home there. The leader of the group, whom I'd never met before, said to me afterward, "Miriam, I believe the Lord can use you not through what you do or say, but by your being. Just by being with you, I can see that the Lord can work through your stable personality." I remember at the time I was bewildered and didn't understand what she meant. More and more through the years, I can understand.

And so instead of putting me on one mission station with a regular coworker, which is the "norm," He has moved me and shifted me about so that I have lived with practically every missionary in Guyana and now starting again in Brazil. I thought Isabel would be my coworker, but it seems as if the Lord has other plans. So again, I am looking to Him to supply the need. I will say, I have profited personally from each one I have lived with, and the Lord used them in my life, probably even more than the other way around.

Despite setbacks, changes in location and coworkers, loneliness, and even discouragement, Miriam knew that God would remain faithful to her. She trusted Him to give her His best.

Chapter Ten

God Transforms

*Don't be like the ways of people on this earth. But
surrender your thinking, letting God change your ways.*
    —Romans 12:2, Macushi Back Translation

*And do not be conformed to this world, but be transformed
by the renewing of your mind.*
                                                    —Romans 12:2

Knowing that her time with Isabel was limited, Miriam plunged
into the work she had planned to do. She began to teach reading in
another Macushi village, Maracanã.

*Today I held my first class in literacy. It was quite disorganized
to say the least. We had five ladies and two men. One man
arrived after it was over, and so I taught him separately. I
think they are all anxious to learn.*

*My men will be the brighter pupils, of course. They are the
ones who get out more, conversing with others and learning
things, so they will pick things up faster. One had just a
smattering of Portuguese before, so he recognizes some letters*

already and can read the first primer very well. My other man knows very little, only numbers up to ten, but he wants to read the same thing as the other one. I'm afraid he will get in the habit of memorizing if I'm not careful.

And so I have begun my life as a teacher.

This work of literacy to which God had called Miriam—preparing, writing, teaching, and learning—would continue throughout the remainder of her ministry, over 30 years. But even in the midst of her service, the daily grind of life continued, as well. Each village held its own challenges.

We've got a livable set-up here at Maracanã. Not quite as convenient as Napoleão. The kitchen is someone else's that we use. The bathroom needs a new one! However, since it's just a hole in the ground, it's a lot cleaner than having a seat that no one knows how to use! We also brought more food this time. We brought cans of meat, enough to have two tins a week. This week we're eating eggs and cheese, so we are saving our meat.

The reading class is going great. I have 19 students on various levels now. I teach from 8 a.m. to noon. It takes that long or longer to get around to each one. Then in the afternoons, I'm busy writing stories for my "star" pupil to read the next day. He finished all three primers the first week, and #4 is not yet written, so I've had to just write stories and try to keep ahead of him. He knows all 16 letters in the Macushi alphabet now. I think it's quite a record for only ten days of studying. Tomorrow I'm going to give him a simple story of the creation to read. It has lots of repetition: God made this and this and this, etc. So I think he'll be able to read it.

He, of course, is an exception, but the other students, the average ones, are doing much better than I expected. They are beginning the second primer, even the slower ones. Then I have three that haven't learned the first page, and I don't think they ever will. But if 16 out of 19 can learn to read, I think it is a terrific record.

One day one of the ladies was in her house reading the primer. All of a sudden, she said, "Puxa! I'm reading!" "Puxa" is an expression like "Imagine this!" So you see, it's kind of exciting to see people like this learn to read. It is something so new and different for them.

Well, I just know the Lord has something in store for the Macushis. This is just a beginning of it. It truly is His work. I'm just glad He's allowed me to be here to see some of it.

At times, Miriam was weighed down by regular, everyday challenges. At other times, the challenges were quite unexpected!

Last night we had a snake in our room. It's the first I've had in any house I've lived in in four years. It was a jararaca, a poisonous one. Very small, but very dangerous. It fell from the roof. I heard a noise and Isabel said, "Oh, it's just a piece of mud that fell." I shined my flashlight, and we saw the snake on the ground in the corner, not far from Isabel's hammock. I ran for a piece of wood and hollered for the boy that lives next door. He came a-runnin' and smashed it in the head. So you see, the Lord is protecting us from a multitude of microbes, as well as beasts—like snakes!

The results of Miriam's first literacy class in Maracanã were fantastic.

We're just finishing up our time here at Maracanã. The Lord surely has blessed this time in the village. I feel the adult literacy class was a success. My star pupil is reading very well now. He reads anything I give him. And now I find out he is from Guyana. He's going to Georgetown next week. He is so excited that he can read; I believe he'll spread the news far and wide. He says he's a Christian, but I don't really know how strong he is. Then I have seven others who finished the third primer (all that I have written) and will be ready for #4, #5, and #6 when I come back. They know all the letters except for three. I have been teaching some of them these three letters, but they need lots of practice before they will read fluently. I have three others who began later that are in the third primer. Of the three that I thought wouldn't learn anything, two of them have learned the vowels, a few consonants, and a few words. So even they have benefited some. Never knew I was a teacher, but it looks like that's my job for the time being.

Miriam's time was not all-consumed with the literacy classes, though it often seemed that way. She and Isabel wrote a Sunday school lesson book, with plans to cover the entire book of Genesis in bilingual format. And she received a special gift from home.

Well, finally your tapes came, and they were worth waiting for. I really enjoyed them. It seemed so strange to hear your voices again. I never realized you all had such accents! Ha! But it really was great to hear all the singing and the wise cracks in the background. Isabel liked it as much as I, though it kept me busy translating into Portuguese all the stuff you said. The jokes were quite difficult and changed a lot in Portuguese! It was great too, to hear the kids, Melody and Joy. I am looking forward to seeing them all again this year.

Miriam's heart overflowed with praise to God for His work among the Macushi. While Isabel served in Field Council meetings and taught Portuguese in a remote jungle village, Miriam stayed in Boa Vista, working at a frantic pace to finish her primers and several other literacy projects. Her furlough date was looming ever nearer.

I am up to my ears in typing stencils. I have two books completely done, the Sunday school lesson sheets are all stenciled, the Bible story book I'm stenciling now, one primer (#5) is ready to stencil, and I'm still writing stories for primer #4. I think I lack about six stories. I think I'll make the deadline!

She also compiled a list of the literacy work she wanted to accomplish before she left Brazil.

While at Maracanã, I want to get lots of stuff on tape. I'll teach in the mornings, but I hope to finish the stories of Genesis on tape and also get some of the old people to give me stories on tape. So I will be busy there. Then, I'll be coming to Boa Vista for June and July. I want to mimeograph the Book of Mark (that's Pat's doing) and his New Testament Bible stories, the rest of Genesis, and a book of songs and verses. So I will be busy right up until I leave Brazil for furlough it looks like.

Miriam returned to Maracanã for the second round of literacy lessons.

We arrived here a week ago today at Maracanã. Everyone seemed glad to see us. They made us a new bathroom and a new bath house (both were badly needed!). My students seem excited still about learning to read, and only a few have forgotten what they learned before. Most are at the same place where I left them, so I feel that's a big step. I hope to teach the remaining three letters and give more practice in discovering new words.

The clinic team came on Friday and picked up Isabel and me to go to Mutum—me to help the doctor and Isabel to say goodbye to everyone there, as she's leaving in June. We had a good clinic there and stayed overnight. There's a good mountain stream there and a waterfall. We went swimming in the natural pool in the rocks—crystal clear water. Then Saturday we came back to Maracanã. We had service and clinic, and I gave immunizations (DPT) for all from Macedonia. Then yesterday we finished up with kids from Maracanã. We gave 52 shots. It's a good thing, as I heard from Doris that they have whooping cough in Guyana right now and already some children have died. So I am glad we gave 52 shots!

Today I am back on our schedule. I teach in the afternoons this time, and it looks like I'll have a student or two at night to study by "lamparinha" (lamp light).

Also, I am sending you a sample of what we've been eating— ants. Yes, this is ant season. These are already roasted and cleaned. Just pop them in your mouth and chew. They taste like nuts.

God's direction and protection were clearly evident in Miriam's life.

One night while we were in Boa Vista, we stayed up quite late, drinking coffee and talking until 2 a.m. We went to bed, and I was just getting off to sleep and turned my head on the pillow and saw a man at my window, looking in. I screamed, "Homem! (Man!)," and ran for Isabel's room. It took a little time, as I had to get out of the mosquito net. When I screamed, however, he didn't run, but rather started talking. I didn't get what he said. I had to shake Isabel, as she is a very heavy sleeper. She came back to my room and shut the window and locked it. We walked back to Isabel's room and turned on the light and saw that he had pulled back her curtain, too, to look in. We were really frightened because it was raining so hard that no one could have heard us at all if we had screamed. It was 3 a.m. Well, we quickly dressed and sat on my bed the rest of the night, waiting for it to get light. Isabel slept some, but I couldn't sleep a wink. The next morning, we found out that he broke a tile in the roof and entered the back bedroom. Fortunately, that room does not have in inside entrance. But everything was sopping wet. Isabel had all her stuff laid out on the bed to pack, and it all was wet from the rain. He did not take one thing.

After several reports to the police and more late-night visits from the neighbors, Miriam and Isabel finally got a good night's rest.

We haven't had any more trouble, but Pat Foster loaned us his gun. I don't know what kind it is, but it has real bullets in it. The first shot is just for noise, but it has two more that are for real. Also he put up two large yard lights to light up the whole yard. The police are looking around here from time to time. Everyone in town knows about it, so I bet everyone is afraid to set foot in this yard.

This event was followed by yet another heartache.

Isabel left last Monday. It was a sad day to see her go. I don't know when I'll see her again. I really think a lot of her and surely do miss her. But I have been enjoying Marilyn here, and she is helping me type. We have two books almost completed now and want to do two more before leaving for furlough.

Miriam had, by God's grace, accomplished her literacy and translation goals for the year. Now she was ready for a time of furlough and visits with her family and friends.

Chapter Eleven

God Grows

But you keep on knowing even more what God has freely given and keep on knowing more of our Lord Jesus Christ.
—2 Peter 3:18, Macushi Back Translation

But grow in the grace and knowledge of our Lord and Savior Jesus Christ. . .
—2 Peter 3:18

Miriam traveled throughout the United States in the late summer and fall and visited her parents in Arizona for the holidays. She also made trips down to Texas to visit her sister and to Mexico, where two of her brothers were missionaries. Finally, she traveled to Oklahoma for more SIL classes.

Yes, I'm really busy now. I am working all day long every day on Macushi grammar. Right now I'm on clauses, afterwards will go to phrases, then to words (if the summer lasts long enough). Around the middle of July, I must stop and begin writing up my findings formally—in a paper that can be published. I have to present it to my class (only four people) and then revise it and have it in final form by August 7th.

I don't have many formal classes. Twice a week we meet together and discuss general topics. I attend evening lectures three times a week on linguistics and literacy. So you can see it's a big job.

Guess my work is going OK. My consultant is encouraged anyhow. And as long as she knows what I'm doing, I guess that's enough! Ha. This week though, I've been better able to see how my paper will go together. I'm going to start out describing basic Transitive and Intransitive clauses and how to make them interrogative, imperative, etc. And then go on to sub-divisions that we have in describing various kinds of Intransitive clauses—like those with motion verbs (coming, going, arriving, etc.). These are all independent clauses, and now I'm just beginning to touch the surface on dependent ones (what makes them dependent, why they are different from independent, etc.).

As the summer classes came to an end, Miriam eagerly prepared for her return to Brazil and her beloved Macushi.

Tuesday is my day to present my work to the class. Then they can tear it apart and say what's wrong with it, and then I put it back together again in final form to turn in.

Yesterday, Rod and Tommy Lewis, our UFM field director now, stopped by to see us, as they are home on vacation. They told me all kinds of news about Boa Vista. Evidently there's quite a bit of improvement there.

The Brazilian girl, Julieta, will be working with us with the Macushi. It'll be good, as she'll be helping to teach them Portuguese. Irene won't be coming to join me until October, so if I want to visit Macushi villages before then, I can go with Julieta.

My first project after going back is to type my texts for the computer. It'll take me only about two weeks though, so I hope to get that done first and out of the way.

But upon her return to Brazil, Miriam experienced an unfamiliar and unwelcome setback: her first serious illness.

Most of this letter will not contain such good news because I'm writing from my bed. I'm sick. I have malaria. Sorry I can't blame my writing on that, but the bum pen they gave me.

But today is my first day of recovering, I guess. I don't have to tell you I feel pretty punk! Monday morning at 6, I awoke because I felt cold. I pulled up the sheet and realized it wasn't enough, so I knew I was sick. The girl who was sleeping next to me (the whole crowd is here for conference) got me blankets and told me I had malaria. Well, I didn't believe her, but she went down to the malaria department right away, and a man came and took a blood slide. They identified it positively as malaria, though the kind was unknown.

Well, we waited for them to come treat me and my fever got higher and higher, so finally Maria, another missionary nurse, started treating me for both types. That was Monday.

Tuesday I was worse, so she called the doctor. He's continuing to treat me for a mixed infection of malaria.

I had between three and four crises of fever per day where my temperature got up between 103° and 104.6°. But of course, each time I was sponged off with alcohol to bring it down. I am at home in my own bed, and one night the doctor thought he'd better take me to the hospital. But he came back later on and my fever didn't go up that high, so he said O.K. My temperature has been normal one morning—yesterday—but was up to 101° in the afternoon. Today it has stayed between 100° and 101°. Nausea is a great problem. I'm still battling with it.

A few days later, Miriam reported to her mother again.

Today I'm feeling much better. My temperature is 99.6°. The doctor came yesterday, and I asked him when this fever would go down to normal. He said very, very slowly. All the medicine I'm taking now is penicillin once a day. My nausea is gone, and I'm enjoying the juices and things they bring me.

So it looks like I'm on the mend, but I really have no idea how much time it will take. Guess the Lord thought I needed a rest. I know it's probably a shock to you, but it was to me, too! I'll try and get this letter to you the fastest way possible. But even so, by the time you get it, I'll probably be feeling really chipper.

Flo Riedle has been taking care of me day and night. There is nothing they haven't done to help me, and everyone has been so good to me. My Macushi friends came to see me, too.

Unfortunately, malaria was not her only problem. The lack of a coworker continued to hinder Miriam's travel and ministry.

Our annual conference is over, and, though I missed most of it by being sick, I've heard it was a really good time. Many needful decisions were made, and we're trusting the Lord for wisdom and strength to carry them out. There may be some changes in my work, and Irene is feeling like she should be helping out Flo with the Wai Wai. I'm not sure if it will be just temporary or if it will be a permanent move. She certainly would be more content to be working where she already knows the language. But it will put me back to the same old problem of how I'm to travel. I cannot travel in the villages alone because there's no radio contact. I may be able to work something out with the two couples. Well, you can all be praying about this now.

And yet another difficulty in the Macushi ministry was addressed a few weeks later.

Pat and June Foster and I have been talking much about the various church problems in the different Macushi churches. As you know, we have no one to pastor these churches. It's amazing to me that they do as well as they do. Anyway, Pat came up with an idea that may help. He's going to talk with the folks at Maracanã (where the church is very weak) and ask if they wouldn't be interested in inviting a couple from Napoleão to come and teach them, preach, and do visiting. They would have to provide his food while he's there, and then the church at Napoleão would have to promise to take care of his fields and chickens while he's gone. We thought of a couple who seem to be very steady. Domingos taught himself to read Portuguese, so he is a very intelligent man. His wife also reads, and I taught her a bit and left her to teach the women's Sunday school class there at Napoleão. I think it has gone well since then, so both of them would be useful at Maracanã.

Pray about this, that both congregations would be willing to try this effort and recognize their responsibilities one for the other. We are thinking about this for a limited time only, like three months, to see how it would work. The biggest problem is that most of the men don't know enough to preach or teach anything. We need to teach them somehow. With translation and literacy work and the medical-evangelistic trips, neither Fosters nor I feel we can do much to meet the needs of five congregations. Each one needs a full-time pastor. Each one has a potential outreach of several other villages. Well, we are asking the Lord to supply the workers, whether they be Americans, Brazilians, or trained Macushi.

Irene has gone back in with Flo, so Flo won't be by herself for a while. In fact, Irene is thinking maybe the Lord wants her in there permanently. She has agreed to wait on the Lord for His move, and when the Lord provides someone to travel with me, then she'll go on back to the Wai Wai.

The last two weeks of May, I'm going to take my vacation and go to Belém to visit Joe and DiAnne Butler. She is expecting her baby then, so I'll go and stay with her in the hospital. They have asked me to come and said they would pay my fare. Cheap vacation, eh?

God Grows

The frustrations of work weighed heavily on Miriam.

I've been doing fine but very busy and not seeming to get much done. Irene's been away with the Wai Wai and just returned Saturday. So I have been alone to answer whatever demands present themselves at my door. All month I've been making daily visits to the hospital (sometimes hospitals) to see my patients from the interior. When they need medical treatment here it is so much work for me, running around shopping for things they need (soap, combs, toothbrush, nightgowns, etc.). Then there are visits to doctors to find out what they are doing for the patients, when they can travel, etc. Then I go to the pilot to find out if he's going in the patient's direction and when, then to find a place for the patients to stay when they get out of the hospital until they can travel. And so it goes. It takes so much time that I don't have time to do my real job! Sometimes I think maybe I should move interior somewhere permanently and use that base instead of Boa Vista. But it wouldn't solve the problem because there would still be people who would need medical treatment and someone who is in town would have to do all that needs to be done.

The other day I listed all the linguistic projects I'm doing at the same time, and there were seven. Of course, that's just the language work, not to mention the medical and the teaching! So, I discovered why I don't seem to get much done. Well, this is what has been going on, and I feel so snowed with work. But the Lord knows I'm only one person, so I'm only required to do the work of one person. It's just that each day I have to decide what doesn't get done, as well as what does!

In addition to the heavy workload, Miriam missed her family.

Just got my draft receipts yesterday, and the Lord is really sending in the personal gifts. Some of it I'm saving to see if some day you can't come down and visit me. I know the Lord can make it possible. So, you be praying about it and decide when and let me know! It's not impossible, and I do want you to visit before you have to come with your canes and rocking chairs! Ha. You don't have any grandchildren down here, but there are lots of Macushi kids.

Miriam and Irene Benson planned to go to Manoá for about six weeks. The local Macushi were supposed to build them a house, but they had started much too late to have it completed in time. Instead, the ladies lived with a Christian Macushi family in the village.

Right now I'm teaching a class in Macushi. I have two students who know how to read and write in Portuguese and are learning in Macushi now. I'm trying to get them to write short stories. We have three who are starting from the very beginning, and three have had some schooling. It's not many, but I am hoping to get some more language work done, more stories written. I made three booklets of stories that my class in Macedonia had written.

I'm looking forward to my vacation in May, but I just got a letter saying that three missionaries are having their babies then and are hoping I'll be there for the "blessed events." It looks like I should study to be a midwife!

Flexibility was an absolute necessity for Miriam, as her plans continually changed.

We are finally ready to go interior. I don't know how long I'll be staying this time, as Irene is staying with me only one week before going into Anaua. So, I'll see how long I can stay alone. I don't think it will be much trouble there because at Manoá, we stay with an exceptional Macushi family. They are exceptionally clean, and they just have one teenage daughter, so the house isn't teeming with kids like most Macushi houses. And they are good Christians, so you don't have to worry about wild parties.

We are late getting ready because we tried to have clinic trips this week, but the radio was off the air, so we couldn't let any of the villages know. We went to Mutum, where they have a two-way radio, and we had advised them of our coming. Flying in, we went over Maracanã and dropped a milk can with a note in it, telling them we would be in Macedonia that afternoon, so they got a little notice. We also took a man back to Napoleão, who had been sick here in Boa Vista, so he told them we would be there on Monday. So it's been a problem this month getting word around.

I was going to pack Tuesday and go into Manoá on Wednesday, but then Irene found out she had to go to Lethem to check out of the country so she could get an extension on her visitor's visa. She had waited till the last minute to see about it, so we had to go Tuesday to Lethem. She doesn't drive either, but Joe and DiAnne Butler said they would go with us. We had a horrible time because she couldn't get her passport stamped until about 7:30 a.m., which made us miss the 8 o'clock ferry, and we didn't get on until 11 o'clock. So that made us rush all day to get there and try to make it back by the last ferry at night (6 p.m.). Well, we got back at 6:15 p.m. and had to leave the car on that side and come across in a canoe in the rain. DiAnne had the children too—a month-old baby in a canoe in the rain! Well, they'll never forget it. The next day, the whole family came down with colds and fever. I didn't though. So anyhow, I'm finally ready to leave for the peace and quiet of the interior again.

Once she did reach the interior, her frantic pace relaxed.

Our classes are going slow here. This week has been a week of review. Most are very slow learners here so it will take longer, but the leader, Enedino, is almost reading alone now. After this month, I think he will be on his own and will be able to read Mark when it comes.

Miriam worked hard for the next weeks, plowing the fields of Macushi hearts, preparing them to receive the seed of the gospel. And, thanks to a packet of notes and articles from Wycliffe about their writing workshops, she had a new plan.

Pat and June have been here all week with their kids, so it's been nice. I'm going to Maracanã for the course in writing. We'll be there three weeks. Don't know how it will go. It's a new brainstorm, but I trust we'll find some real talent for writing to help produce more Macushi literature.

Much to Miriam's delight, the results of the writing conference were outstanding.

We had 14 students. We had the cream of the crop—really smart fellows. They were all enthusiastic about it and got up early in the morning to study. And they usually studied after we went to bed at night. We heard some good sermons from these students. Two of them preached from the book of Mark, one about the parable of the sower. He told how the man went to sow papaya seeds. (It was translated that way because papaya seeds are the only ones the Macushi sow by scattering. All others they plant one or two at a time.) It was great to hear the way these folks are reading Mark.

Our whole course at Maracanã went better than I expected. We made a book right there with the students helping. They wrote true experience stories, fiction (legends), teaching things like describing an elephant or describing a machine they saw, and also testimonies. We picked out the best thing from each student and included it in the book and entitled it What Macushis Wrote.

Before the writer's conference, the mission's field council held a meeting. Unfortunately, their conclusions did not help Miriam much at all.

They were discussing my need of a coworker. It really wasn't a very profitable discussion. It doesn't make much difference because there isn't any prospect in any direction. Well, the Lord knows and will supply. If my confidence were in the field council, I'd go home <u>tomorrow</u>! I never was one much for organizational procedures and rules, etc. Pat was teasing me and said he thinks I should be on council next year. I said I'll arrange another case of malaria first! Ha!

Yet God was working when Miriam and the field council could not see. His timing is always perfect.

Chapter Twelve

God Settles

We all want you to strengthen those who are fearful, that
they be not afraid.
—1 Thessalonians 5:14, Macushi Back Translation

Now we exhort you, brethren, comfort the fainthearted.
—1 Thessalonians 5:14

In September 1974, after years of praying and waiting, Miriam received a ray of hope about a possible coworker.

I received a letter today from Jane Burns, who is on furlough from the Belém field. She asked me what I thought about her coming down here and helping me next term. Well, I just answered her letter and said come right on down! She's a top-notch nurse and a real go-getter. She's had special studies in lab work and tropical diseases. So, I am praying that the Lord will work out all the details and bring her down. She already speaks Portuguese and has her visa, so there will be no hold-up as far as that is concerned. She's had lots of health problems, which are common to those who live in the jungle, but is being treated now at Sinai Hospital in Chicago (tropical disease place). I already know her and know we can get along. She lives in Michigan. On furlough, she's taking some Bible school courses.

But that hope was soon crushed. Although Miriam desperately wanted and even needed Jane to come help among the Macushi, her letter never reached Jane. And the reality of mission work continued to wear on Miriam.

I went out to Pat and June's tonight. We got talking about the problem of witchcraft among the Macushi, and Domingos, the fellow from Napoleão we have here now, told us of the real situation among the Christians. The way witchcraft works in Macushi is that a witch doctor is called to the house of a sick one at night, and he has his "things" (these are usually small white stones and tobacco). He makes a drink from tobacco and drinks it and goes into a trance. Then he calls his "people" (spirits of plants). He tells them all the symptoms and problems of the sick one and asks the spirits what to do. Then a spirit will come up with a certain "taren" (a procedure to follow to bring about desired results). Sometimes the spirits will say they don't know what to do, so then someone will suggest the witch doctor call back the spirit of an old, famous witch doctor who has died, so he may come and give them a new "taren."

Domingos says there are hundreds of different tarens. Usually, it's something you say or do in a certain situation—like you take a certain weed and beat it around the house, calling different words—and this will keep spirits from entering.

There's something else you do when you get a cut to keep it from bleeding.

Now when Macushi become Christians, <u>most</u> of them realize it's wrong to go to the witch doctor and call on the spirits, but most of them feel it's perfectly all right to use different tarens. You see, anyone can use the tarens, you don't have to be the witch doctor to use them.

So Pat's wrestling with the problem of translating Scripture concerning this. All the words used to describe these practices are so hard to understand in English and then to try to find an equivalent for them in Macushi! We know "taren" is wrong, but where is the Scripture? Chapter and verse. Divination and astrology are foreign to Macushi. They have no problem with these things. They don't ask the spirits about the future; they could care less! So all those things don't apply. I think "medium" could be translated into their word for witch doctor, "pia'san," because he does contact the dead at times. And I think the word "magic" applies to <u>some</u> of the things involved. But we <u>really</u> want the Word to be <u>clear</u> and <u>correct</u> to Macushi readers.

I think the Lord is beginning to teach them some things. Yesterday I saw something for the very first time. Iracema, Domingos's wife, was studying with me, and her little boy (two years old) started to do something she told him not to do. She told him again, and he still persisted. Then she told him she would spank him if he didn't stop. He stopped. She looked at me and said, "Just recently we've started spanking them." No Macushi ever spanks their child!!!

But at Maracanã, it was Domingos who started asking questions in Bible class about discipline of children. So I was really thrilled to see this beginning in following the Word.

Domingos and Iracema are really a great Christian couple. They are both very quiet and shy, but both are anxious to serve the Lord. He says he feels guilty about staying at Napoleão all the time and wants to go out preaching to other villages, only he doesn't know how. I know women shouldn't teach men, but I just can't see sitting by doing nothing to meet this need. I think I'll teach both women and men until the men learn enough to learn on their own and teach others. You have to start somewhere.

I still need to learn more Macushi. I need to discipline myself to learn more of the complicated stuff that I'm not sure of. Iracema is helping me with this. She doesn't speak much Portuguese at all, so she speaks to me only in Macushi. She understands enough Portuguese so that I can tell her the Bible lessons in simple Portuguese and simple Macushi, and then she tells me in good Macushi. We are doing lessons of pardon and repentance. I'm making a file of all the Biblical terms and the ways we say them in Macushi. Like there are two ways for saying "humble" and about six ways to say "proud." So, I'm learning slowly.

Continue to pray about teaching Macushi. There's so much to teach, we don't know where to start. Tonight Pat and June and I were talking about needful topics to teach like: What is a Christian? What is a church? Leaders, prayer—it's not magical words like the witch doctor uses! The Bible is not a charm! They don't know anything about a Christian home or raising children.

Last night in our missionary prayer meeting, we were talking about the "fullness" of the Holy Spirit and what it is. The illustration "full"—like filling a glass with water—makes no sense whatsoever in Macushi. We would have to use terms like "be controlled by" or "possessed by." In fact, in Portuguese, it sounds funny to use "full." To say "You're filling me," means that "I'm fed up with you," or "I can't take any more of you." So you see some of the problems of saying things we're so accustomed to in a meaningful way to someone who has never heard of it before.

It didn't take long for Miriam to see that God was indeed teaching and growing the Macushi.

One Macushi man told how he had read the translated portions of the Word on "What God Says about Witchcraft." He said he learned that God doesn't want His children to practice "taren," so he said he was giving up even the few practices he'd held on to since becoming a Christian. He's a converted witch doctor and no longer consults the spirits, but now has even given up his charms, as well. His elderly father has done the same. Praise the Lord for changed lives!

Even as she struggled through these various issues and questions, Miriam continued to trust the Lord for the future.

I have been praying for a long time for a partner in the Macushi work. On Thanksgiving, a new missionary arrived from Canada who has been appointed to work with us. She is a nurse and apparently a top-notch one. With all of the stations but one needing a nurse, I hardly dare hope that she will be assigned to work with me. However, I am going to pray that way. Will you pray with me that the Lord may make it possible for Lois to join our Macushi team?

At the same time, we had a couple, who just finished up language school, arrive here to begin, and they lasted only a month. Their first week in the jungle, they announced they were leaving for home. This was a great discouragement to all of us, after all their preparation. The need here is so great. But the Lord is in it all, and I know He will provide.

Having fellow-laborers arrive on the field, only to announce their intention to immediately leave, must have been a discouragement. Yet once again, Miriam chose to trust God's perfect timing and plan for her life. He would never fail her.

Jane

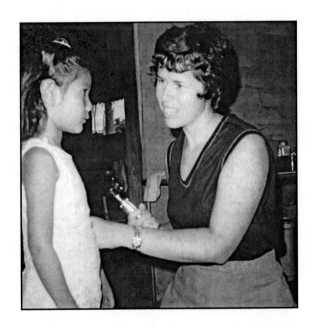

Chapter Thirteen
God Calls

How can they make Him true when they've never heard His news?
—Romans 10:14, Macushi Back Translation

How then shall they call on Him in whom they have not believed? And how shall they believe in Him of whom they have not heard?
—Romans 10:14

Jane Burns was born on May 16, 1946, to Christian parents, Earl and Betty Burns. She grew up in Redford, Michigan, a suburb of Detroit. Her father's family was originally from Scotland; they immigrated to Canada and subsequently to Michigan. Her mother's family was from Marion, Indiana. Jane had one brother and one sister, who were three and four years younger than her, respectively. She attended Redford Union Township schools for her early education.

While growing up, Jane's father was an elder in the church, and both of her parents were Sunday school teachers. Jane's mother often led her family in devotions in the home and ensured that they faithfully attended services at Covenant Community Church, led by Pastor John Drummond. This church helped start Michigan Theological Seminary and participated in the Missionary Internship Program located in Farmington. They frequently hosted missionary speakers and interns. In this way, Jane's attention was focused on missions, and her mother remembered that as a child, Jane had pointed at a globe and announced, "I want to be a missionary to Africa!" (She really liked the Tarzan movie.)

At age seven or eight, she led her best friend, Nick, to the Lord while swinging on a swing set. Sometime later, she and Nick stole some apples from an orchard, and then her conscience kicked in. "We can't do this, Nick. This is a sin. We have to throw the apples away."

"But can't we eat one first?" Nick asked.

"No, we have to throw them away!" Jane replied. And so they did.

Jane was saved at age fifteen during revival meetings at Covenant Community Church. The Lord used the messages of the evangelist to bring conviction upon her life. Jane, who had already memorized a number of verses on salvation, quoted these to her counselor, prayed, and received Jesus as her Savior.

From an early age, God began preparing Jane for service to Him. As an elementary student, Jane was asked to teach the Sunday school lesson when her elderly teacher was unable to do so. As a teen, several families relied on her to regularly babysit for their children. These experiences worked to mature Jane and help develop character and responsibility.

Frank and Jane Severn were an especially influential couple in Jane's life. As an active part of the Missionary Internship Program, they led her junior church class and taught her the importance of serving the Lord.

For several years, Jane served as the president of the young people's group. She was responsible for helping plan activities ranging from holiday parties to hospital visits and occasionally was called upon to give a devotional. Her class mates voted her to be the vice-president of the Voice of Christian Youth club at her school, as well. God expanded her influence and granted her many practical life experiences.

At 16, Jane felt called to missions during her daily Bible reading. Romans 10:13–15 arrested her attention: "For 'whoever calls on the name of the LORD SHALL BE SAVED.' How then shall they call on Him in whom they have not believed? And how shall they believe in Him of whom they have not heard? And how shall they hear without a preacher? And how shall they preach unless they are sent? As it is written: 'How beautiful are the feet of those who preach the gospel of peace, Who bring glad tidings of good things!'" She never had confirmation from any other source, but she knew without a doubt that God had called her to be a missionary!

Chapter Fourteen

God Prepares

*Don't make forgotten what God told you to do, because He
gave you knowledge in order that you do it. . .*
      —1 Timothy 4:14, Macushi Back Translation

Do not neglect the gift that is in you. . .
      —1 Timothy 4:14

While in high school, Jane wrote reports on several careers: doctor, nurse, and lawyer. She felt confident that nursing would enhance her ministry on the mission field.

Even though she had earned an academic scholarship, Jane had need of additional finances for her studies. Therefore, she worked as a lifeguard and horseback riding instructor at a YMCA camp. From 1964-1967, she attended the Henry Ford Hospital School of Nursing, an elite program of the time. No student from there ever failed her state board examination, although many quit the program before they advanced that far. The hospital was also known for having their nursing students work many hours. Thus, Jane was a full-time student with a full-time job.

During her college years, God tested Jane's commitment to Him. She seriously dated a young man who determined that the Lord had not called him to missions. Once she realized that, Jane had to choose between her call to serve God and her love for the young man. After several months of struggle within her heart, she chose to break up with her boyfriend, dedicating her life to God's service.

Upon completion of her nursing degree, Jane attended Bob Jones University to study Tropical Medicine under Dr. John Dreisbach, a veteran missionary in Africa. Unfortunately for Jane, the university discontinued the program before she could finish it. So, in 1968, she went back to Michigan and attended Detroit Bible College for her Bible training.

As part of the Tropical Medicine course, Dr. Dreisbach invited Jane to join his team for a short-term mission trip. She readily agreed and spent her summer in St. Lucia, an island in the West Indies. This trip prepared her well for the challenges and responsibilities she would soon face as a missionary.

We made it! All 19 members of the team, Project Compassion, arrived at our destination. This may not sound fantastic unless you have ridden the small propeller plane which brought us here.

The team consists of one doctor (and family), two medical students, nine nurses, three teachers, and one ministerial student. We are divided into four family units. Each family lives in a house in a different part of the community. We have centered our work around and in the town of Chioseul. My family consists of four girls, two teachers, and two nurses.

God Prepares

We live isolated from the rest of the group on the top of a mountain in a small village called Mongouge. We operate and live in a small clinic building constructed by the government. Each clinic is open for four hours in the morning. This leaves the afternoon free for evangelization.

The Lord works in strange ways His wonders to perform. We had been in St. Lucia seven days, our barrels of medicines not yet through customs, when a seeming tragedy had beset us. One baby of ten months came to us with whooping cough, progressed into pneumonia. Another young boy came with an infection and high temperature. Then late that afternoon, about 25 people headed toward our little clinic with an old woman carried on a homemade stretcher. On questioning the relatives, they summed up the entire case as "she fell sick." The woman was very ill. Our entire medical stock at that point consisted of aspirin and bandages. We sent her home with aspirin and prayer. We continued in prayer throughout that evening for all three of those patients. The next morning, the doctor came with supplies, and we immediately left to see the patients. Each patient had not only lived through the night but had shown a significant improvement. The old woman, Mistress Pierre, was sitting up upon our arrival, stating she was better than she had been in weeks. Mistress Pierre turned out to be a prominent member of the community. After presenting the gospel to her on several occasions, she is telling everyone that Jesus must have sent us. This has really given us an opening to the people.

This last Sunday, we presented the gospel to about a hundred people. One of the medical students on the team came to do the preaching. We had at least thirty men in the audience. There were no conversions, but great interest was shown. Our children's Bible classes have been well-attended, too. We hope to have a fruitful ministry among the children.

By the end of the summer, God's power was evident in St. Lucia and in Jane's life, as well.

How glad I am to be home again in America. I'm sure none of us realizes how precious our country is until we've been abroad for a while. America's faults dwindle more and more the longer you're away. The depravity of the people is not my point of reference now; it's the vise-like grip the religious system of St. Lucia has on them. The government, schools, hospitals, and cemeteries are under its control. Pressure can easily be applied, as it was this summer and even more previous summers. However, the Lord interceded. On the right day and perfect time, these verses were revealed to me: 2 Corinthians 4:8–9 "We are hard-pressed on every side, yet not crushed; we are perplexed, but not in despair; persecuted, but not forsaken; struck down, but not destroyed." Sometimes it seems a verse was written centuries ago for me alone.

Now for the report on this summer's activities. Our team, though medical, viewed its major objective as spreading the "Saving Knowledge of Jesus Christ." At our clinics, a gospel message was presented every morning. In addition, one of the men on the team mingled with the crowd spreading this "Saving Message." Each team member witnessed while they worked, showing their love of Christ. At our Mongouge clinic, we saw sixteen hundred patients, and at the Chioseul clinic, 2,650 patients. Two dentists came down for a week each and pulled a total of 1,330 teeth. Every day after clinic, if time allowed, the doctor pulled teeth. Even at ten to fifteen people a day, he pulled four hundred teeth. As we worked from clinics this summer, we had no hospital available for deliveries. We delivered 26 babies! All of these babies were delivered at home, and we had no complications! I made my first delivery on this trip—a set of triplets!

The true fruit of our work came due to the daily children's classes and street meetings. Every Sunday, we held eight services, each in a different area. We had a total of fifty converts. One of these was the Mistress Pierre. (I had requested prayer for her conversion.) PRAY again for her and the others that they may stay strong in the Lord. Each of these conversions was followed up. One point we particularly tried to stress was the importance of Christian fellowship. As a result, upon our departure, the new Christians were making plans to buy land to build a centrally located church. We hope this will be a light house of faith for this end of the island. Previous to this time, there has been no Christian witness in this area.

From St. Lucia I traveled to Surinam before returning home. There is a great need there, but all fields are ripe for harvest.

Where, when, and with whom are the big questions now. PRAY that I may know His will for my life.

Step by step, God did show Jane His plan for her life, and He prepared and equipped her to fulfill it. Now it was time for her to step out in faith and experience His power and faithfulness.

Chapter Fifteen
God Strengthens

I can stand everything that comes upon me because Christ gives His strength to me.
—Philippians 4:13, Macushi Back Translation

I can do all things through Christ Who strengthens me.
—Philippians 4:13

After working for a summer with Dr. Dreisbach in St. Lucia and another year in Bible school, Jane joined Unevangelized Fields Mission. The Lord directed her steps toward a ministry in Brazil among the Amerindian population.

Shouting for joy describes my feelings very accurately. I've finally made it to Brazil! As most of you know, I had been waiting for quite a while for my visa. Then when it was granted, everything happened at once. On May 28th, just eight days after receiving word of my visa's arrival, I left for Brazil.

My flight to Brazil was a very nice one. I flew from Philadelphia to Miami, then from there to Brazil. The whole trip only took about seven hours. My first impression upon stepping off the plane was that the whole country was one big "sauna bath." The humidity and heat combined were quite stifling. There were several people there to meet me at the airport, despite the fact it was 3 o'clock in the morning. I had no problems with customs and was immediately taken to the mission compound. I am now located in the city of Belém. It is a small, older city; however, I'm living in luxury compared to other areas of Brazil. We have plumbing and electricity— what more could you ask for?

Three days after arriving, I started language school. I was late for the beginning of it; however, I've been able to catch up. There are two couples and two single girls, besides myself, studying together. I'm enjoying language study very much so far. Pray that the Lord will enable me to memorize accurately, as I feel this is a large part of language study. The first week in August, we will have our first exams. For this, I am required to memorize Psalm 23, the Lord's Prayer, and the books of the Bible in Portuguese. Of course, much more is required in other areas.

Most of my time is spent in language study; however, once in a while I have time for a swim in the "Mighty Amazon." I've also had a few opportunities to use my medical knowledge among fellow missionaries. One of my patients was a large German shepherd. He is the mission's watch dog. He had quite a number of ailments and was ill for nearly two weeks. I had never given a shot to a dog, but I sure learned fast!

At the Lord's clear direction, Jane Burns had finally begun her life as a missionary in Brazil! What excitement and joy she must've felt at reaching this goal. Her first item of business was to learn Portuguese, which took her about eight months.

I have just finished my second semester of language school as of October 15th When I left for our three-day holiday after exams, I felt that if I heard or spoke one more word of Portuguese, I would bust. After a rest from the language and a change in environment, I'm finding I really can cram more into my head. I'm now entering my third and last semester which ends December 31st.

Actually language study is coming along quite well. I'm making the usual "funny" mistakes and getting the same odd stares that all language students receive. So far, I've made a salad with girls (moças) instead of apples (maçãs). And one time I invited a Brazilian to dinner and then followed up by saying that she was to be eaten. We all agreed later that the "pizza" was a lot better than she would have been. Pray with me that the Lord will renew my zeal for the language and thus facilitate my study.

As the date January 13th draws closer, I'm becoming more and more excited. This is when we have our annual field council meeting. This year we will have one hundred adults and eighty children. At this meeting, we make plans for the future year, as reports are given from the last. It is at this meeting my assignment will be decided. First, I will be assigned to a Brazilian work to practice my Portuguese. It will be after this year that I will go to an Indian station. This is a good plan, as the thought of beginning to learn another language at this point is rather overwhelming, besides the fact that my Portuguese would suffer until it is more a part of me.

Jane's advisory council set the plan in motion for her future.

After Christmas, I finished language school and did well in all of my exams. After exams, I took a three-day holiday and returned just in time for field conference. I am presently in the process of packing up and moving out of base headquarters to my first allocation.

And what is my first allocation? I've been assigned to a traveling ministry with Jean Bradshaw and Phylliss McLean until June of this year. Their traveling ministry consists of literacy classes in interior congregations, thus enabling Christians to read their Bibles. Spiritual growth is difficult without daily feeding from the Bible. Right now, they are located in Portel, a town of about eight to ten thousand people. They are carrying on a full church ministry, waiting for a missionary couple to return from furlough. When the couple returns, possibly in March, our plans are to move on to another congregation for literacy instruction.

Then, after June, I am assigned to work in Gorotire, one of our five Kayapo Indian stations. This station is our largest and oldest, consisting of about four hundred and fifty Indians. I will be living with a Brazilian missionary couple. My primary objective there will be to continue my Portuguese study and take over the medical work. I am extremely pleased about the possibilities of learning Portuguese well by living with a Brazilian family.

So, as you see, if things go as planned, in the Lord's will, I will be moving three times this next year. I'm asking for prayer for health and strength during this next year of adjustment and learning. I, as yet, have many things to learn about the Brazilian language and culture.

With language school behind her, Jane looked forward to starting her medical missionary work in Brazil.

Miriam standing on bumper of WWII-era Jeep

Miriam teaching Macushi students

Miriam and Jane resting during one of their interior visits

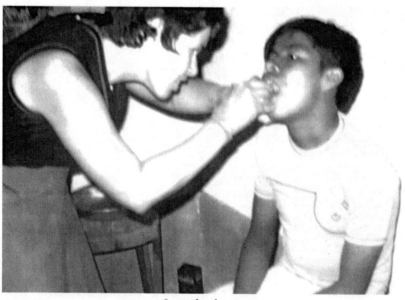

Jane, the dentist

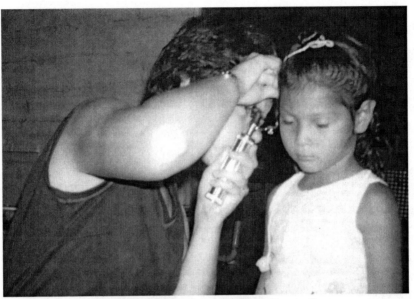

Jane used medical work to prepare the way for
spiritual ministry among the Macushi.

MAF planes and pilots were vital to the medical clinic ministry.

People came from miles around to receive medical help.

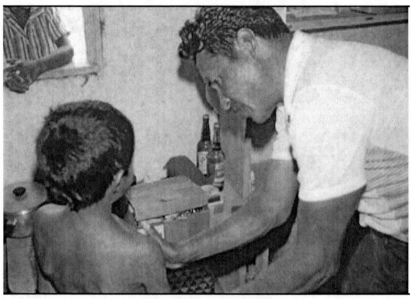
Medical attendant, Adolfo

Inside a Macushi clinic

Jane teaching others to continue the medical work.

Miriam crafting a Macushi alphabet

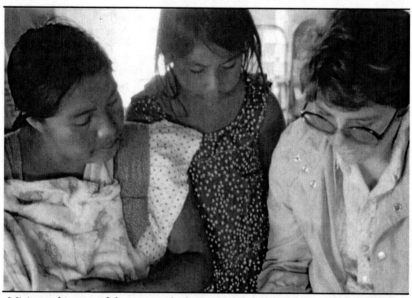

Miriam taking careful notes on the language while talking with a Macushi lady

Miriam instructing Macushi pastors to read and write in their own language

Miriam working with her primary translation helper, Waldemar

1942
December 6 – Miriam's date of birth

1954
Salvation, baptism, and surrender

1960-63
West Jersey Hospital School of Nursing,
Camden, NJ

1963-66
Glencove Bible School,
Rockland, Maine

1966
UFM Candidate School

1967
Internship, Juniata Baptist Church, Vassar,
Michigan
November 4 – Left Philadelphia for George-
town, Guyana, South America

1968
Moved to Parishara, Macushi village

1969
January 2 – Guyanese Revolt

1970
Summer – SIL, Oklahoma

1971
January-July – Portuguese Language
School, Belém, Brazil
November – Began teaching
Macushi literacy

Miriam

Jane

1946
May 16 – Jane's date of birth

1962
Salvation, baptism, and surrender

1964-67
Henry Ford Hospital School of Nursing

1967-68
Bob Jones University Tropical
Medicine Program

1968
Summer – St. Lucia missions trip

1968-69
Detroit Bible College

1970
Left Detriot for Belém, Brazil, South
America

1971
April 9 – Portel house fire

1972
Moved to Gorotire, Kayapo village

1975
Returned to Brazil and became Miriam's
coworker among the Macushi

1976-77
Served as UFM Boa Vista field treasurer

Important Dates 1942-2002

1977
May 17 – moved to Napoleão

1980
Moved to Manoá

1981
Miriam began Macushi grammar

1982
Moved to Maracanã

1983
Moved to Serra Grande

1986
Moved to Flexal

1995
The Luke Film completed in Macushi

1996
April – Catherine Rountree approved
New Testament translation

1997
April – Dedicated the Macushi New
Testament in Brazil
Started Project Bethel

2002
Moved to Pickens, South Carolina

Georgetown

Guyana

Santa Elena
Mato
Grosso
Mt Moriá
Caju
Flexal
Blue Creek
Macedônea
Maracaná
Lethem
Parishara
Boa Vistá
Manoá
Nappi
Serra Grande
RUPUNUNI
Fonte Nova
Pium
Kanashen

Rio Branco
RORAIMA

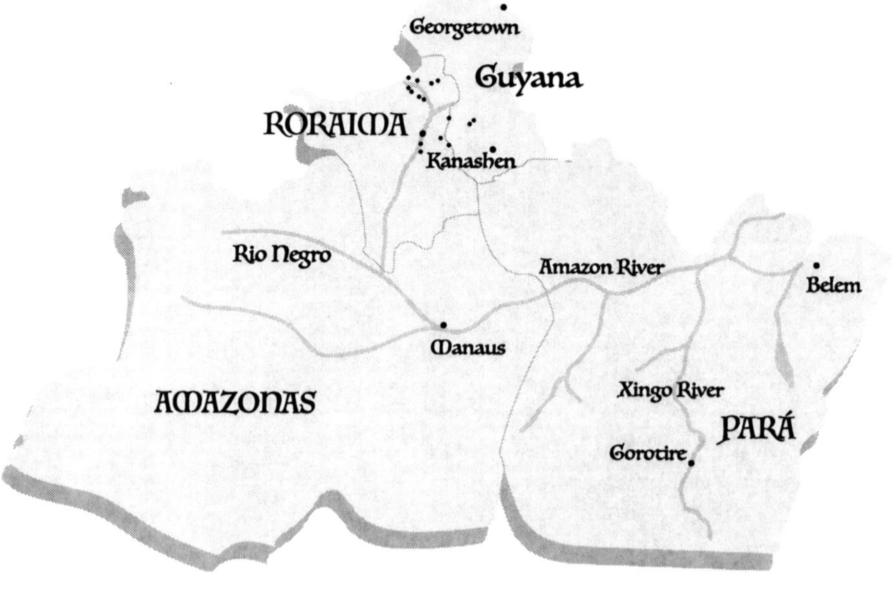

Georgetown

Guyana

RORAIMA
Kanashen

Rio Negro
Amazon River
Belem

Manaus

AMAZONAS
Xingo River
PARÁ

Gorotire

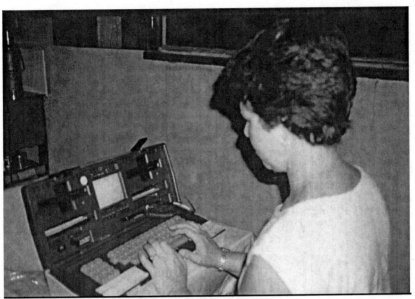
Jane was trained on special computer software for the translation.

Miriam teaching the youngest Macushi.

Macushi pastors studying the Word together.

Macushi church leader, Domingos, with his wife and family.

Macushi Bible school graduates

Jane learning to record radio broadcasts.

Jane travelled to bring the Luke Film to Macushi villages.

Jane Burns

Miriam Abbott

Jane Burns and Miriam Abbott, God's servants to the Macushi.

Macushi pastor, Waldemar, baptizing a new believer

Chapter Sixteen

God Trains

I received all strength in heaven and in earth.
   —Matthew 28:18, Macushi Back Translation

And Jesus came and spoke to them, saying, "All authority has been given to Me in heaven and on earth."
   —Matthew 28:18

Jane eagerly began her first assignment in Brazil.

Well, this has certainly been an eventful few months. I arrived in Portel the last part of February to begin my work with Phylliss McLean and Jean Bradshaw.

In Portel I've been helping with literacy classes, teaching a children's Sunday school and Saturday Bible class, speaking occasionally in the church or for ladies' meeting, and of course, visitation work. It has been a time of language and culture absorption.

Jane remembered the earliest days of her ministry in Brazil.

The only way to get to Portel was by boat. It was a little two-

story boat, and when it sat in the water, it listed to one side. But it had never sunk up to that point, so we felt that we were safe enough. Being very frugal with funds, we always traveled in the poorest class, sleeping on the deck in a hammock. If we splurged on a cabin, a little room the size of a cot, we were just able to sleep with the door shut, instead of the chickens and people and pigs all walking around us. My coworkers felt that was too luxurious.

There were typically fifty or sixty people on the boat, with one little outhouse for everyone's use. People frequently stuck animals that kept running away there. So when we went to the bathroom, a chicken or pig was often in the outhouse, too. But we made do.

We usually brought our own food on the boat, but my coworkers didn't bring their own water. I knew that that was an unsafe practice, so I brought my own water. The first time I traveled on the boat, I ran out of water because I didn't realize how long the trip was going to be. I then drank some ship water, and I became quite sick. I contracted an ameba, and because it was rainy season and we were tromping around in the mud most of the time, I also got hookworm, which left me anemic and with intestinal distress. So, I was trying to get used to the heat and primitive living circumstances, and I was very sick.

To add to my distress, the other missionary girls felt that I needed to learn certain "primitive" skills. Our language students often brought us presents because they were grateful for learning to read and write. One time, we received a duck, which created quite a mess in our back yard. The other girls decided that this duck had to die and that since I was going into Indian work, it would be a good experience for me to kill and pluck it. That duck was stronger than it looked, but I managed to kill it!

Jane wasn't in Portel long, when a tragedy beset her and her coworkers.

April 9th, Good Friday, six weeks after I arrived in Portel, we had a fire in our house. Phyllis was filling our butane lantern from a larger tank of gas when the valve failed. The kitchen filled with gas and a spark from somewhere ignited it. I was standing on one side of the tank and she, the other. The explosion blew me out the door and blew her back into the kitchen. She was caught in the burning kitchen, but I was outside. My face and hair were slightly burned, but Phyllis received second and third-degree burns on both arms and legs. She was immediately flown into Belém for treatment. I accompanied her on the flight; Jean came into Belém a week later. Phyllis was in the hospital one month and then moved into the mission home in Belém. She is just now beginning to walk a little. It appears she will be in Belém under treatment until the end of June.

I stayed in Belém three weeks helping care for Phyllis and undergoing medical treatment. I hadn't been well while in Portel due to a couple of intestinal parasites. (I had lost twenty pounds in six weeks.) I'm feeling much better, due,

I'm sure, to your prayers.

I am rejoicing that "The Most High Ruleth in the Kingdom of Men" and that He has permitted these incidents in the last few months for a definite reason. With this in mind, I know He will rule tomorrow also!

Because of the fire and Phyllis's injuries, Jane needed a new place to live and work.

The mission decided I should go back to Portel by myself and live with the head deacon and his wife. That way I would learn more Portuguese, and I could continue in the work. I don't remember how long I was there, but it seemed like a long time. I was very lonely. I was just learning to speak Portuguese, and no one else knew English, so it was very hard living there.

I tried to keep busy. The deacon's wife had a birthday party for her little girl, and she wanted me to speak at the birthday party. How difficult that was! I did write the whole thing out and get her to correct it, but of course, there's a limit to how much you can memorize. I tried to make it a good time. Brazilians always like long, flowery prayers and long sermons, but I couldn't manage that yet at that point. I was a bit of a disappointment for the birthday party entertainment.

Finally, the mission decided that this arrangement wasn't going to work out. There was a couple waiting for me to come and work at their station, the Kayapo village of Gorotire. The Uchoas had been doing medical work, along with missionary work, because it was expected by the government. Neither one of them were medical personnel, so they promised the mission that if I would come and work on their station, they would continue my Portuguese learning. So the council decided that would be the best way for me to finish my internship (since I was going there when I finished anyway).

Jane happily made the move to Gorotire, eager to see how God would use her among the Kayapo.

Chapter Seventeen
Life and Death

I will never desert you at any time. Therefore, let's search to stand strong with our speech. We will say to others, "God is our helper. Therefore, what are people able to do? Nothing!"
—Hebrews 13:5b-6, Macushi Back Translation

For He Himself has said, "I will never leave you nor forsake you." So we may boldly say: "The Lord is my helper; I will not fear. What can man do to me?"
—Hebrews 13:5b-6

Many have never heard of the Kayapo tribe by name but know them for their protruding lower lips, which are stretched out by disks. They typically shave the tops of their heads and paint their bodies. Clothing is optional; men often wear only G-strings. They are primitive and aggressive. Three missionaries were killed during the initial contact with this tribe in 1935, and the remains of their bodies and equipment were found at the foot of Smoke Falls, a well-known waterfall in the area.

With the approval of the mission board and the government, Jane was permitted to live among the Kayapo as a nurse in 1972. Also living among the tribe was a Brazilian couple, Durval and Miriã Uchoa.

The Kayapo, according to their cultural traditions, adopted Jane into their tribe as a member of the Koko family, giving her the name "Kokoränti," which means "tall, flowering palm tree." Since Jane was a nurse, she was "adopted" by the only female witch doctor in the village and was considered by the Kayapo people to be a witch doctor herself. Of course, she did not practice spiritism or witchcraft but only used those practices that she had learned in nursing school.

The Kayapo's animistic beliefs led them to attribute each illness to a specific spirit. For example, the Kayapo believed that a patient who had convulsions or seizures had offended the wild boar's spirit. Other common spirits included snakes and bobcats. Traditionally, each witch doctor held a special relationship with a certain spirit, making him more effective in treating illnesses caused by that spirit. If a witch doctor's practices failed, that witch doctor was blamed for the death of his patients; he could pay for his error with acts of hatred directed toward him, with shunning from his community, or even with his own life. The Kayapo believed that Jane possessed power over death because her modern medicines and treatments, empowered by God, were often effective in saving lives. However, if a patient died, the Kayapo held Jane responsible.

Jane did not approve of being associated with the spirit world of witch doctors and the tribal superstitions, yet this appointment resulted in her acceptance in the Kayapo community. Jane struggled to communicate with those in her village since she spoke no Kayapo and only limited Portuguese because of having just studied it. The native people were suspicious of her white skin and her foreign approach to treating illnesses, although they didn't hesitate to demand her help at any hour.

They had a little house for me to live in by myself. It was a typical, old-fashioned missionary compound, with a fence all the way around. The Brazilian couple never locked the fences, though. The Indians had access to us day and night. I asked that the fences be locked at certain times because I never had a full night's sleep, but they didn't feel that would be good for relationships.

I was trying to make the medical work a little more organized. I vaccinated and de-wormed everybody. Since it was just one village, I was trying to control what among the Indians is endemic: tuberculosis and malaria. It was hard for them to understand my ways. The Brazilian government workers said to the Kayapo, "You have to get used to her. She's not used to bending very much."

And I guess I had to learn over the years to bend, but there are certain rules about giving antibiotics. You have to give it on time and complete the whole course of antibiotics, and they didn't understand that. Being fresh out of nursing school and from Dr. Dreisbach's preaching about creating resistance to medication, I was trying very hard to do things correctly. There were a lot of adjustments. I was not a well-loved individual in the beginning.

It was frustrating because I couldn't communicate clearly in Portuguese to the couple, and I couldn't communicate at all to the Indians. I didn't have any cultural background in what they believed, what they thought about illness, what caused it, or any of these things. So, it was a very difficult time trying to adjust to everything new around me.

Jane continued to serve because she felt her medical skills might be just the key to unlock the door of the Kayapo's hearts. She communicated this to her prayer supporters.

My responsibilities right now are medical work and language study. And quite often, I'm afraid, more medical work than language study. The Kayapo are now being exposed to modern man's diseases. In the month of October, I was caring for 50 patients per day as a result of a flu brought in from civilization. Since my arrival in August, I have had three deaths. It was hard to accept the deaths of these three children (ages 3, 11, and 17 years), yet I must realize that the Lord is in control of every circumstance.

Yes, I'm starting on my third language. The Kayapo have the Gospel of Mark and The Acts of the Apostles in their language, along with several smaller Scripture portions. The Kayapo Church is a young, growing church with new Christians added every month. There are 100 believers; 59 of these are baptized.

Initially, the Kayapo were not eager to welcome another foreigner to their village, but when they learned that Jane's tools and medicines could heal their wounds and make them well, they asked for her help. The door for ministry was open.

I had some difficult experiences in the beginning. I had an eight-year-old die of snake bite. He was bitten by a huge rattle snake in the morning but wasn't brought to me until the afternoon. So even though I had the antivenom and gave it immediately, the child died during the night.

I was blamed for his death. I'm the one who sat up with him, and I had to wake his parents up and tell them that he had died. Because of the time between the bite and when they brought him to me, I couldn't get a vein to give him any of the medication intravenously. The second quickest place to absorb medicine is in the abdomen. So I gave him the antivenom in the abdomen, which they'd never seen before. The Kayapo decided that I'd punctured his liver, and I had killed him. Of course, I gave it all subcutaneously, which was very far from his liver, and he was bleeding before they brought him to me, but none of that made any difference. They believed I had killed the boy.

They didn't understand me, and I didn't understand them because of the language and culture barrier, and now my first serious patient had died. Things were a bit rocky. The only thing that kept me there was that the family was not a very influential one in the village, and they couldn't sway a large number of people against me. So, I continued with medical work.

After that, I had several successes. Specifically, one of the more acculturated women let me deliver her baby. Up to that point, no woman from this village had ever allowed an outsider to be with her at the birth of a baby. But this woman was not really Kayapo, she was Xikrene. The Xikrene were a very small tribe, and there weren't very many left of them. Because they were near the Kayapo, even though they were a different tribe, the government just threw them in the village together. They considered themselves to be a higher class than the Kayapo. This woman could speak Portuguese and talk to me.

Their language was close to Kayapo, so she was able to communicate with the other women also. She told them that she felt wonderful, and she gave me an "A" on my delivery! All of the mothers then wanted me to deliver their babies. The Kayapo tradition was the one who delivered a child also named that child. So, I gave each baby a Bible name. Imagine finding a Moses or Esther in the middle of the Amazon jungles!

The Lord gave other opportunities for Jane's ministry.

I did manage to save a witch doctor from dying of snake bite, which was an interesting circumstance because he was the witch doctor that treated all of the Kayapo's snake bites. Someone carried him on their back to me because he was an old man. Another witch doctor also treated him, which I was against. But the missionary convinced me that if the patient died, he would die without Christ. He didn't yet understand anything we were teaching. Since he didn't have the background to make a decision to choose between Christianity and paganism, I treated him. And he survived.

Of course, the other witch doctor got the acclaim. But the people did ask him why the snake bit him when he was the snake witch doctor. He simply responded, "Does the snake have eyes?" I never understood that, but it seemed to satisfy everyone else.

Probably my work with the Xikrene woman and my success with the witch doctor's snake bite were keys to opening the doors to work with the rest of the Kayapo people.

Being alone, scared, and overworked, it didn't take long for Jane's exhausted body to succumb to illness; she contracted hepatitis.

YELLOW! That's how I ended the old year and started the New Year. About six days before Christmas, I started feeling sick, tired, and generally miserable. It was just two days before Christmas that my case was diagnosed by a nurse friend that was in the Indian village with me. I have hepatitis (yellow jaundice). The day after Christmas, I was flown out of the Indian village. Then on the Friday before New Year's Day, I flew to Belém. I have had laboratory tests here which have confirmed the diagnosis. Pray with me that the case will be a light one and that I won't be laid up more than a few weeks. Right now I am confined to bed.

Several years later, Jane discovered that her hepatitis had not been the common Hepatitis A from drinking contaminated well water. She had actually contracted Hepatitis B, a serious and potentially fatal disease, probably from a local dentist's needle. Yet God answered prayer in allowing Jane to fully recover from the illness and to return to Gorotire, the Kayapo village. He also sent Jane a coworker to help carry the burdens of ministry.

I want you, my prayer partners, to get to know my new coworker, Beth Ann Smith. About the only thing we have in common is Christ, but I believe that our contrasting talents and personalities will make us even more useful to each other in our service for Him.

The two young ladies made a good pair, and Beth Ann's knowledge of the Kayapo language and culture proved vital to Jane.

Every year, the Kayapo went into the jungle to harvest Brazil nuts for the government. They compensated the Kayapo with trade goods. The Kayapo had their own tobacco and hand-made cots, but the government did bring in hammocks and blankets and other goods to trade for the Brazil nuts.

The government wanted just the men to go in to harvest the nuts, but the men took their families. The wives and children wanted to eat! They were largely gatherers and hunters, so they didn't have planted fields. If the men were gone, where was the food to come from? Therefore, everyone went into the jungle. As soon as someone became sick, they all came back to the village to get medicine.

In order for me to get permission to go into the jungle with the Kayapo, I went as the government nurse. I wasn't paid, but I was ordered to go into the jungle with the Indians while they collected Brazil nuts and to treat them when they were ill. This was difficult because I didn't want to go by myself and the logistics of going into the jungle with my Brazilian coworkers were often difficult.

After we began working together, Beth Ann went on several trips with me into the jungle. The government gave us a canoe and an Indian boat driver. We traveled up and down the river, stopping at all the key positions to treat those that were sick.

While we were in the jungle one day, the boat broke down, and we had a very sick child in the boat. The driver didn't know how to do anything but pull on the motor cord. He pulled until he could pull no more, and the motor wouldn't start. So we just stopped by the side of the river and camped in the jungle on the ground.

During that night, the child died, and I was blamed. Her father was very angry at me. He came after me with a club and threatened to kill me. Beth Ann spoke the Kayapo language, and she managed with the Lord's help to calm him down enough so that he backed off. But he was determined that he was going to get revenge for his daughter's death.

I still had to sleep there that night with the same group of Indians and the angry father. During the night, someone passed me a piece of meat in the dark. I found out later that it was the mother of the child, who understood that it really wasn't my fault that her child had died. It was encouraging to realize that someone was beginning to understand that I really did not have control over life and death. Only God has that power.

Jane survived a year in hostile, Kayapo territory, but she suffered throughout it. Illness, exhausting hours, loneliness, and threats to her life and her property all took their toll. Although God allowed Jane to be challenged in Gorotire, she chose to remain and continue the work there. In God's strength, she accomplished several things.

It seems the Devil has been working overtime to discourage us and deter the work here in Gorotire. The government has been applying pressure in respect to my medical work. A group of Indians decided to blame me for the deaths of three children, and I was almost expelled from the village. Then because of exhaustion, I have had one cold after another and had another attack of malaria.

But with the Lord's help, I have been able to (1) vaccinate the Indians here against tetanus, typhoid, whooping cough, diphtheria, polio, and tuberculosis. (Previously they had been vaccinated against smallpox and yellow fever.) (2) Begin laboratory diagnosis and medical treatment of tuberculosis. (3) Start an obstetrics program—I am doing the larger part of all the deliveries. (4) Do fecal exams for the intestinal parasites present among the people and administer medication to the entire village. (5) Become officially recognized medically before the Brazilian government by doing several internships.

I am in desperate need of language study. After a year among the Kayapo I speak almost nothing of the language. With all the problems and sickness, there has been no time for study. Pray with me that in August in our Indian committee meetings my problem will be understood and solved. I want to be a nurse and a missionary.

Although God did send another missionary to work with the

Kayapo, Jane's struggles continued. Her life was again threatened, this time by the Kayapo chief.

I was out of the village for a time being treated for illness. The Kayapo people at that point had begun to have a good deal of faith in me.

The chief's granddaughter fell out of a tree onto a stump that punctured her abdomen and intestine. (This is what I am deducing from the stories that I heard afterward.) The chief felt that if I had been there, I could have saved her life. Because of that, he blamed me for her death. This was the second of the chief's grandchildren to die since I had moved to the village. So while I was away, the people went into my house and stole everything that I had. Some Indians lived in my house, and they dirtied it with urine and feces. The chief said that if I came back to the village, he was going to kill me.

Uncertain of what to do, Jane looked to the Lord for direction.

Eventually, the people put so much pressure on the chief that he said I could come back to Gorotire. They missed the medicines and services I could provide for them. The Uchoas told the chief that I couldn't come back without my things. So the people returned many of them. Some of the Kayapo Christians said they took my things to save them for me. That could have been true. They were in a little bit better condition than others. But you can imagine the condition of my clothes after the Indians had been wearing them with paint on their bodies. But I washed them and wore them with stains. What else could I do? My curtains had been made into clothes by that time. I was given back as much as they felt I needed. As I saw my things in the village, I would go to the chief and tell him that somebody had something of mine, and it was his responsibility to get it back for me. But this chief didn't like me, so it didn't always happen.

For a short time at the end of my term, I did return to work with the Kayapo, but it wasn't for long. Most of the feelings, at least on the chief's part, weren't very favorable to me at that time. I was pretty discouraged.

Although Jane was committed to serving the Lord faithfully, she was unsure whether or not she should return to Gorotire or the Kayapo after her furlough. The challenge was great, her authority there had been diminished, and her competency questioned. She left Brazil discouraged, but waiting upon God for His clear leading in her life.

My future is still a question mark. Pray with me as I continue to seek the Lord's will for the future. I am actively looking into new opportunities for service, yet without excluding the work in which I was previously involved. The Lord has confirmed nothing to me as yet. Please pray.

Little did Jane know that there was another single missionary, serving in another needy Amerindian ministry, desperately praying for God to send her a full-time partner. God would soon answer both of their prayers.

A note from Jane's friend Carol Morrill, who speaks about Jane's ministry and life:

Jane and I first met while she was on furlough after her first term in Brazil. I was amazed listening to Jane describe her first term. She had just returned and was struggling with the knowledge that she would be going back to the jungle at the end of her furlough. The fact that she survived her first term physically is God's grace. I know God used that time in ministry to the Indians in preparation for her later work. It made Jane the very special servant she is.

Part Two

God at Work: Providing

"Beginnings"

Oh Lord, when do I begin?
Is life just a series of endless preparations?
Of false starts, setbacks,
Assignments, delays?
I know there is value in learning new skills,
Accepting changes, gaining flexibility,
And each new phase of life
Has in some way prepared me
For the task You have ahead.

But time is so short, Father.
An important job awaits me,
A task that would serve You
And have lasting value.
Is there no end to delays,
Incidental tasks,
Interruptions,
Preparations?
When do we stop?
When do we begin?

My child.
What do you know of beginnings?
Were you there when I spoke the word
And all creation burst into
A glorious beginning?
Were you aware when I breathed life
Into your mother's womb,
And you began?
The task you so eagerly long to start
Was begun in my mind
Before the foundations of the earth.
And I, who have begun a good work in you,
Will complete it.
But I have not called you
To a glorious future task.
I have called you to walk with me,
Today.
What you call obstacles,
Time-wasters, delays,
Do not block progress toward my goal.
They are the goal.
What you call the means,
I call the end.

So do not concern yourself with beginnings,
Or ends,
But with me.
I am Alpha and Omega,
The Beginning and the End.

Mrs. Heidi Coombs
Missionary to Peru

As Thomas Fuller noted, "The darkest hour is always just before the dawn." This was certainly accurate for Miriam and Jane as they struggled to serve God, each in their own set of difficult circumstances, each alone. Yet they knew that they were never truly alone, for God had promised to be with them always. They simply trusted that God had a good plan for the future. Just as He promised, He provided.

Chapter Eighteen

God's Good Plan

*Look, we all know that everything that happens to those
who are lovers of God, and that God works in order to do
good to them.*
—Romans 8:28, Macushi Back Translation

*And we know that all things work together for good to those
who love God, to those who are the called according to His
purpose.*
—Romans 8:28

Miriam spent the first part of 1975 at Napoleão teaching a Bible
study on 1 John, which Pat Foster had recently translated, and
caring for many who had contracted measles. Along with these
duties, she struggled with an enormous disappointment. Because
of problems with the postal service, her letter never reached Jane
Burns, and therefore, Miriam assumed that Jane would not be
coming to the Macushi work after all. And yet, God was working in
Jane's life to lead her to ministry with Miriam among the Macushi.

*I went home rather discouraged from my first term. I doubted
that the Lord wanted me among the Kayapo, especially with*

the Kayapo not wanting me back again after the difficulties we had over the chief's granddaughter's death. So, I started looking for something else to do. I actually went and talked to a military recruiter because the Vietnam War was on, and they were desperate for nurses. I looked into all different types of nursing where I could serve the Lord.

I was having trouble with headaches every day. I felt it was just because I was so concerned about the future. I wasn't getting any answers from the Lord.

One day, I chose to fast and pray and read the Word to see if the Lord would give me an answer. Finally, the Lord brought to my attention that I needed to be willing to go anywhere. Not anywhere but to the Kayapo. But anywhere. So I surrendered that matter to the Lord. I got a great sense of relief, and I stopped having headaches.

But I still didn't know where I was going. It was getting closer and closer to the end of my furlough, and I didn't know what I was going to do unless I went back to the Kayapo. I thought, "I'm sure, now that I've said I will go back, He's going to send me."

I had previously signed up for a conference that MAP (Medical Assistance Program) held for missionary doctors and nurses. They helped provide medicines and medical equipment with up-to-date information for those on the foreign fields. So, I went to that conference and enjoyed it. But still all the time in the back of my mind, I wondered where I was going to serve.

There were hundreds of people from all over the world there. We sat down for lunch, and a couple, John and Madel Payne, sat down with me. They had just come from a visit to Boa Vista, Brazil. Madel's father was the field leader there, Neill Hawkins. John Payne was a doctor. One thing they were very impressed with in Brazil was Miriam Abbott's work. In fact, John said that if he ever went to the mission field, he wanted to do the same type of clinic work that Miriam was doing.

I thought afterward that it was certainly a big "coincidence" that this couple would sit down and eat with me and talk to me about this work, with the myriad of other people that were at that conference. And then I started praying and asking the Lord if this was what He wanted me to do—go and work with Miriam Abbott. I hadn't ever considered it, previous to this point. I knew that we had hit it off when we saw each other before, but that wasn't enough to base a decision on. So, I prayed to the Lord like Gideon. I told Him that I would go if He would confirm it at my mission headquarters.

I had to check in with the mission office before I left for my second term. So, I went and told them the difficulties of my first term, and, of course, part of it was that I was working by myself so often. They said that if I didn't want to return to the Kayapo, that there were other areas that needed my expertise. They mentioned Miriam Abbott, and as I talked to them about it, they seemed to think it was a really good fit.

They said, "We want to give you time to pray about it, come back to us, and tell us how the Lord leads." I knew that this was a confirmation from the Lord. So, I told them, "I'm going with Miriam Abbott. I know that this is what the Lord wants me to do."

Just a few days later, Miriam learned the good news.

Another breath-taking item—Jane Burns has decided to come to this field and work with me among the Macushi. I had been thinking that any new missionary that would come here would never get assigned to work with me because all the other stations are yelling for people, too. So, I thought, unless someone says, "I came to work with Miriam among the Macushi!" then I would never get a partner. And that is exactly what Jane said!

She's planning to come in June—but I'm still going on vacation in July. Pray for her, that everything will work out. I'm still not getting my hopes up too much until I see the whites of her eyes!!

While Miriam rejoiced in God's provision of a coworker, Jane shared the good news with her supporters.

I'm so happy to be able to write this letter. It's one I never thought I would be writing when I first came home. But after a visit to mission headquarters in Philadelphia the first of April, preceded by months of prayer and self-searching, I expressed my desire to return to Brazil with a change in location and ministry. I have been assigned to work with Miriam Abbott, also a nurse, among the Macushi Indians in the north of Brazil. These Indians are semi-civilized, spread over a large savannah region in Roraima territory, and are about five thousand in number. Miriam has been hindered in her ministry for several years now for lack of a partner. I know it is of Him that I join her. We will be doing a traveling medical-evangelistic-literacy ministry.

So, this is a happy ending to a busy and fruitful furlough.

Jane also personally contacted Miriam's mother.

I'm really anticipating working with Miriam. We know each other from language school in Belém. I finished in the class before her. We really became quite good friends, and I'm delighted that the Lord led in this way. Last term I worked without a partner among another tribe of Indians. I know how difficult it is. I believe that this is a direct answer to her and my prayers.

I just wanted to drop you this little line, as I know my mother is much comforted by the thought that I will have a partner. I'm not sure if Miriam even knows yet. The mission wrote her field immediately, and I in turn wrote her. I'm anxiously awaiting a reply from her.

By mid-May, preparations were well under way for Miriam to welcome Jane to the Macushi team. Miriam cleaned and re-arranged her house, and she updated the vaccination and financial records to turn over to Jane. Much to Miriam's relief, Jane arrived on June 11, 1975.

Well, Jane came in on Friday. She's all full of ideas of stuff she wants to do and is really looking forward to working with the Macushi. She has permanent permission from the Brazil

Health department to carry on a lot of things, like an extensive TB treatment program in the interior, plus malaria control. She also knows a lot about lab work, has a microscope, etc. So, I can see already that there is a lot for her to do among Macushi. She says though, she won't start any major project until she learns the language. I've got to teach her!

Jane will be traveling around visiting the jungle stations and seeing all the aspects of the work here while I'm on vacation in Rio. Then when I get back in August, I'll be taking her interior to stay for a while. Don't know how long, nor where yet.

Despite her excitement over Jane's arrival, Miriam continued to struggle with a heavy workload and physical exhaustion.

Just a note this week, as I'm very busy and tired. It really has been fun having Jane here. I keep waiting for her to leave though, as I'm not used to anyone staying. It will take a while to realize she is really here to stay. I was so glad you had written her. I know you must have given me a build-up. You have to 'cause you are my mother!! Ha. She's got lots of big ideas and is full of pep and energy. She makes me tired just listening to all her plans.

Seriously, I've been extremely tired this whole month—so tired I have to lie down mid-morning and mid-afternoon. I'm really fed up with it because it's really hard to try to get things done that way. Pray with me about it, as I don't know if anything is wrong physically or not. When I go south for vacation, I'm going to have a check-up and at least get de-wormed.

Already I've turned over a lot of responsibility to Jane. She says she's floored at the amount of work, but I assure her I have plenty left to do. She's come to the conclusion that I was doing too much. I told her I haven't had time to write anyone but Mother and Aunt Miriam for some time now, and I probably won't have any friends left at all when I go home on furlough!!! But it really is a BIG relief to have someone to share work with. And it is wonderful to know that it is the Lord who chose her and sent her because He knew what we needed. Jane is an up-to-date nurse who pulls teeth, does minor surgery (even on herself), does her own laboratory work, plus can make up a lot of her own drugs herself. She worked with the Kayapo Indians her last term, down on the Xingo River, and they are an aggressive tribe to say the least. Anyway, she's had her experiences and is looking forward to a somewhat tamer situation among Macushi. Already this afternoon, she has to pull a child's tooth that broke off. Word gets around fast.

Upon her arrival in Brazil, Jane found a very weary and discouraged coworker. Miriam was over-worked by anyone's standard, and she was physically paying the toll. Shortly after Jane arrived, Miriam left on a much-needed vacation. She returned to Boa Vista in August with renewed energy for the future.

Jane Burns, the answer to our prayers, will be traveling interior with me from now on. I know many of you have been very faithful in praying with me for a coworker to make our ministry more effective. Praise the Lord with me for sending Jane, the one of His choice, who already wants the

Lord to use her among Macushi Indians. She will be taking the medical responsibilities, including the clinics, but I will be accompanying her as interpreter until she learns the Macushi language. Our first interior visit will be to Maracanã to be with our new Guyanese couple, Lionel and Iris Gordon. I shall try to teach Jane and the Gordons the Macushi language. Pray that I may know how to make up a language course to teach them. With all this extra help now, I am looking forward to having more time to work on literacy and train Macushi teachers. Also pray that I may be able to teach more and more Bible classes in the various villages.

From their earlier experiences, Miriam and Jane both knew they needed a teammate to share in the work. Together they found that God had answered their prayers above and beyond what they had asked.

Jane and I have both been busy! She still can't believe that I did everything by myself. But somehow I still seem as busy. I'm a lot more rested though since my vacation, and all my tests turned out negative. Didn't even have worms.

We had clinics together Thursday and Friday, and it's much better with two of us. I like the way Jane treats—she's very sensible and uses drugs very sparingly, which I like. So we get along even with medicines. This is usually hard for two nurses. In every way, the Lord knew what I needed in a coworker. She's already been through a lot—she suffered a lot her first term, so the Lord has more than prepared her for all she'll meet here. She's 5'7", so quite a bit taller than I and quite a bit taller than the Macushi. I tease the Indians,

*telling them she is my servant and I make her cook for me.
This sends them into peals of laughter, thinking of little, short
me telling someone so big what to do!!!*

Although Miriam and Jane knew that their ministry would
continue to be demanding, challenging, and full of hard work, they
praised the Lord for allowing them to face the future together.

A note from Joe and DiAnne Butler, who were missionaries
that worked for years with both Miriam and Jane. Their
memories of the ladies reflected humor, respect, and love.

*Two little girls played in the back seat of the old station wagon
as they traveled around the country with their missionary
parents doing "depuzation." They started their favorite game,
"Jane and Mircy (two-year old version of Miriam)."*

*"I get to be Jane because I'm the boss of you," says 3-year-old
Sarah. "But Mircy's a nurse too!" answers 2-year-old Lisa.
"Yes, you are. But I'm the main nurse, and I'm the one that
gives all the shots!" Thus begins another episode of a visit to
the Macushi clinic treating doll-patients with various cuts,
breaks, and illnesses requiring bandages, medicine, and lots
and lots of shots!!!*

*We are the Butlers, Joe and DiAnne, with 3 kids—John,
Sarah, and Lisa. We went to Guyana with UFM in the
summer of 1968, before we had any kids. We stayed for a
year. After finishing Bible college studies, we went to Brazil to
join our UFM colleagues for the next 18 years.*

Our first memory of Miriam Abbott was when we were staying in Lethem at the MAF home in 1968, when Miriam drove up in the oldest Land Rover you could imagine. I wondered if it was left from World War II. A cute little petite brunette hopped out and introduced herself. She said she was going to take us out to Nappi Station, the missionary outpost about 20 miles out of town. I know that Joe was amazed when Miriam had a little trouble getting the Rover started, so she climbed up on the bumper, lifted the very heavy hood (with a big old tire on top of it), and said, "I just have to jiggle something on the carburetor like Pat Foster told me to do." Lo, and behold, that old engine fired right up. She said she would do some shopping, pick up some Macushi folks, and we would head back. We finally got all the stuff and people "overloaded" into the old clunker and started the trek to Nappi around 4 p.m. We traveled dirt roads, barely passable wooden plank bridges, and lots of bypasses down even worse tracks to drop people off. The sun goes down just after 6 p.m, so we soon found ourselves in the dark, and believe me, when you are in the interior, dark is really dark. One old lady couldn't seem to remember exactly where her turnoff was. We made several dead-end attempts requiring precarious turnarounds. Finally, we found her house and got to Nappi around 10 p.m. How many times I saw Miriam driving that old clunker around and admired her courage and skill!

Our first memory of Jane Burns was when we finally finished all our schooling, candidate school, raised mission-required financial support and travel expenses, and we were cleared to go to Belém, Brazil, a large city at the mouth of the Amazon

River. We started studying Portuguese at the language school at the mission base. We were also getting used to the heat and the culture. One day, Joe was walking up to the big house, when he met up with a tall, young American woman. She introduced herself: "Hi, I'm Jane Burns, I got bit by a dog yesterday in a village. I cut off the dog's head and have it here in this plastic bag." Joe asked, "Why?" She answered in her most reasonable voice: "I started the rabies shots yesterday, but I don't want to get all those painful shots in my stomach unless I can prove the dog actually has rabies. So, I brought the head in for testing." From that point on, we learned to never question Jane's motives for anything medical. She should have and could have been a doctor. Who knew that Jane would eventually join our friend, Miriam, in Boa Vista to partner up for many years of successful ministry?

I had no sooner arrived in Belém when I discovered I was pregnant. We had brought our 3-year-old Johnny and 8-month-old Sarah with us. Having another baby so soon was more than a shock. I had terrible morning sickness but kept trying to learn Portuguese. I wrote to my dear friend, Miriam, of my struggles, never expecting her to come to my rescue. She wrote back that she would use her vacation time to come to Belém from Boa Vista (that is like a trip from Seattle to New York) to be with me when it was time for the baby's birth. She was true to her word and was with me all through labor and delivery. I was afraid of the hospitals and nursing care, but when God brought Miriam to be with me, I had total peace. I will always be so thankful for her loving care as we brought our little Lisa into this world.

Moments in time:

Miriam, do you remember that night we got back from Lethem and missed the ferry (before there was a bridge) and rode across the Rio Blanco in a small boat with each of us clutching a baby girl and Johnny between us with the wind blowing on that dark night???

Jane, do you remember telling me that I was going to fill in for you on clinics when you went home for 3 months, and I said I couldn't, and you said I could, and you trained me, and I did it????

Both of you, do you remember Joe coming out to Serra Grande so many times and driving that crazy tractor around and clearing brush and bringing building supplies?

We admire these two strong women so very much. They have been an example of perseverance and spiritual strength.

Chapter Nineteen

God's Coworkers

Everything that you do, when you do it, do it very happily.
Work well for the Lord, not only for people.
— Colossians 3:23, Macushi Back Translation

And whatever you do, do it heartily, as to the Lord and not
to men.
— Colossians 3:23

As they got to know one another, Miriam and Jane adjusted their shared responsibilities. Jane repaired their household items, cars, lights, and anything else that needed to be repaired. They both agreed that Miriam's food tasted better, so Miriam became the regular cook. They traveled to Maracanã for their first interior visit together, where Jane lived up to her reputation as a dentist.

Well, this is my first stay interior with Jane. It __really__ is different. Very nice. She's civilized! She doesn't let me do all kinds of stuff like I used to—like skip meals and baths, not use a mosquito net, etc. We even wash our dishes, rinsing them with boiled water! Actually, I'm enjoying being more civilized. The hard part is that we are running out of supplies.

I bought the stuff based on what I usually use. Jane uses much more, so next time we'll have to bring more. We're using the last of our kerosene now. We're also running out of alcohol and toilet paper! Also coffee! It will be interesting to see what happens.

Jane has been making a name for herself with her teeth pulling. Saturdays are the days for the "dentist." I'm kept busy holding heads and boiling needles. She's treated <u>lots</u> of tooth abscesses, too. I'm really glad she's able to do this. She wants to teach me, but I'm afraid if I learn, I'll have to do it!!! She ran out of Novocain, and so the Macushi have been out scouting the ranches to see if they can get more. One came back yesterday with about 20 shots. So, they are really interested in keeping her pulling teeth.

After arriving in Macedonia, she pulled 25 teeth that day. We stayed Sunday, and on Monday, she pulled 14 more before we left in the afternoon. We had a really good visit there. I spoke in church on Sunday, two times.

Jane often found herself in humorous predicaments as she provided medical and dental help to the Macushi all across the savannahs of Brazil.

I didn't like pulling teeth on clinics because my time in each village was limited. If a patient had complications, I wasn't there to help him. Occasionally, when I had enough people that needed to have their teeth pulled, I would set a day and do them all at once. While we were living in Maracanã, I experienced one of my first day-long teeth-pulling adventures.

There is a mountain in between the two villages, Maracanã and Macedonia. The Indians skitter back and forth across the mountain all the time. But it was quite a walk for us, and I wondered how I was going to make that hike and pull teeth afterward. As we started walking, the Lord sent a cowboy along. We started talking to him and he said, "Well, I'm going to Macedonia to have my teeth pulled."

I said, "Oh, you are? Well, I'm the dentist!"

He looked at both of us, turned to Miriam, and asked her if she wanted to ride his horse. She definitely refused to take the horseback ride! So, I quickly said, "I will!" I thought, "O Lord, you've sent someone along so I don't have to arrive in the village so tired and then pull teeth all day long."

I jumped on the horse, and I rode off into the wild blue yonder. The horse didn't want to walk as slowly as the people were walking. Then the cowboy casually mentioned to Miriam that a couple of weeks earlier, no one could even get near that horse because he was so wild. "But," he said, "look at how tame he is now!"

Well, I found out just how tame he was! We came to a stream, and he did not want to cross that stream. And I, not knowing that he was still pretty wild, decided to encourage him by digging my heels in and flapping him with the end of the reins. Well, that was enough to set him off, and he started bucking. I knew that it was improper protocol in riding horses to grab on to the saddle horn, but I grabbed anyway. I found out to my dismay that the Macushi saddles have no saddle horns! So, I had nothing to grab onto but the horse's mane. But because the Macushi don't like to comb their horses' manes, they also cut off the mane. So, there wasn't too much there for me to grab onto. I did manage to stay on the horse, and we got across the stream. Despite that horse, I was able to pull teeth all day long.

As the interior trip ended, the ladies rejoiced in all that God had accomplished. Jane had pulled a total of 116 teeth! But more importantly, the Macushi people had accepted Jane and grown to love her already.

Chapter Twenty

God's Grace

But He answered my word, "No, I will not take it out, but
I will continue to help you in order for you to endure it like
that." What He gives to you is enough.
  —2 Corinthians 12:9, Macushi Back Translation

And He said to me, "My grace is sufficient for you,"
  —2 Corinthians 12:9

Before Miriam and Jane could settle their plans for the future of
the Macushi work, an unexpected setback blindsided them. The
mission needed a full-time treasurer to handle the finances for the
entire Northern Brazil field.

This week has been full of training sessions with the treasurer.
This is because the current treasurer is due for furlough in
March. We are really praying that the Lord may provide
someone else to be treasurer, because Jane won't be able to
get any Macushi work done for a whole year if she's treasurer.
That means I won't be able to travel interior alone (my same
old problem). So, I hope you all will pray that the Lord will
provide someone else to be treasurer.

This time, however, God's answer to their prayer was, "No."

In March, our mission had their annual conference, and many decisions were made for this coming year. As usual, we were confronted with the amount of work to be done and the lack of workers. Jane was elected treasurer to replace our current treasurer for the year she's on furlough. This will hinder our travels considerably, but maybe the Lord wants me to do more translation this year. I'd like to do Old Testament stories, but with everything else on the schedule, time for it will be a problem.

Jane's responsibilities as treasurer did create some problems, the most obvious being the time involved. Jane had to be at the Boa Vista mission office for two weeks every month, making travel to villages impossible for Miriam. To help Jane, Miriam would stand in the slow lines at the bank or add up long columns of numbers from the books. Jane always felt torn between her obligation to the mission and her desire to be in the villages. But the ladies continued Macushi work every chance they had.

The immediate goal of the Macushi ministry was to establish literacy programs and medical clinics in each of four villages, with newly trained leaders in charge. When the ladies finally made it back to Napoleão, the first village scheduled to set up a medical clinic, they found that the promised clinic had not yet been built. And the teacher, Waldemar, had just left for Boa Vista with his wife, who was very ill. The chief of that village opposed their literacy strategy, especially the teaching of the younger children, and finally, many of the spiritual leaders had left the village to visit their relatives.

Rather than letting these circumstances discourage them or stop the work altogether, Miriam and Jane made the best of things. Miriam taught the adults and the school children, grouping them by their progress so that Waldemar's job would be easier upon his return. Jane dealt with whatever medical conditions she could, knowing that when she returned to Boa Vista, she would be occupied with the treasurer's work.

Rainy season came with a bang this year and caught everyone by surprise. The Indians were caught with their fields unburned (their method of plowing and preparing for planting), which means less planting this year for them. We've never seen so much rain at this season of the year before, and it has meant many changed plans for the pilot and for us. Our clinic trips were postponed to later dates; air strips in the jungle have been muddy and dangerous. But the Lord has granted protection and wisdom in it all.

Due to our added responsibilities, we have been unable to spend more than one week per month interior. In April, we went to Napoleão and in May to Maracanã. In Maracanã, there was much sickness, which kept us busy.

June and July hold more responsibilities for me, as I am the buyer for all the jungle stations during these months. Each of us has to take our turn as we have no one full-time to do this job. June is also a busy month for Jane, as the American draft (our money) comes, and she has to process it all. If we get it all done in time, we can go interior.

Despite the heavy workload at the Boa Vista office, God continued to use the ladies to help others.

Two missionaries from Venezuela, who had visited once before, came for more language help. They arrived Thursday noon—Jim Berryhill and Bob Nasker. We worked Thursday afternoon, Friday morning, and Friday afternoon. They just fired questions at me about Macushi grammar, as the Arecuna language is <u>very</u> similar. They took back the stories I did in Genesis and another story on Zacchaeus in the New Testament. I gave them a copy of my grammar paper, too. They said that cleared up a <u>lot</u> of problems they were running into. I encouraged them to come back after Pat Foster returns to talk with him further.

Miriam and Jane diligently continued the work God had given them to do. For Jane, that meant the bookkeeping and money-handling for the mission. Miriam, meanwhile, conducted business for the missionaries that couldn't get to town for various reasons. Bad weather was the primary deterrent to travel, but also mechanical problems with the airplane kept many families out of Boa Vista. Miriam considered the struggles of the ministry to which she and Jane were called.

It seems like missionaries are not going into Indian work anymore. The trend is to go to the "crowds" and to areas where there is great response to the gospel. Nobody wants to shut himself up in the jungle anymore for 20 years, working with Indians. It takes a special kind of patience and faithfulness to the Lord. If you hear of an accountant and a handyman, we sure could use them down here.

Although Jane's service as the field treasurer was not what they had planned, Miriam and Jane were faithful to serve the Lord day in and day out.

Chapter Twenty-One
God's Itinerary

His taught ones went every place to tell His news.
—Mark 16:20a, Macushi Back Translation

And they went out and preached everywhere.
—Mark 16:20a

As soon as Jane completed her term as treasurer, she and Miriam made plans to move interior on a more permanent basis.

Last year at this time when Jane was elected treasurer, we wondered how we would ever keep up with the Macushi work. And now as we anxiously await the return of our treasurer from furlough, we praise the Lord for His undertaking in all the work of this past year. May 16, Jane's birthday, is our date for moving out of the city, back among the Macushi, to do language study and translate Old Testament stories. We have chosen Napoleão as our home since the church there has some of the strongest leaders, with whom we hope to work. We praise the Lord for the willingness the believers have shown in fixing up a house for us: building a bath house, a well, and an outhouse; repairing the roof and floor; and building several pieces of furniture. We look forward to living close to these friends.

The first trip to Napoleão to prepare for their eventual move began with a plane crash. Thankfully it was not serious, but it did ground the plane for some time. In the midst of the chaos, very little work was accomplished.

Thursday: plane crashed—Indians had to watch.

Friday: fixed the plane—Indians had to watch.

Saturday: started to dig a hole for the bathroom (outhouse). Worked one hour, then all went fishing. Came back in after-noon and worked an hour, then all played football.

Sunday: no work on Sunday.

Monday: really worked all day. Made bricks for outhouse and bath house.

Tuesday: laid bricks and made more (didn't make enough on Monday to finish).

Wednesday: "borrowed" leaves from somebody in village for roof of outhouse and finished it, except for a door. Also patched holes in walls of house, inside and out. Jane and I painted the doors and windows. We left Wednesday after-noon.

The return to Boa Vista was via truck, as the plane was still out of commission. When the chief's wife went into labor on Wednesday morning, Jane determined her baby to be transverse. So, they took her with them to town. With the expectant mother in the truck cab, Miriam and Jane rode in the bed of the truck.

The roads weren't bad, but I have never seen so much dust in all my life! It was like talcum powder. I kept trying to wipe it from my glasses and discovered it was on the inside of my glasses! I told Jane to stop licking her lips because she was making mud. We were white from head to toe with dust. I said, "It's almost like flying—all you can see is clouds (of dust)!" We couldn't see a foot in front of our eyes.

The move to Napoleão was finally accomplished safely, if a little differently, than most.

We moved in on the 17th of May. We had three flights to get everything in. The first flight, Ken (the new pilot) and Clair (the MAF carpenter) worked for two hours the day before, getting as much as possible in the plane. Clair had made us a sink with a Formica top, using an old aluminum sink. So the sink and some real tall shelves (for food in the kitchen) went in that first load. They packed boxes and boxes in and around the bulky stuff. I never knew they could get so much in one plane. The second load was the refrigerator and Jane with a bunch of little stuff. The third load was the stove, motorcycle, me, and the dog. I guess we're settled in now.

After finally completing the move, Jane and Miriam laid out their plans for the upcoming year.

While here in Napoleão, this last year before furlough, we have various goals. Miriam hopes to finish translating Old Testament stories, which she wants to print while on furlough. Jane would simply like to learn the language. This year was slow-going while she was in the treasury department. Then too, we'll be working with the church. Miriam will be starting a Sunday school program and training the teachers for it. Jane has already started a Saturday night Bible study. They hope to do a complete New Testament survey this year.

Village life is certainly different from city life. Now it is planting season. The corn has been planted, and the caterpillars are eating the new shoots. Then yesterday, practically everyone in the village walked a whole day, climbing three mountains, to pick a palm fruit that is in season. Upon their return, they shared the fruit with us. So today, we made popsicles from it for the children (in our ice cube tray).

Weekly fellowships were another attempt at getting to know the Macushi.

Tonight, Saturday night, is social time. We usually have games, etc. You know how I hate parties, but guess I have to go. It's interesting to see how a hilarious stunt or game can fall flat with the Macushi, and something you don't even think is funny, they will just roar with laughter! Guess I'll never understand Macushi!!!

As Miriam and Jane adjusted to village life, they learned anew to trust the Lord for everything. A two-way radio was the most important need for their new home. Without that, they had no contact with Boa Vista or the rest of the world. The cost was steep: $700.00. But God did provide.

ASAS (the Brazilian arm of MAF, whose acronym means "wings of help") Napoleão is now on the air! We finally received permission for the radio the Lord so wonderfully supplied. We now have contact with Boa Vista, where we can get help in case of emergency.

Jane's mother came for a visit in November 1977. Jane and Miriam prepared for her coming by bringing in to a Macushi village the first toilet seat ever. Someone in the mission made it for Mrs. Burns, who suffered from severe arthritis, and the MAF pilot delivered it for her to use during her stay with Miriam and Jane.

Really enjoyed Mrs. Burns' visit! Did I tell you about all the clothes she gave us? She gave me three dresses and three gaucho pants and a blouse! Imagine! She made all but one of the gaucho pants and the blouse. She made them for herself to wear here and then left them for me. She made some for Jane, too! So now we're all decked out! I was really surprised to know I've been wearing my dresses about six inches too short! (The styles of five years ago!)

We took her back to Manaus by plane and saw her off on her plane to Miami. Then we shopped a few days, and Jane bought me a watch for Christmas—her mother had given her half the price! Then we came back to Boa Vista by bus. It was a 17-hour trip, and we saw nothing but jungle. It was a good trip, but dusty. We were red dirt from head to foot!

Throughout their years in Brazil, Miriam and Jane lived and worked in many different Macushi villages, always eager to share the gospel with the people. All told, they lived in five villages, Napoleão, Macedonia, Maracanã, Manoá, and Flexal. In their day-to-day lives, the missionaries became friends and mentors to the Macushi people. They went where the Macushi went, ate what the Macushi ate, and did what the Macushi did. They learned from the Macushi how to survive and thrive on the savannahs, and in so doing, they earned the people's trust.

In 1980, Miriam went to Surinam for a translation workshop. Jane had no trouble keeping busy in Manoá, the Macushi village where they lived at that time. The care that the Macushi showed Jane was evidence of their respect and love for her. Jane relayed this to her supporters in a prayer letter.

> *You ever feel like a priest? Maybe it sounds funny, but that's what I feel like these days. You see, our Macushi people have very little money, so instead of bringing paper money to church and putting it in an offering plate, they bring us a portion from their fields. From Boa Vista, I brought chicken and hamburger to eat, but since then have received liver, wild pork, fish, and whole beef filet, besides various other cuts. Of course, none of that includes the coconut, pineapple, watermelon, grapefruit, oranges, bananas (cooking and regular), papaya, and lemons I receive. My vegetables include sweet potatoes, corn, and squash from their gardens. (My own garden produces onions, lettuce, collards, tomatoes, green beans, and green peppers.) I could also freely receive rice and beans, but I already have that in store. I feel like an*

Israelite priest living off the tithes of the people! I believe the Lord blesses them for their generosity.

For the last month, I have been alone—at least in the sense that Miriam is not here. But surely not alone—I have almost constant visitors! If I leave the house to visit someone, I have three or four people complain afterward that they came to visit, but that I wasn't home. When the people here learned that Miriam had traveled to Surinam, their immediate response was: "Poor thing, so far away all by herself. So, you came back here with us so you wouldn't be all by yourself." After this busy month, all I have to say is a hearty, "Yes! So, I wouldn't be all by myself!"

It has been a busy month. Besides the usual medical work and my language study, I've been helping with the youth group. Also, I have been working closely with the Sunday school teachers (10) and preachers (7) to help them in their preparations (a job that Miriam usually does).

It took about a whole month for me to receive my first letter from Miriam, but now they're coming pretty regular. I think for the first time Miriam is realizing she really <u>enjoys</u> language study. I had already realized it and was hoping she would pretty soon.

After Miriam completed the translation workshop in Surinam, she returned to Brazil amid the rush of Christmas to find that Jane's sacrificial service to the Macushi had taken its toll.

I'm sorry I let so much time pass without writing. But when

I returned from Surinam, Jane was in a terrible condition. (By the way, Jane's mother doesn't know and is not to know how bad she was!) She was so weak from malaria, she could hardly do anything, and yet she had tried to keep up with everything! She'd get out of her hammock shaking with chills and fever to go bathe an Indian baby who was convulsing with fever! There's just no way you can say no to a mother who comes for help like that! Anyway, I put her to bed practically and wouldn't allow her to do any physical work. She took a nap morning and afternoon for a couple weeks, and by the time Christmas conference was over, Jane was feeling a lot stronger.

There were other responsibilities for Miriam to fulfill, as well.

Our new missionary family, the Teeters, and I arrived here in Maracanã last week. I'm helping them to get settled in and start learning the language. Everything is so new and different for them. It's amazing how much I've come to take for granted! But they are doing well.

Teeters are living in our house at Maracanã, and I'm eating with them, but I'm sleeping and studying in the old clinic building. The first night I woke up with rain splashing in my face! So, I had to get up and move my hammock over to where it didn't leak.

Even though they never complained, living in Macushi villages and constantly working under high pressure cost Miriam and Jane physically. After a series of difficulties in 1986, a vacation was in order.

This vacation has been the most restful Jane and I have ever had! We are really enjoying the cool climate up here in the mountains. Our daily exercise is going up to the waterfall to take our bath. It's a half-hour walk one way. But the rocks are beautiful and the water is crystal clear.

Jane seems to be better now. Hasn't had any heart symptoms since we've arrived. However, she has been bothered with malaria. Thankfully, it's a light case! So, we hope we'll both be able to get back to work in better conditions.

The difficult living conditions never discouraged Jane but rather fed her hunger for primitive living and adventure. She wrote a rare letter to her mother about her activities.

I bought two horses from one of Messias's daughters. I'm very happy with them. One is all white and the other is a white speckled with brown. I ride the white one, as he has a very nice trot. The other one is older and needs a lot of encouragement to keep going. I travel every week to Mt. Moriá to give two Bible studies, and then on Sunday morning I give a Sunday school lesson using the chronological studies. (A study of the whole Bible from cover to cover. . .I use pictures, so it's popular.) I usually have an Indian girl go with me. It's good for building discipleship relationships. I go Friday afternoon and come back Sunday afternoon. We're getting to have quite a bit of night life here. Tuesday and Thursday nights Bible study, and Wednesday and Sunday nights church.

During the week in Flexal, I give four Bible studies. The two evening sessions are a group studying the Life of Christ using

213

Matthew. The two afternoon sessions are a group studying basic Christian doctrines, for new Christians. I am doing the same studies in Mt. Moriá, but only one study for each group. It's the people that have chosen the times and frequency and have been very faithful so far. In Mt. Moriá there is a total of 16 studying and in Flexal a total of 13.

Since Elizabeth has been here, we've, of course, spent two days in Manaus. One day we spent shopping so Nancy (Miriam's sister) would have souvenirs to take home. Elizabeth didn't seem too interested. The next day we took a tour on the Amazon River on a ship. We went to the "meeting of the waters" where the Rio Negro flows into the Amazon and stopped a couple of times along the way to see rubber trees and other interesting sights. The same day we washed clothes and shopped in Boa Vista. The next we took them to Serra Grande to meet everyone and see our house. Then we went to Flexal. Nancy, Miriam's youngest sister, spent about a week here before she went out on a clinic flight to return to the US.

Since we've been here, we've taken them on several walks to see Indian life. I took Nancy on a horseback ride to a nearby village. Elizabeth went with me to Mt. Moriá by horse (three hours unless you want to trot, and then you can make it in two hours). Needless to say, she didn't want to trot. She can't remember ever having been on a horse before, so she spent most of her time just holding on to the saddle. She survived the trip but says it was the most dangerous thing she's ever done in her life.

I hope you like the gifts I sent to you. The crystal was a present that the chief of "Nova Vida" (New Life) gave to me after I treated his grandson for pneumonia. The wood for Dad is called "purple heart" for which Brazil is famous. One of the Indians is making me a rabbit hutch and "just happened" to use this wood for one of the cross beams. It's a very expensive wood. I thought Dad might want to sand and varnish it and set it out for use as a paper weight. I would have done it myself, but the wood is still green and needs to dry out a bit.

I mentioned about the rabbit hutch. I have four chickens for fresh eggs as well. They lay very well, so we're well-stocked in eggs. One of our Brazilian missionaries is doing a rabbit project among the Wai Wai Indians and it seems to be working out very well, so I decided to try it here. There is a lack of meat in the area so I want to increase it perhaps by rabbits.

I am really enjoying my time here. The weather is great (we always sleep with a blanket at night, yet the days are warm). I enjoy the work, mostly teaching with a touch of nursing when there is a more serious case. I have five medical attendants here, so it keeps the load off me.

Miriam told me to tell you "HI." She really enjoyed the M&Ms, gum, and Life Savers. My specialty was the "Pringles." But we made a mistake and opened things while our company was here, so everything went all too fast! We still have that cake to bake though. You've really caught on to all the things we really enjoy.

I forgot to tell you about Miriam's hobby. She has started to *plant a garden again. She was transplanting today (tomatoes, onions, collards, parsley, lettuce, and Chinese lettuce). I'm looking forward to the fresh vegetables. Then with chicken, eggs, and rabbit, what more do you want for a balanced diet?*

Clean water was a constant need in the Macushi villages, which meant there were always wells to be dug and lessons in hygiene and cleanliness to be taught. Outside of translating God's Word into their native language, this was perhaps the greatest gift that the missionaries gave to the Macushi people.

This is a very dry year, and besides praying for rain, we are having our well dug deeper—so far, no water. But Jane is busy with the "deep" subject. Mr. Swain, a retired electrician, came to spend two weeks with us and is working with the Indians to help them close in their wells.

Since we had our well dug here in Flexal (over a year ago now) many of the village people have been using it and, as a result, see how convenient and clean the water is. So now Jane's encouraging as many as possible to dig their own wells. Presently three wells are in the process of being dug. We are hoping that this will make a real difference.

A later report documented that eleven wells were dug between the villages of Mt. Moriá and Flexal. As they showed the Macushi how to find clean water for their daily physical needs, Jane and Miriam also demonstrated how the Living Water would meet their spiritual needs.

Elizabeth Kereji, a friend of Jane's from her home church in

Michigan, was a pharmacist, and she visited Brazil several times to encourage Jane and Miriam.

I was at Covenant Community church when Jane was there giving a report during her first term. I learned that her mother was going to visit her. I figured if she could do it, I could do it, too. So, I spent 4 weeks with Miriam and Jane the first time I went. It was hot and steamy. I traveled with Jane, visiting villages and observing her teach health courses. The government wanted Jane to give health classes so the Macushi could learn to care for themselves. Of course, very few of them could read, so Miriam was preparing the Indians with literacy classes. I remember vividly seeing Jane's love for the people, especially the children. It was evident that they needed a teacher, and God sent them Jane and Miriam.

Throughout the course of Jane's ministry in Brazil, various politicians questioned her motives. But they were always pure. Once they realized how good she was, they wanted her to do a lot for the Indians. She qualified the Indians to help their own people by teaching them basic first aid, hygiene, wound care, etc. Jane's love for the Macushi really set her apart.

One time in the village she was living in, they brought a baby to Jane with a bad fever and some kind of rash. The child's head and face—everything—were red and swollen. Hideous, actually. When they treated the baby, nothing happened. But Jane prayed for God's help, and the Lord *healed the baby. It was a triumphant time. God allowed Jane to have much more credibility both in her medical practice and in the teaching of the gospel because of this.*

Another time, on a Sunday afternoon, we went over to a village that was without a missionary. The Christians there wanted a church. When it was time to go, Jane said we would be going by horseback. . .uh-oh!!! I had never ridden a horse before. When we came to a small river crossing, I thought, now what?! As the horse went down the river bank, I had to lean way back to keep from falling off. My shoes got wet, but I made it! We hung our hammocks in the church for the night.

There was a diamond miner with many daughters (Messias at Blue Creek). Jane and Miriam took me to see the mission station near his house. The family was very glad to see the missionaries. When I asked to use the outhouse, I learned that it wasn't quite finished yet. No one else seemed to have a problem with it! Then they told me that I would have to take my bath in the river. What?? And that they had found a snake in the river just that morning. I was terrified until they said they were just kidding—about the snake, anyway!

We visited another village of a tribe different than the Macushi. We ate our own food there. The Macushi village was not all that far away, but such a difference in the cleanliness. I wondered for a time what had caused these changes. I know it was because many of the Macushi were Christians. The men were good to their women and children. Mothers cared for their children's physical needs. I was glad to go back to the Macushi village to sleep.

After I first went to Brazil, I felt that everybody should go to the mission field and visit their missionaries. After a while, I decided that not everyone should go, especially if they would complain about the hardships of the field and discourage the missionaries. But I'm thankful that God let me go visit Jane and Miriam.

Chapter Twenty-Two
God's Birthday

The angel said to them, Don't be afraid. Don't be frightened.
Because I came to tell you good news, in order that you and
all people would be very happy.
— Luke 2:10, Macushi Back Translation

Then the angel said to them, "Do not be afraid, for behold,
I bring you good tidings of great joy which will be to all
people."
— Luke 2:10

The annual Macushi Christmas Conference was a memorable tradition for Miriam and Jane. João Batista, a Brazilian evangelist, had started this special event for the Macushi people a year before Miriam came to Brazil. At that time, there were very few believers, and they were scattered throughout the various villages. For the Macushi, Christmas was only celebrated with drunken feasts. The missionaries felt that it would be a good idea to gather all the Christian Macushi in one place to celebrate the true meaning of Christmas, as well as to encourage and edify one another. And it was a tradition that everyone was happy to continue.

For me this was the busiest Christmas conference ever. I left early the 23rd, and, after a very rough flight, we landed in the "wind tunnel" at Maracanã, in the mountains. From then until I left at 1 p.m. on the 27th, I didn't stop. I had to help with the organization of 101 little things, though my main responsibilities were a women's class in the afternoons and the medical work (all day long). Neill needed me to tell him how his messages were being translated and if they were getting across all right. In between all the services and meals, Neill and I were both kept busy counseling people who came for help with problems. The Macushi can never solve anything quickly; each one involved has to have their own say. The last day I had a session with two sisters, and it took all morning. Neill was running around packing up my things so I'd be ready for the plane. But the Lord seemed to work in many hearts.

Neill said it was 30 years ago this Christmas that he first spent Christmas with the Macushi in Contão. There is a long way to go yet before all Macushi will hear the gospel; there are still 85-90% of the Macushi here in Brazil, as well as 5,000 Macushi in Guyana and still some in Venezuela. Will it take 30 more years? I hope not!

But the ladies did continue to work with the Macushi for another 30 years. And throughout that time, Miriam and Jane spent nearly every Christmas somewhere in a Macushi conference. The events always involved hard work and busy schedules, but they also resulted in spiritual renewal and leadership development among the Macushi.

For me, the month of December is a busy one with lots of correspondence (because of Christmas and my birthday), as well as the yearly Christmas conference with the Macushi. Jane and I are planning together this year (a big help), and it's a lot of fun. I've already taught Bible lessons to a Macushi lady (Iracema) for her to teach the women at the conference. Jane has been preparing materials for the children's program. Jane and I will be leaving December 19th for the conference and stay afterward 'til January 7th, so we'll have a week or so where we can get some work done.

As they used the Christmas story to give the gospel to unsaved friends and family members, the Christians also took steps of faith and obedience to God. Weddings were often performed, as well as baptisms. God commissioned new missionaries and called men to preach during these special events. The multiplying of the Macushi church was evidenced in the growth of these conferences. Over time, the Macushi assumed the preparation, preaching, teaching, and counseling of the meetings. God used this annual tradition to strengthen and encourage the Amerindian people and the missionaries alike.

The important part is always the SPIRITUAL BLESSINGS, as we see the Lord do His work in the lives of the Macushi. This year was especially blessed as we saw around 12 Macushi make decisions for salvation, and many others made things right in their lives. Many of these we had been praying for. Eight were baptized, and around 80 baptized believers partook of the Lord's Supper.

We heard the testimony Domingos gave as he told how God called him to leave his village of Napoleão and preach the gospel. He obeyed and went to Manoá, and there the leaders of that church made him "the teller of God's Word" (preacher). God has blessed his testimony there with new converts in that church. Pray for him, our missionary from Napoleão to Manoá.

One night, Raimundo preached in both Macushi and Portuguese and gave his personal testimony. That night several accepted Christ as Savior. His testimony maintains a good influence among unsaved relatives and friends there in Napoleão.

Another highlight of each Christmas conference was hearing the Macushi themselves give testimony of how the Lord had been working in their lives.

Each year, new Macushi make decisions for the Lord as a result of the faithful witness of Macushi believers throughout the year. This year it was outstanding to see the leadership that has developed among the believers. Each evening of the Christmas conference, different Macushi preached or gave their testimonies. We had several of the women do counseling with those who came forward to make decisions. Two women taught the women's classes in the afternoons, and two teenage girls taught the children's classes.

One girl, who was baptized by Lionel Gordon, the Macushi church leader, told me how her life had changed this past year. She said, "I never wanted to do what my parents told me, ever since I was ten. But now my thinking has changed, and I don't get mad anymore at what my parents tell me to do." Believe me, only the Holy Spirit could bring about a change like that in the life of a teenager!

Christians are greatly encouraged as they hear of the Lord's working in many lives during the past year. Arlinda, the leader's wife at Macedonia told me after counseling a new convert, "This is better than going hooking (fishing). We're not catching fish, but it's our brothers and sisters that are increasing!" Another girl, a teacher at Maracanã, told me how the Lord has worked in her heart in making her ask forgiveness of those she has held grudges against, her own husband included. She has shown much growth in the Lord, as has her husband. Continue to pray for growth in Christians' lives.

Raimundo's testimony was of the Lord's protection of his family at Surucucu (where he was helping the missionaries for two years) when the Waica Indians came barging in, demanding guns and ammunition, threatening them with cutlass, bows, and arrows. Raimundo told how the Lord kept him calm, and as he prayed aloud, the Indians also calmed down somewhat. The missionaries there said he took cheerfully the "spoiling of his goods." Many of their household items were stolen.

But occasionally, the plans for the Christmas conferences were changed due to weather, drought, or other emergencies. One Christmas was especially memorable for Jane.

The day before Christmas, I found myself in the village of Kaxmi, which is a Wai Wai Indian village. We had decided to spend that Christmas in Napoleão, a Macushi village. Miriam and I had the responsibility of giving the Christmas conference along with the Macushi there. Well, as we were trying to get everything ready, one bright morning, the airplane flew in to tell me that the administration had decided that I was not going to spend Christmas in Napoleão, but rather that I was going to Kaxmi to help with a malaria epidemic. So, I climbed into the airplane with my plans completely changed. I left Miriam there by herself to carry on the Christmas conference, and I flew off to Kaxmi.

When I got there, things were pretty dismal, so I started my regular routine of taking slides of every person in the whole village. When the health department saw what a high percentage of the people actually did have malaria, they sent their own team into the village to help us.

One big problem was that the malaria strain the people had was resistant to the drugs we were using. The health department team came with quinine. Taken repeatedly, quinine causes hearing loss. If taken during pregnancy, the baby is often miscarried. So, we hesitated to use that. But if a patient didn't respond to the initial treatment, then we had to use quinine.

We were so scared because the majority of the people had a form of malaria which can be fatal. Initially, when people were the very sickest, we had a shelter (without walls) which we used as a makeshift hospital. As the patients lay in their hammocks, we gave medicine through intravenous. Then we prayed. After their lives were out of danger, we continued giving the oral doses of quinine for the rest of the ten days.

There wasn't much intravenous quinine available, and a health department employee had been assigned to guard the supply. Therefore, every time I wanted to give someone quinine, I had to request the medication based on positive slides.

The renowned and revered chief of the Wai Wai, Elka, had a daughter that came down with malaria on Christmas Eve. I was called, and I found her in her hammock in a coma. Advanced cases of this strain of malaria can produce stroke-like symptoms, often resulting in paralysis or death. I realized that this was a life and death situation.

Instead of dragging her out to the shelter in the middle of the village, I decided to treat her there. It was late at night, and we didn't have light anywhere anyway. I got an intravenous started on her and began giving her the IV quinine. Usually, we get a fairly quick response, but we didn't with her. I prayed and prayed for wisdom to know what to do with her, as I was very concerned. The believers there prayed also.

The Lord seemed to tell me to give her a higher dose of quinine, even though I knew that could be very dangerous. I asked for one, and with a lot of hesitancy, the health department employee did give me an extra amount of quinine for her. As soon as I started the higher dose, she woke up.

Of course, I had already spent most of the night before Christmas by her bedside. When she woke up—and we were all ecstatic that she did wake up—she looked around. Her husband was there with a very concerned look on his face. She started yelling at him, asking about their kids, and wondering what he had done with them, just as if she'd never been unconscious! To her, it seemed as though she'd been there all along with us. She continued yelling at her husband as she had been beforehand, concerned that he wasn't taking care of the children right: giving them enough food, getting them to bed, etc. All of us just sat there roaring with laughter after this woman woke up.

The Wai Wai really considered it a miracle from the Lord, as though she'd been resurrected from the dead. In their language, they use the word for "dead" when speaking of someone who is unconscious. So, we had a resurrection on Christmas morning! Praise the Lord!

Only God could transform entire tribes of people so that their Christmases were spent in celebration and worship of the Christ Child, rather than in their former drunken stupors. What a glorious transformation Miriam and Jane witnessed!

Chapter Twenty-Three
God's Hope

Remain at waiting for Him happily, endure your sufferings with strength, not being sad, but keep on praying without forsaking it.
—Romans 12:12, Macushi Back Translation

Rejoicing in hope, patient in tribulation, continuing steadfastly in prayer.
—Romans 12:12

As Miriam and Jane finally settled into a work rhythm, they found that trials of every sort, even life and death, assaulted them and their Macushi friends.

On Monday afternoon, Hidelbrando from Mutum came in with his 11-year-old son, bitten by a snake—a rattler. He died just a few hours after arriving in Boa Vista. He had been bitten Sunday afternoon late, coming back from their field with his father. His father saw the snake first on the trail and jumped away, hollering, but the boy was right behind him and stepped right on top of it. Needless to say, the father was very broken up about it. They are a Christian family, but the teenagers are not living for the Lord at the moment. We trust this will have an effect in their lives.

Also, Paulo Silas and his wife, Brazilian missionaries, lost their newborn son early Tuesday morning. He lived just two days. So, we went to the cemetery together and had a simple service (Pat led it) for the two families. Don and Barb Borgman went and were a real comfort to them. Don told Hidelbrando his son was buried in the same cemetery; he also died of snakebite.

That same day, in the afternoon, a small plane (air-taxi) caught fire and exploded. They were returning from Tototobi, a New Tribes station. They had taken some Indians back, left them off, and were returning to Boa Vista. On board was Dr. Vicente from the FUNAI (Indian agency) and Dr. Ruth from the malaria department. I had been talking with Dr. Vicente the day before, and he told me about their trip in to Tototobi. He was looking forward to it, as he had never been there, and offered to take in anything I might want to send to the missionaries there. Well, it was a real shock to the whole town.

On top of such intense struggles, finances were a continual concern. Brazilian governmental policies produced an unstable economy, which affected everything for the missionaries, from food to travel to ministry.

We cannot let the ministry we have at present go—we need to continue with the medical and spiritual assistance to these scattered villages. (We are serving eight villages on our monthly clinic trips.) And we also feel the need to branch out in faith. The Lord is supplying personnel among our Brazilian missionaries, but how can we think of expanding when we are behind financially? We feel this is an opportunity to trust the Lord and really seek Him concerning the Macushi work. He is the One who has blessed in such a way that we must expand. Therefore, pray, and trust Him with us to supply financially.

1985 was a particularly difficult year for those ministering among the Macushi, starting with Jane's return to Brazil from furlough.

It sure was great to see Jane return. She had a terrible trip—worst ever—everything happened that could possibly happen. (She's not telling her folks, so don't mention it!) She had to change planes in Chicago, as well as Miami, and they refused to check her baggage through, so she had quite a hassle in every airport (10 pieces of baggage!). The plane couldn't land in Manaus because of rain, so they went on to Belém. Was a big hassle there—went through customs and all, got on TransBrasil line, and they mistakenly tore off her ticket—the passage to Boa Vista. So, when she finally arrived in Manaus, she had no ticket to Boa Vista. They made her buy another passage. Said they had no proof that she had paid for a passage to Boa Vista. Then she got hung up in customs. They took the computer, two solar panels, and the printer (that goes with the computer). Well, to make a long story shorter—a missionary from New Tribes is working with a "dispachante" (a go-between) to get the things released. Reams of forms had to be filled out stating the use of it. Well, Jane finally arrived at midnight on the 11th, completely worn out. She'd been up for 36-40 hours without sleep and spent every meal time in an airport hassling! So, she was also famished! By the time we got her baggage back to the mission and got to bed, it was pretty late.

While another malaria outbreak kept both nurses busy for several weeks, the computer situation had a happy ending.

Finally, Joe Butler made a trip to Manaus and succeeded in getting everything out of customs with no cost except for our "dispachante," our go-between, who kept working on the process. It took a month.

This is the first day that the computer has been in use, and you are the first ones to get a letter on it from Brazil. Joe Butler got back with it from Manaus the day before yesterday. . .I guess the Lord knew we wouldn't have time to do anything with the computer until now. So, to help us so we wouldn't be frustrated, He let it stay in Manaus for a while.

As various missionaries moved to new locations or returned home, the need for workers in the Macushi field grew more desperate. At least five unreached villages were pleading for a missionary to come help them. While it was not possible to start anymore new works, Miriam and Jane wondered what could be done.

What are God's economics? He tells us of the Good Shepherd leaving the 99 and going far into the night to reach the one.

But he didn't have to pay the high cost of air travel!

In 1985 what are the opportunities around us that we will miss (for very good reasons)? And in 5 or 10 years, when we have the resources of personnel and funds, will these villages still want us?

Discouragement fell on both ladies. Miriam had a bout of malaria while taking a few days of rest, and Jane came down with it, too, just before a scheduled clinic trip. Miriam was able to postpone the trip for a few days and travel in Jane's place. She stopped at Maloquinha, a small village that had extended a special invitation for the missionaries to come. Several people made decisions for the Lord, including the chief's wife. Upon returning home after the clinic visits, Miriam found Jane still not well.

On the 10th of June, shortly after receiving her last dose of medication, Jane went into shock. She was rushed into Boa Vista, all of us believing it was due to the malaria medication. On the 11th, she was released from the hospital, feeling weak, but much better. Then on the 13th, she had another attack, which at that time she recognized as her heart. This was later diagnosed as supra ventricular tachycardia, a hereditary condition. When this occurs, the heart beats very rapidly, but ineffectively, so that there is insufficient oxygenation to other parts of the body. The cardiologist here was able to bring the attack under control but felt more testing should be done as to the cause of these attacks. Due to the superior equipment available in the US, Jane left for testing June 23rd.

Miriam was concerned and overwhelmed. She had an automobile accident while Jane was in the hospital. All the pressures and demands of life and ministry were mounting up, but both ladies knew that God was in control.

Thankfully, Jane responded to medication and within a short time, she returned to Brazil and her usual work. But the problems continued: the computer began having trouble and the MAF flight program was grounded while being investigated for smuggling precious gems! But Miriam and Jane never quit.

We made a trip by car this month to Maracanã to take supplies to Dan and Marge Teeter. We also took medicines along to leave in some of the villages we thought we could get to. We left Monday morning and went by one road—shortest route—but there were four bridges out. We managed (with difficulty) to go through three of the creeks, but the fourth one was just too deep. So, we turned back and tried to enter Napoleão on the return trip, but the mud was too bad, so we turned back from there. We took the long way home and on the way, a pebble hit our windshield and broke it. The glass shattered all over us. Jane jumped from the surprise and got a terrible stiff neck. But we got home—dead on our feet! Tuesday we got a new windshield put in and we started off again on Wednesday—another route. No bridges out, but terribly bumpy! The rain has really destroyed all the roads this year! Terrible conditions. We made it in good time—about 3 p.m. Dan and Marge were really glad to see us and treated us royally. We stayed Thursday and started back Friday, stopped in Araça to leave medicines, treat people, and pick up two students to come back with us to study. Again, we arrived home at 11 p.m. exhausted.

Guess I'm not as young as I used to be, and I dread these trips, but guess we have to do it.

At times, it seemed that Miriam's sense of humor was the only thing keeping them going.

We didn't plan on rain in dry season (the day before traveling) on our return trip from Manoá. We took the students and other passengers out to the road to catch the bus and went back for the cargo. Due to the rain, the creek bank was slippery, and we didn't make it up the bank but got stuck in the mud. We spent from 10:00 a.m. to 3:00 p.m. working on ways to get out, during which time it poured rain. Finally, one last attempt was made, we got out of the hole, and we slid back down the bank into the creek. By this time, the water had risen enough to cover too much of the truck's exhaust pipe. That's when we discovered we had a Presbyterian truck that didn't want to be immersed. A kind horse and a dozen men pulled us out backward, and we spent the next day changing the oil and drying everything out. We finally had just started on our return to Boa Vista when we met the "search party" the mission sent out for us. Pat Foster came looking for us in another truck, and the pilot flew over us on the road as we were approaching Boa Vista. We felt quite important!

Despite a year filled with difficult trials and hardships, they had accomplished much, and several souls were saved through the power of God and His Word. Their love for people and for the Lord was the motivation for Miriam's and Jane's service.

Miriam took a much-needed, six-month furlough in 1986. On June 23rd of that year, she returned to Brazil with her niece, Melody Smith.

> *Jane and I have really enjoyed Melody. I guess she'll tell you all that happened. I feel badly that it's been so rainy and wet that we couldn't really take her anywhere by car. We did make a flight to Messias's, a special one—Jane needed to get away after six months of working alone, so we went up and stayed overnight. Melody took Jackson (her puppet), and we translated for her. I translated Melody's speech and Jane translated Jackson's. Sunday, we went to two Sunday schools. She told a story in the opening exercises of one and in the closing of the other. Tomorrow she'll speak at kids' club.*

Miriam and Jane were not the only ones who benefited from this visit. Now a missionary herself, Melody remembered her time in Brazil with fondness and thankfulness.

A note from Melody:

> *I went to Brazil for three weeks the summer after my freshman year in college. Since I was young I always had a desire to "be like" Aunt Miriam, a missionary nurse. Though the Lord changed that desire (to be a nurse) before I went to college, I still wanted to be a missionary and I*

thought that perhaps the Lord would call me to Brazil, so I wanted to visit. Miriam and Jane were happy to have me come. I had a great time and learned so many things while visiting. Of course there were many memorable experiences, like seeing a tarantula my first day, hearing the screaming monkeys in the jungle, eating a large rodent (that was given to Miriam and Jane by a native, and they "couldn't waste good meat!"), flying in a small plane that had to land on the top of a mountain, visiting a baby with malaria, having roasted pig at a Brazilian's home, helping with little projects, eating the best mango I've ever had, seeing a diamond mine, using an outhouse, etc.!

But two things "stick out" to me the most. One was a conversation I had with Miriam about missions. I told her that I was majoring in Speech and did she think that was ok, or did I need to major in "missions" or Bible in order to be a missionary. She said, "Well, a missionary has to know how to communicate with people, so I think it's fine you are in that major." And that was a real blessing to me.

The second thing that impressed me so much was how Miriam spent her "siesta." I was usually pretty tired by the afternoon and would lie in the hammock and take a nap. But I found that Miriam was resting on the couch with a box full of letters in her lap. They were letters from missionaries all over the world. I asked her what she was doing, and she told me, "I'm praying for the missionaries that sent these letters. You see, God has said, "Go ye into all the world," but I can only physically be in one place. So, by praying for each of these missionaries I can fulfill that Great Commission." What a lesson!

The Brazilian economy continued to wreak havoc on the missionaries' finances over the years. MAF flights and medicines were especially difficult to afford. Extra money donated for the expansion of ministry had to be used instead to pay for medicines.

> *Guess you've heard about our new government and the new economic policies. This time it's affecting us US missionaries because the dollar dropped in value. In one day, the exchange fell from 69 to 29 cruzeiros (Brazilian money). Prices have decreased, but not enough. What has happened in <u>practice</u> here in Roraima is that there is not much to buy and no cruzeiros to buy it with.*

> *We've had the lowest support rate of any country in the world except Guyana for many years. Now I think it will have to change. MAF is now charging us $1.10 per mile. It's been 75 cents for 10 years and was 10 cents for 10 years before that. So, you can see how costs are rising.*

Buying a vehicle was another lengthy, expensive process for the missionaries. Yet, Miriam and Jane were always encouraged to see God provide.

> *What is giving us real problems now is our car. It's really getting quite costly, and we want to sell it. But it's very difficult to get anything else. <u>So,</u> we went into the dealer and got put on the waiting list—#50. And they only got in 15 new pickups this <u>year.</u> So, Jane called her brother (ham*

radio) and asked him about their friend at GM who helped us get the Chevy pickup. Well, he said he could still help even though he's retired. He called São Paulo and Jane has had two calls so far from the head of the factory there asking about specifications. The latest word is that they have a diesel truck like we want, but they needed information as to why it should leave the factory "High Priority" marked for Jane. She told him all about her work, and he said that gave him more than ample reason to request high priority. So, he'll let her know when it's on its way and approximately when to expect it in the agency here. If we really do get it, it sure will be a miracle.

Thankfully, Miriam and Jane served a God who specializes in miracles.

Well—we finally got our truck—a Chevrolet diesel pickup—called a D-20. It arrived the week they said it would. Jane was getting phone calls from São Paulo about the truck all the way along. But when it arrived, the agency here changed the bill of sale (that was in Jane's name) and sold it to the Catholic priest in town, who has been waiting for a truck. We went in to see about it, and they said it wasn't ours, even though the Bill of Sale number was the same. So, we just called São Paulo. Well, I guess they made a lot of trouble for the Agency—told them it was ours and they'd better get the receipt back from the priest. The agency was really in a fix, between GM on one side and the Catholics on the other! Anyway, they finally got it resolved by promising the priest another pickup "at cost." So, we got our truck—at last year's price. We ended up selling our Toyota for 120,000 cruzados, and we bought the new one for 134,000 cruzados! Unbelievable. We sold the cruzados to the mission for dollars—it came to 8,500 dollars, and then when we cashed the money again to pay for the new truck, we only needed 6,500 dollars—which paid for licensing, insurance, and everything. We made about 2,000 dollars US through this transaction. Who but the Lord could do that?

Through many such difficulties, the ladies learned to rely solely on God. And He never failed them.

The latest thing is we are being sued! One of Jane's medical attendants is suing the mission for about 6,000 dollars because he says we never paid him anything. Well, we never hired him nor any of them. They are working for their own villages. They were chosen by the chief and the church, and we only trained them and provided medicines for them. Yesterday, Pat Foster and Jane went to court. We had a prayer meeting during the time they were there. Our lawyer showed up drunk and made the judge mad by repeatedly interrupting him, so the judge refused to hear the case. He said he couldn't judge it impartially, so he put it off till they appoint a new judge. So now, their lawyers are trying to get us to settle out of court. They asked for 1,500 dollars yesterday. But we don't feel we can give anything because it would be setting a precedence and all the others could demand the same thing. But we feel bad about the fellow and his family. We feel he was likely manipulated into doing this.

It's been very hard on Jane especially. She had been having more trouble with her heart, especially while I was gone. She's beginning to feel better these last few days now, but we're not sure how much longer she'll be able to control her heart with medicine. She's taking the highest dose now that she can take.

The heavy workload, lack of funding, and needy people all weighed on the hearts of Miriam and Jane. Yet they knew that God was in control and would work things out in His perfect way and time.

The Lord has answered our prayers.

After a number of setbacks and changes in the court case, we were summoned to appear in court. So, we again had to work on our defense. The church in the medical attendant's village had written in their records that he was chosen by the village (not the mission) and also when he left, moving to another village. With this document and the testimonies of the village chief and the present medical attendant, the judge ruled in our favor, stating that the medical attendant's testimony was proven false—he had not worked the hours he said, and there existed no agreement of employment with the mission.

We praise the Lord for this answer to prayer and ask that you continue to pray with us for this man.

Faithfully, God continued to meet Miriam's and Jane's needs. As they trusted Him, He expanded their ministry among the Macushi.

Part Three

God at Work: Producing

"Not Home Yet"

As the ship came in from sea, crowds gathered on the shore.
Bands were playing gustily, and the throng began to roar.
Then people clapped and banners were raised, and they all shouted with glee.
And I could only stand amazed that they had remembered me.
For God called me, the gospel to sow in a land of pagan night;
So that men the Saviour might know, and be called into His light.
But still I who am nothing was humbled by the cheers.
Though I was herald to the King, the sight brought me to tears.
Then a man on board waved to the crowd, because for him they came that day.
And when he came they cheered aloud. Then he left, and they went away.
Hurt, that my work was not regarded and that by crowds I was not met;

One came and said, "Don't be downhearted, for you are not home yet."

Mr. Jim Bjur
Missionary to Chile

The more a person knows of God, the more he recognizes that everything around him is orchestrated by God to fulfill His highest purposes. Missionaries especially know this to be true. While they get a front-row seat to God's divine appointments, His methods, and His plans, they can take no credit for what is accomplished. Rather, they worship God all the more, for they see His power, sovereignty, faithfulness, and love through a magnifying glass.

Chapter Twenty-Four
God Uses the Medical Work

And He sent them. They were to tell of God's coming to be everyone's boss and for them to heal the unwell ones.
—Luke 9:2, Macushi Back Translation

He sent them to preach the kingdom of God and to heal the sick.
—Luke 9:2

As Jane took over the primary responsibilities for the medical work, she had a very specific plan to reach out to the native people with medical care and the gospel.

First, she continued the monthly clinic trips to various villages. The trips were expensive and difficult to schedule since Jane was dependent upon MAF for transportation and since there was no way to contact the villages ahead of time. But they proved to be vital in making new contacts.

BURABBOTT—that's the name we've chosen for our station! (For bookkeeping accounts, every station must have a name. So, the combination of Burns and Abbott

247

gave us this!) Since my return to Brazil in June and my first time in Boa Vista, Roraima, I have certainly done a bit of traveling. I have visited our four jungle stations, gone on three (two-day each) clinic trips, and spent five weeks in a Macushi Indian village.

I have joined Miriam Abbott in her work here. Up to this point, she has done nursing, literacy, and Bible teaching. Now I hope to help in the Bible teaching and take over the nursing ministry. This will leave her freer for literacy, teaching, and reading material production.

Our work schedule consists of monthly visits to five different villages via airplane to hold short half-day clinics. These visits occupy three days monthly; we are the only medical assistance available. In between clinics, we spend time living in different villages. We recently spent five weeks in the village of Maracanã. The month of November, we plan to spend in the village of Manoá and December in Napoleão.

Jane, and occasionally Miriam, continued the monthly clinic flights for years. The goal was to supply each village with medical care and medicines, as well as to encourage them spiritually through evangelism and discipleship. They were continually looking for new villages that they could reach through the medical ministry.

We did go to Caju yesterday. We went right to Messias's home, one of the few Christian families in that area. He lives at "Blue Creek." It's a beautiful place, kinda like story-book land, in the mountains. You can just tell he and his wife and eleven daughters are real hard workers. He's a Brazilian man married to a Macushi woman (Their wedding was held during Miriam's first Macushi Christmas conference.), and he was a Communist before João Batista led him to the Lord about five years ago. Since then, we've been having clinics in his area to try to win others to the Lord and to encourage him. We've never had time to spend there with him, but he has really grown in the Lord.

Messias wants to build an airstrip closer to his house so we can come and visit easier. The closest strip is a 45-minute walk away, crossing two creeks. He had the pilots look at a place he's chosen, really the only one in the area, on top of a mountain. He wanted to know if it would be long enough. They looked and said yes, but he'll have to flatten off the two high parts of the mountain and fill in the valleys! With a shovel! He said he's not afraid of hard work! His wife told me "it really won't be much work!" Can you imagine!

They are going to build a clinic with an extra room on it for us to visit. They already took out 3,000 leaves and are going to take out 2,000 more. His wife and daughters do that! The girls do as much work as he does. They work with the cows, building and repairing houses, and they even re-plaster their house with mud every year! It's the neatest, cleanest house interior I've seen!

Isabel trained one of his daughters to be a teacher, and she's taught the rest of the girls to read and write. They listen to Trans World Radio every morning at 4:30 a.m. and have sent away and taken every correspondence Bible course available! They are just such an amazing family. I sure wish you could meet them. Jane and I will go spend a week with them in April, as they want to build the clinic "just the way we want it."

Blue Creek was a strategic location for a clinic due to the villages nearby that still needed to hear the gospel.

This month we're starting a new outreach. On our clinic day (when we normally visit each clinic and supply them with medicines), we're going to make our last visit at Blue Creek and stay overnight with Messias's family. The next day we will go with them to two new villages where we haven't been before. We hope to do this each month. There are as many as 12 villages that we know about that we could visit, so there are probably as many more. We'll be picking up a Macushi preacher to go with us each month to preach in these new places. Also, our medical attendant will be treating the sick there. Pray with us concerning this new effort.

What were these clinic trips like? A "clinic" was certainly not like an American doctor's office! Miriam's sense of humor and gift of writing allowed supporters to experience a clinic trip with her and Jane.

"KVW taking off from Boa Vista, destination Manoá. Five people on board." This is a direct translation of the pilot's radio talk, as he begins our three-day clinic trip. First stop—Manoá. He leaves off our month's supply of food, medicines for the next month, and sick people that are now well and

returning to their villages from the hospital in Boa Vista. Oh yes, he'd better not forget our mail!

Miriam hurriedly sorts the mail, sending on lots of letters for various Indians from their relatives in different villages. Jane directs the Indians carrying cargo to and from the plane. She has already spent the previous week packing the medicine boxes for each village on the clinics.

"Don't forget your lunch!" That lunch is three-days' worth of food, complete with a live chicken! Without refrigeration, he keeps better that way.

The plane is finally off and the pilot asks casually, "Where are we going?"

"Well, let's see, the plane is too heavy now to land on the horrible strip in Pacu, so we'd better go to Napoleão." Jane stocks the clinic with medicine there, talks with the medical attendant about difficult cases, and corrects mistakes he's made.

"No, you don't give that medicine for a scorpion bite. It's only for a woman in labor...Yes, I know scorpion bites hurt!"

After a couple hours, KVW is off again, this time with a Macushi preacher heading for Mato Grosso, where we have an evangelistic service before Jane treats the sick. We've been making this visit for a year now. It's hard to know how much of the gospel they understand.

On to Blue Creek to spend the night. The airstrip is on top of a mountain. Down below, Jane restocks the clinic and enjoys a special dinner prepared by Messias's wife, who is a very good cook. After a good night's sleep, all feel rested—until we climb the mountain to the plane.

Today, the first stop is Flexal, another new village where an evangelistic service is held. Ivo Uchôa is staying in this village this month, so the pilot goes to get him at a neighboring village while Jane and the Macushi preacher begin the service. Ivo's glad to get his mail and supplies, as well as catch up on all the news, as he has no radio contact during the month with Boa Vista or other missionaries. The people in Flexal seem to be very interested in the gospel, and Ivo is excited at the prospect of teaching them this month. He has a service each day where he teaches the Word.

After all the sick have been treated, we're off to Macedonia to spend the night. Since the medical attendant died, Jane has had to treat the people there when she visits. Here is where we lose one passenger—the chicken! He makes a good greasy stew to eat with rice and cassava bread!

The next morning we're not in too much of a hurry as the remaining villages are just quick stops. However, upon arriving in Pacu, the medical attendant tells Jane of a sick man, unable to walk to the airstrip, that he doesn't know how to treat. Jane, wanting to be economical with time, borrows an Indian's bicycle to go treat the man. After she goes, the Indians all start laughing. The pilot asks why.

They said, "She doesn't know it, but the path is all uphill."

After resuscitating Jane upon her return, we took off for the next village. At Araça, a surprise awaited us: two sick people who needed to go on to the hospital. In order to accommodate the extra weight, the pilot suggests a Coca-Cola! We were all ready for one, but he was talking about taking half of us to a larger airstrip, coming back to Araça to get the rest, and picking us up again at the larger strip where he could take off with more weight. That's a pilot's coca-cola!

Jane was exhausted when she returned to Manoá and was ready for the hot meal waiting for her. All over for another month, except the reams of paperwork needing to be done to turn in reports to the Health Department and Indian Department. But probably more than 600 or 700 people have been treated during the month with those medicines by Christian medical attendants who treat them with no remuneration, but because they love the Lord and want to serve Him.

But over time, the clinic flights came to be more of a burden than a blessing because of financial challenges. It cost a lot of the missionaries' money to pay for the airplane and the medicines, both of which were necessary to the clinic trips. Changes were inevitable.

Those of you who have contributed and prayed especially for the medical ministry will rejoice to know that this year we are terminating the clinic flights as they have been in the past. We will just be supervising the full-time village clinics and supplying medicines. We are encouraging the Macushi leaders and medical attendants to make evangelistic trips to new areas, as we have done in the past. We will be opening one more clinic this year in the Caju area. It is now under construction, and we will be training the attendant in May. Pray that the change-over may be smooth, as we try to put more and more responsibility on the Macushi.

We are still making one quick trip per month by plane, visiting four villages, just to supply them with medicines. This allows only about 1 hour and 45 minutes on the ground at each village. This is a difficult change for some of the believers to accept, as it throws more responsibility on them. Pray for them during these first months of change. We would like to see the church be responsible for services on the day people come from afar to receive medical treatment, just as the medical attendants are accepting the responsibility to treat them physically.

The training of Macushi medical attendants was the second step in Jane's plan. She wanted to help the Macushi become as independent as possible by establishing clinics in each village. Jane described the root issues that had to be addressed in order to accomplish this goal.

I had the vision that Indians could learn to treat their own people. I had started among the Kayapo giving a few simple things: aspirin, something to put on a cut, and little things like that. I tried to explain to them about how you decide the root cause of a symptom because everyone wanted to treat the symptom and not the cause. For example, if you had a cough, they would give you cough medicine. They don't think "Why do you have a cough? Do you have tuberculosis? Do you have whooping cough? Do you have bronchitis? Do you have pneumonia? Do you have worms?" Obviously, you can't just grab a bottle of cough medicine every time someone comes for a cough. So how do I get the Macushi to understand that you have to ask more questions?

Miriam found out very early that the Macushi didn't understand questions in the same way that we do. They had a way to ask questions, it seemed. But why would you ask questions if you already knew the answer? Asking questions to ascertain if you understood something was not part of their culture.

Also, their witch doctors told patients what was wrong with them when they went to them. The patient didn't have to tell the witch doctor. So, when you went to a witch doctor, he would have to ascertain which spirit was afflicting you.

So, I saw that working with the Macushi attendants wasn't going to be just a matter of paperwork.

To begin, Jane held medical attendant's training courses in various villages. She would train a handful of people at a time, beginning with very basic healthcare and hygiene. Then she would give them hands-on training in the areas they had studied.

We're both busy preparing for our course in February.

Jane has completed two books for the medical course. One is entitled Let's Take Care of our Health *and the other is* Let's Understand the Medicines. *The first one is written in both Macushi and Portuguese. It gives a list of complaints people have, a list of questions the attendant needs to ask the patients, and a list of sicknesses that could be diagnosed. Then the treatment is listed for each sickness.*

Our schedule will be full. We'll have four class hours, plus Bible. Jane's medical course schedule will be half lecture and half practice.

Jane believed that the training courses were successful.

I sent the four trainees home from that first conference with a task. Each one of them was to get their community to choose a location to build a clinic. I would supply nails, paint, hinges, windows, and doors, and they had to supply the rest. When it was all built like I wanted it (Actually all of them had their own models, but it had to have a door, a table for them to work on, shelves for their medicines, and a window or two.), I would come and bring them the medicines. I stayed there working with them. I gave them medicines that I felt they were capable of using at that time.

Initially, I started them off with simple medicines. I had no idea in the beginning that they would end up giving intravenous or that they would end up suturing. I figured I was going to have to teach them to give intermuscular injections, but I had no idea how extensive I was going to have to become because of the necessity and because of the medicines being given to them.

I tried to get them together at least once a year, if not more than that, so they could talk over all their problems, and so I could teach them a little more each time. It was a long process to get all four clinics going because it took a very long time for some villages to actually build a clinic.

We finally got all four going and each one was functioning at a little bit different level, depending on the ability of the medical attendant. Those four stuck it out a very long time, in comparison to later attendants. They would get discouraged because the idea was that the community would help them in their fields because their medical practice often took time out of every single day. That didn't always work out very well. But these four were very determined men, and they did continue with their jobs. Later ones quit very quickly because people would talk bad about them.

At times, the training was discouraging. I remember one village where there had been a death. I said, "What did the man die from?"

"Oh, he died from Kanaima," was the response.

Kanaima is a spirit. If you see this Kanaima, the Macushi believe you will die. That is one reason why the Macushi never go anywhere by themselves and why they close all their doors and windows at night, even though it's well over 100 degrees because they don't want Kanaima to get in. They believe they are more likely to see him if they are alone. So, they don't ever stay by themselves. But if they see Kanaima, they believe they will die.

I said, "So you couldn't help him? Just tell me what his symptoms were."

The attendant told me that the patient had vomiting and diarrhea and fever. I said, "Do you know any disease in your book that has those symptoms?"

He thought, and he thought. Finally, he managed to come up with bacillary dysentery. And I said, "You never thought to give him that medicine so he would get better?"

The medical attendant replied, "No! Because he saw Kanaima, and he was going to die."

So that's the way it went a lot in the beginning. They had more faith in what the spirits could do than in what God or the medicine could do. So, it took a long time to convince them.

But God used these village clinics and Jane's training to help many, many people, physically and spiritually.

The four attendants, Sebastião, Odilon, Adolfo, and Francisco, are doing their job as unto the Lord. Sebastião has already successfully treated a snake-bite case. Francisco has saved a woman's life who was hemorrhaging. Adolfo has battled an epidemic of flu, treating many children and old people for pneumonia. And they have all had their share treating colds, diarrheas, skin infections, worms, etc. PRAY FOR THESE ATTENDANTS, that their Christian testimony may be pure and true as they minister for the Lord. One lady arrived in Napoleão and asked Odilon for medicine, saying she was not a Christian and had no right to come to the "Christian" clinic. But she was very sick and needed help. Odilon explained that the Christians were there to help everyone, and his services were available to all.

As time passed, the medical attendants became more confident in their abilities to help patients. They also realized that their role opened many doors to share the gospel.

This month on clinics we were very encouraged at how our attendants are doing. In two villages (Napoleão and Macedonia), they were asked by another village to come and bring medicines and preach. Waldemar and Odilon (from Napoleão) are going this month on their first medical-evangelistic trip. They are really excited about it! Pray for them that they will have an effective witness there.

We are continually amazed at how the Lord is blessing the medical ministry. People appreciate the help and dedication of the attendants. Sebastião went to another village with his father-in-law. They held a service first and afterward treated the sick (just like we've done for years). He treated 32 people that afternoon. So, it seems like there will be more and more villages open up to the ministry of the Macushi churches. We feel even a greater pressure to teach these believers, so they will know better how to minister.

Slowly, the Lord allowed Jane to expand the medical work with more attendants and clinics. She furthered the attendants' training to include dentistry, midwifery, and minor surgical procedures, and she taught the entire community basic hygiene, prenatal care, and child care practices. Miriam, too, came to the training sessions and taught the attendants how to read, teach, and preach Scripture. This was a very effective method in reaching many Macushi for Christ.

I've also started women's classes to teach hygiene and prenatal care. One Sunday afternoon, my midwife and I went around to all the houses by bike and invited the women to the first class on the 11th of October. I expected about 50—we had over 100—men, women, and children! Pray that the Lord will use these classes to win many to Himself!

Jane was pleased as punch upon hearing the news that the midwife she had trained here (Luciola) had successfully diagnosed and treated an expectant mother with toxemia of pregnancy. Luciola has more than gained the confidence of all the women in the area—wives of Brazilian ranchers, as well as the Indians. We pray the Lord will continue to use her testimony as she has contacts and opportunities we would never have.

Later, Luciola delivered a baby for the school director's Brazilian wife, as well as a complicated feet-first delivery. She attributed the successful delivery to the Lord, as He brought back to her memory the exact page in her textbook that explained how to safely deliver a baby in that position.

Jane and Miriam did not stop with just training the Macushi, but they eventually expanded the medical training courses to include other Amerindian tribes. This also increased the outreach and influence of the gospel across the savannah.

In the village of Manoá, Jane and Miriam held a course to train medical attendants. Twelve students were taught, and, by God's strength and grace, all twelve also passed! It was the largest number of students ever because we accepted three Wai Wai Indians and two Maiongong Indians. It was more difficult to teach because of their various levels of Portuguese comprehension. Flo Riedle, a nurse, accompanied the Wai Wai and interpreted for them. They all will receive follow-up in the practical areas as they return to their villages. Jane went to Kaxmi, a Wai Wai village, to work for three weeks with the Wai Wai who studied. Pray that these students will be effective as they begin to minister to their own people, not only physically, but also spiritually.

Besides the routine medical trips and attendant training, there were often emergencies and epidemics during which Jane and Miriam were called to serve. Jane went to minister to the Wai Wai during a particularly difficult malaria epidemic. So many people were ill that there were few healthy people left to care for them. The medicine supply was dangerously low, and Jane knew that God would have to intervene if lives were to be saved.

The malaria epidemic is the worst I've seen in 16 years! Now the same people are being re-infected and coming down sick again. I took 25 slides to the lab yesterday, and only five were negative. One of those negatives is burning up with fever and vomiting. Jane has her on IVs today! I don't know how long Jane can stand this pressure. And the quinine will run out Tuesday! I just don't know what we're going to do. Please pray for us.

God did bring healing to the majority of the Wai Wai. Jane was thankful for the opportunity to teach her attendants medical practices and spiritual lessons, despite the high cost of personal exhaustion. As the crisis finally passed and she prepared to leave Kaxmi, one attendant commented, "I'm going to miss Jane. She's like my mother."

Frequently, as Jane traveled for clinics, she would find remote villages that were without medical or spiritual help. The physical demands were high, and often it seemed that the most important need—spiritual instruction—was neglected. But without fail, God always worked in the hearts and lives of those who sought Him.

Last month Jane went to Agua Fria, a village near Bananal. She said there were so many people there. She treated 94, besides giving vaccines. Can you imagine! She said she was so busy she hardly had any time to talk with anyone, and as she was getting into the plane, one lady told her she wanted to join "our belief," but she didn't know how. Jane didn't have time to talk to her but told her just to talk to God about it and next time she'd explain it to her.

Jane has been praying for a long time that a door would open up in one of our northernmost areas. Two months ago, we visited a little village of about 50 people called "Aro'mata" (the place of the frogs) and were welcomed with open arms. We can really tell that the Holy Spirit has gone before us and prepared their hearts. This little village is nestled between three large villages that have previously rejected our visits. Pray that Aro'mata will become the "gospel light" for this whole area. Already twelve have made decisions for Christ.

There were times when Jane left Brazil for furlough or medical needs of her own. At such times, Miriam continued the medical ministry. During one of Jane's absences, the financial situation in Brazil became quite precarious, and the funds were no longer available to purchase medicines for the Macushi. Yet God had already planned to supply the need. Jane reported to her supporters.

Medicine

That word has been following me around lately in my personal as well as my professional life. As many of you know, I'm home now on a short medical furlough. The "short" was supposed to be "shorter" than it actually was. I stayed a total of six weeks to be properly regulated on my medication. For right now, I've been given a clean bill of health which includes unrestricted activity.

The other side to the word "medicine" has to do with the medicine shortage we have been experiencing in Brazil due to the runaway inflation problem. Since the month of May, we have been unable to continue our monthly medical/ evangelistic outreach to the Macushi Indians. We make them bi-monthly now as the funds available will no longer buy sufficient medicine to make the trips profitable. The price of medicines has risen 200% since May. A lot of the basic medicines are no longer available.

But the Lord has answered our prayers through three supporting churches. They were able to assist during my short time home, which has enabled me to take back 300 lbs. of medicine. I've also ordered medicines through MAP, Blessings International, Compassion International, and International Aid to help supply us in the future. I want to thank these churches for their liberal contributions which have made this possible. Pray with us that the Lord will continue to provide the funds necessary to continue this ministry.

Even though they were beyond busy, Jane and Miriam patiently and faithfully served in their various roles while God gave grace and help in each situation. They continued to hold clinic in many villages, and Jane taught another medical course.

Well, I just got back from eight days of clinic trips. It was longer this time because we had two dentists from the south of Brazil. It was quite a week! We've never had one so disrupted as this one. Because of MAF's plans, the pilots were changing constantly. We had five in on this trip. And to top it all off, it rained so much we were left stranded in the villages 'cause the plane couldn't get back to get us! Jane, the dentists, and a preacher were on one team; Flo, a preacher, and I were the other team. Because the dentists were new in this area, the pilots tried to get them to a decent place to sleep, so it was our team that got left. We went to a village I had never been to before, and two boys came to meet us. The airstrip is some distance from the village, and we had to cross a river. It was full of rapids, and the current was fairly strong. Of course, the canoe wasn't there (someone had taken it off up river), so we forded the river. It came up to my armpits in the deepest place and the rocks were slippery. Raimundo, the preacher from Maracanã, helped us across. We fell only once! Then I stood on the other side watching an old man and a woman carry all our stuff across! Amazing! All on their heads and nothing dropped in the river. Medicines, hammocks, books—it all crossed safely.

Well, we ended up spending 24 hours there. Then we spent 24 hours in Aro'mata where it poured rain every hour on the hour! So, in between times, people straggled in for medicine. We usually treat 50-60 people there in 2–3 hours' time. This time we treated less than 20. Who wants to go for an aspirin in the rain?!!!

Despite her knowledge of tropical illnesses, the rare diseases of the Amerindian communities sometimes puzzled Jane. But the Lord always answered her questions and met the Macushi's needs.

We've been finding more and more cases of Kalazar among the Indians. That's a tropical disease transmitted by the bites of sand flies that causes damage to either the skin or the internal organs. We've had several deaths; it is hard to differentiate from malaria, as the symptoms are similar.

We have a little girl here with us (11 years old) in treatment now, and she seems to be responding well. Her spleen has diminished in size, and she hasn't had fever for seven days now, so we're very encouraged. The treatment is very hard on the organs too, and the literature says a patient may drop dead at any stage of treatment. So, we are just praising the Lord for this girl's healing so far! She's the one I gave blood to several months back, remember? We thought it was malaria. Well, it looks like the blood kept her alive long enough to diagnose it! I tell her that her eyes will change to blue now that she has American blood! Ha.

With the help of Dr. Frank Davis, Jane traveled to the villages affected by Kalazar, where she tested nearly everyone for the disease and euthanized the animals that were carrying the disease. She walked to many of the villages and then commandeered Jeeps, horses, and even an airplane to make her rounds. Thankfully, the epidemic passed without further loss of life.

The main goal of the medical ministry, of course, was to reach people with the knowledge of Jesus. The exhaustion, financial hardship, and frustration were all worth it when a person received Christ as Savior.

On these clinic trips, I had found out that if I arrived too late after my scheduled time, the people who had traveled a long distance to receive medicine would go home and not return. Because of this, I often refused side trips.

As I completed the clinic in Mato Grosso and was preparing to leave for the next village, a young teenage girl came to me and told me that her employer, a rancher's wife, wanted me to come over for dinner. The teenage girl had been telling the rancher's wife about Christ. The woman was very interested, and she wanted to hear about Jesus. I tried to very carefully explain to the girl why I wanted to continue on to the next village, but I told her that I would help her know how to explain the plan of salvation to the rancher's wife. Since the teenage girl was a Christian, she could explain to someone else how they could become a Christian. That's what Jesus wanted us to do! Well, she didn't seem very convinced that she could do it, but we had a good talk. I then said goodbye.

As we flew off, some clouds appeared that the pilot had not previously noticed. When you are flying in a tiny, little plane, the rule is that you don't fly through a cloud because you don't know what's in the middle of the cloud or what's on the other side. We were traveling through a mountainous area; some were very high. You had to be sure you flew over or between the mountains, not through them! So, these clouds appeared, and they were very dark ones. We were trying to fly around them, and it seemed like everywhere we turned, there were more dark clouds. We realized that we were surrounded by dark, thunderstorm clouds! We found ourselves just flying in a circle.

After about 15-20 minutes of this, the pilot said to me, "We can't continue this, or we won't have enough gas to complete the rest of our trip. I'm going to have to go down low and start looking for an airstrip or place to land."

So the pilot lowered our altitude, and there was an airstrip almost right below us. We praised the Lord for that! The pilot did not know about this airstrip; it wasn't on his map. So, we were very happy to find one. He landed just in time because the heavy winds started up.

We weren't too far from a ranch, and that's probably why the airstrip was there. He told me to start walking to the ranch house and see if we could possibly stay the night there, while he tied down the airplane. He literally had to tie the aircraft down to prevent it from turning over or blowing away.

As he was doing that, I walked over to the ranch house. As the Lord had pre-planned, the woman that came out of the house greeted me and told me she was glad I could make it! Supper was all ready for us! This was the woman that the teenage girl had told me about, who wanted to know about Jesus. The Lord had decided that despite my schedule and what I thought I should do, He wanted me to tell this woman about Jesus Christ. So, after supper, we talked about Jesus.

At the time, I don't know if she understood exactly what I wanted her to do. I explained to her that she needed to make a decision for Christ if she wanted to be a Christian. She didn't pray; she probably didn't know how to pray. I prayed for her, but in her mind, she had made a decision.

She didn't tell me that she got saved, but everyone in the area later told me that she was a Christian and that her life had changed drastically.

Through the temporal work of medicine—clinic trips, medical attendant training, epidemics, accidents, baby deliveries, and more—God provided an eternal harvest. Nothing could have pleased Jane and Miriam more!

Chapter Twenty-Five

God Uses Literacy

"Do you understand that which you are reading?" The man answered, "How can I while no one is telling me?"
— Acts 8:30b–31a, Macushi Back Translation

"Do you understand what you are reading?" And he said, "How can I, unless someone guides me?"
— Acts 8:30b–31a

As Miriam arrived to work with the Macushi in the 1960s, she learned that the Macushi spoke an unwritten language. Early in her career, Miriam's field leaders targeted her to tackle the writing of the Macushi language. Thus, literacy became her job and her passion. Not only did she want to help missionaries learn to speak Macushi, she wanted to help the Macushi learn to read and write their own language. Pat Foster had analyzed the language very well but had never written anything out formally. When Jane took over the medical work, Miriam happily devoted more time to this endeavor.

We're busy preparing for our course in February. I'm working on my revised primers and a teacher's manual to go with them. Also a list of teaching aids for the teachers to use.

So with all this preparation, I have about 50 stencils to make, and Jane has about 30. I'll probably have some to do for Lionel's course for preachers. And then we must run them all off on the mimeograph. You see why we want an electric mimeograph? It has been purchased, I heard, and it just has to get here now. May take another year. Also, we're trying to get an electronic stencil cutter, which will reproduce photographs even. It's the best thing going outside of printing.

These courses were often held simultaneously with Jane's medical attendant training course. The preparation for this particular course had not been easy for either Miriam or Jane. It seemed trials beset them on every front.

We're getting ready to leave tomorrow for Maracanã for our training course. I believe the devil doesn't want us to have it. Lionel has been so rushed, trying to get his part ready. I've been fighting a cold for more than a week now, and I'm still blowing my nose and coughing. Jane had a bout with bursitis in her shoulder (I told her not to pull so many teeth!) but is over it now. She had to go to the doctor for the severe pain. We had clinics last week which were especially tiresome, as we gave vaccines.

Our schedule at Maracanã will be full. We'll have four class hours, plus Bible. I'll be having an hour lecture on how to teach; then we'll have an hour where the students will practice what they've learned. The third hour, I'm teaching "how to teach writing," and I will let them practice as well. The fourth hour will be practical, where they'll make their own teaching aids. They will make their syllable chart and flash cards that they'll take home with them for their own classes.

The time invested into training Macushi leaders paid off. As Miriam helped the Macushi to read and write their own language, they would take that knowledge back to their villages.

Our teachers are doing a good job, too. Theirs is perhaps the less spectacular job, but Macushis are arriving from other villages, asking for teachers in their villages, too. The government Indian agency is interested, as well. Waldemar especially has a real good class and told me of a non-Christian who is studying with him and marvels, saying, "Who would have ever thought I could read my own language!" Of course, it's the children who are learning the fastest, and it's especially fun when they can outdo their own parents! PRAY FOR OUR TEACHERS.

Our training course in Maracanã was a real blessing to us, as well as to the 22 students who attended. We taught a Bible class each day, teaching the stories of Daniel and Esther. For all but one student, it was the very first time they had heard those stories. We gave tests on the material, and it was surprising how well they did, considering the newness of the material. Jane taught the lesson in

Portuguese the first day, and the second day, I taught the same lesson in Macushi, explaining the difficult Portuguese words. It seemed to go well that way, and it is a help to them in learning Portuguese, as well.

Yesterday I took my reading materials to the Education Department for approval to start teaching Macushi in the government schools. We have three Christian school teachers who are interested in teaching the children in their own language. The supervisor of interior schools was very enthusiastic about the whole idea and said he'd present them to his superiors and have our permissions very shortly. This is a beginning of a bilingual approach to education. We, of course, are interested so that the children will be able to read Scripture in their own language with understanding.

Throughout her years on the mission field, Miriam continued teaching the Macushi not just the alphabet and phonics of their language but how to write it expressively as well. As she progressed in her learning, she recorded her findings for future generations.

This year (1981) I've accepted the task of writing up a comprehensive grammar for the Macushi language. This is a big job and will probably take 1 1/2 to 2 years' work. It should be a real help to me in knowing Macushi! Joe Hill told me the other day he got a letter from Bob Hawkins, and Bob said, "After 30 years, I think I finally know how to translate into Wai Wai!" So, I guess I have a long row to hoe! I'm just starting!

Many years later, Miriam reported on the progress of the grammar study.

> *I'm planning to go to Porto Velho for another Wycliffe workshop. I hope to finish up the grammar analysis (I've been working on for years) with a missionary there who knows Carib languages. I just hope I can finish it and get it off my mind.*

> *Desmond Derbyshire, the one who did the New Testament in Hishkariana (relatives of the Wai Wais) wants to have it published in a book about Amazon languages. He's doing a comparative study and wants Macushi included because it has many things very different from Wai Wai and Hishkariana. It's called The Amazon Language Project. It will be in two volumes, and mine will be in the second one.*

The book was published in 1991 with Miriam's paper included. On furlough, back in the United States, Miriam often attended SIL (Summer Institute of Linguistics) to further sharpen her linguistic skills.

> *My courses are very difficult. The first couple summers here, I studied how to analyze the grammar and sounds of a language. This summer, it's how to analyze meaning in a language, and how languages differ in using various kinds of grammar to express the same meaning. For example, in English, we use a lot of abstract nouns like salvation to express a whole clause—God saves us. We learn why we do that—to put into one concise noun the whole topic of our speech. So, we analyze language to find all the meaning*

components in a certain word or phrase. That way we can better put it into another language without being bound to grammar patterns of the original language.

The more Miriam understood about the Macushi language, the better she could teach it. However, those in authority didn't always share her enthusiasm for bilingual education. But slowly, over many years and with much prayer, the Lord did open up doors of opportunity for Miriam to teach the Macushi language.

For years we have prayed concerning the teaching of reading and writing in the Macushi language. I had taught some adults to a limited degree years ago, but the majority did not care to learn. What good is a translation of the Macushi Bible if there are no readers?

In July, I was invited to another seminar with Macushi school teachers. The first one was in March helping to develop a primer. I prepared a transition booklet (from Portuguese to Macushi) and taught five teachers how to read and write their own language. I also gave lectures on Macushi literature (what kind of books are needed) and taught a bit of grammar and punctuation.

We were very pleased with the interest all five showed, as well as their abilities in writing. This is an answer to many years of praying as we see the Lord opening up this opportunity to teach reading.

Again at the end of July, I have been invited to lead a bilingual education workshop with Macushi teachers. The new state director of indigenous education is a believer and a friend of the mission. He is very anxious for all the help he can get from the linguists in our mission. He wants me to help with a bilingual survey in each of the Macushi villages. Pray with us about the ongoing program of bilingual education that through it many may be able to learn to read Macushi and that the translated Scriptures would have a wide distribution. We're praising the Lord for this opportunity to work with the village school teachers. They have a lot of influence in the villages, and we long to win them to the Lord.

Of course, the primary purpose of Miriam's linguistic work was to be able to present the clear gospel to as many Macushi as possible. The teacher's training course provided an excellent opportunity for that.

I just got back from a week at Contão, a village where the Baptists work. The school invited us to have our seminar there with the school teachers. It really was a very positive time. We had four teachers from Maturuca, the strong Catholic village. They were all super-friendly, and one talked with one of our Christian teachers and said he's thinking about "changing churches." So, we're praying for them all. Rosalita, another teacher, says she has learned to speak Macushi (she grew up speaking only Portuguese) from reading the Macushi Scriptures.

The director of the school, a Believer, is interested in studying linguistics in Brasilia in January. He's not a Macushi, but was saved through the Macushi believers and now wants to work with them. I told him he should get a transfer to teach in a village in the mountains where there are no schools. He's seriously considering it. So, if he gets some training, I can turn over the coordination of the bilingual education program to him.

Also, an ex-nun, a Macushi girl who speaks only Portuguese, really got excited about learning Macushi. She also told me about the recent death of her brother from Kalazar. I told her what we are trying to do to help in this epidemic and also told her I'd help her learn Macushi. She was very impressed with the Contão church. She attended all the services and seems to be thinking quite a bit. We have lots to pray for now as a follow-up of this course.

As word of the written Macushi language spread, God began to open more doors for this avenue of ministry.

I have to get materials ready for the last week in November when a Wycliffe consultant is coming to help me. She is a Bilingual Education expert, and I need help in the organization and implementation of a program in the Macushi schools. I really need to get it going while the opportunity lasts. It's what I've waited 15 years for!

She's coming November 26th to stay for a week. I want her to see all my materials and tell her where I have problems, etc. and get her opinion and help. I also want to introduce her to the Education Department here and have her help "sell" bilingual education.

Miriam set a new goal for Macushi literacy: a bilingual dictionary. This Portuguese-Macushi tool, she felt, would be readily accepted in the schools and would greatly assist students in learning and understanding their own written language. With the help of several Macushi teachers, Miriam began this enormous task.

I spent one week in Maturuca and taught 27 school teachers more about Macushi grammar, and we worked on the dictionary project. Now I have to get it all on the computer and come up with a book! All this I feel is important in order to have Macushi who can and will read their language. They were from 19 different villages and only three Christians in the group, so we were definitely a minority this time. But I feel it went very well. I had four or five Catholics ask me when the New Testament was going to be done! Even a Catholic priest asked me. So, if I can broaden the distribution of the New Testament, the Word will be available to many more Macushi than just in "our" churches.

Dave and Grace said they will help me get the dictionary published. They will put all the new words and corrections I got into the computer. I told them maybe we'd better mark a month's time later in '92 for us to spend together and get the thing ready.

Upon its completion, however, the dictionary was not bilingual, but rather trilingual: English, Portuguese, and Macushi. In this way, the dictionary served the Macushi in both Brazil and Guyana.

Miriam's faithful work in linguistics ultimately afforded her the highlight of her entire ministry—her return to the Macushi in Guyana, 33 years after she had been forced to leave because of the revolt.

Miriam's Homecoming in Guyana!

That is how I felt as I was driven to an interior village in the north Rupununi region of Guyana. 33 years ago, Dr. Frank Davis, Pat Foster, and I visited these villages providing medical assistance with the help of the MAF pilot and plane. At that time, there were practically no believers in the area. But last week, I visited a thriving church in the village of Annai. They planned a special service just for me and invited two neighboring churches to come. There was much special music, both in English and in Macushi. What a joy to my heart to see what the Lord has done over the years. Many remembered our visits and asked me if Pat Foster could come back for a visit. They even remembered some of the jokes Pat told in Macushi.

It was a big day as dignitaries of Guyana gathered to launch the Macushi Language Project. The Ministry of Amerindian Affairs and the Ministry of Education each gave their support to implementing bilingual education in the Hinterland schools of Guyana. I saw it as a dream come true after all the linguistic work that's been done in the Macushi language. The program will begin with the Wapishana and Macushi languages, and we trust it will expand to include the Akawaio, Patamona, and other Amerindian languages.

The Lord made my trip possible through an invitation I received to teach Macushi in a workshop sponsored by a couple of international aid groups working in the area. An anthropologist is encouraging the Macushi to research their history and culture to preserve it. Of course, that involves the language, so they invited me to teach the researchers (14 Macushi women) to read and write Macushi. It was a wonderful time meeting so many Macushi, and I could spot the believers in the group. They were from 13 villages. They have a small local radio station in the area, so one afternoon they did a special program about the workshop, and, of course, wanted me to speak Macushi over the air.

After three days, we went to another village where we did the same thing, teaching about 20 Macushi school teachers to read and write their language. About half of them do not speak their language, although they understand it. This made their learning rather slow. However, all seemed anxious to begin using their language again and producing materials in Macushi. We have planned another workshop in August, and they will bring stories of the history of their village, so we can put together a history book.

I took over a big box of Macushi tracts, literature, and New Testaments. They went like hotcakes! Praise the Lord. Pray for the believers of Guyana, that my visit would give them encouragement to continue their efforts among the unsaved there.

When I first went to Guyana 35 years ago, the Macushi were ashamed of their language, and it was difficult to get them to speak it to me. There were occasions when children were punished for speaking it in the schools where English was taught by teachers from the coastland.

Though bilingualism has increased over these years, there has been a significant change of attitude towards their own language. We trust this will continue and that the New Testament in the Macushi language will be used more and more in years to come.

Miriam recounted another special visit to Guyana.

It was quite an experience to be invited back to Guyana. I got the invitation from the Brethren Church that the pastors wanted me to come over and teach them to read and write in Macushi. So, it was a wonderful experience going over and carrying on a course. Jane and I went over to Lethem, just right over the border. A whole group of pastors were there. We met every day underneath a tree and taught them how to read and write in Macushi. I was trying to get them to write more songs, as well, and become more independent in their use of the written language. It was a joy to see so many pastors of churches that had started up in that area. When I left Guyana in 1970, there weren't any churches at all, except right there in Lethem. But now there were churches all over in many areas.

Afterwards, I was invited by an NGO (non-governmental organization) group to teach reading and writing to a group of women who were interested in keeping their language alive in their villages. So, they flew me into the center of the country, a village near Annai. I stayed at a resort area that had sprung up there and slept in a cabin. They had invited the Macushi women to come from different villages, and we studied there. I gave them the trilingual dictionary I had done. I was called back two or three times to work with those women. The last time, it was actually just to show the authorities that these women were very capable of managing on their own with the dictionary—able to revise it, use it, and publish it the way they wanted it.

During that time, even though I worked with the education department and these NGOs, it was a joy to see just where the churches were in these areas. So many churches had been formed in all of these villages we used to visit. Years ago, there weren't any at all. The Lord truly worked among the Macushi.

When Miriam came to Guyana in 1967, she believed that her primary work among the Macushi would be medical in nature. But through her willing and teachable heart, God brought a written language to an entire tribe of people. He used Miriam to demonstrate His love and fulfill His plan of bringing the knowledge of Himself to the Macushi.

Chapter Twenty-Six

God Uses Translation

Because God caused men to write His Word, all of it, therefore, it is one that teaches us well about rightness. It is good also as a corrector, and it is one that causes us to live rightly very well.
—2 Timothy 3:16, Macushi Back Translation

All Scripture is given by inspiration of God, and is profitable for doctrine, for reproof, for correction, for instruction in righteousness.
—2 Timothy 3:16

Miriam first went to the mission field as a nurse, happy to be done with school and with no further educational pursuits on the horizon. But within just a few weeks, she accepted the task of writing a language course for new missionaries. As the years progressed and she continued learning through SIL courses, her linguistic skills improved. She began translating brief passages of Scripture or hymns so that she could use them in teaching. But she soon realized that the Macushi desperately needed God's Word in their native language. How else would they ever know God or learn to live in a manner pleasing to Him? Therefore, she pursued several translation goals over her years of ministry.

In 1975, shortly after Jane had joined her in ministry, Miriam wrote:

> *I have a year and a half yet before furlough, and if the Lord makes it possible, I'd like to translate Old Testament Bible stories. I have those in Genesis done, so from Exodus on, there are 148 stories. That means I'd have to do two per week in order to get them done before my furlough. I should be able to do it if the course in February is a success, and we can interest enough teachers to teach Macushi reading in the villages that I won't have to have literacy classes. While on furlough, I can revise the stories and get them ready for publication. Pray about this with me. It's a big job, but the Macushi should have at least the Old Testament stories in their language.*

She did not reach that goal by her furlough, but she persistently continued working. By 1978, she reported to her supporters.

> *The Old Testament stories have been completed! The Lord has enabled us to write 160 stories of the Old Testament in Macushi. The women here in Napoleão have given of their time faithfully each week to help in this project. We trust the revision and correction won't take so long now, and it can be ready soon to print.*

The Old Testament stories were printed while Miriam and Jane were on furlough. Jane's family, who owned and operated a print shop, was a great help with this big project.

At this time of year when the days get shorter, it seems there is too much to do in the time we have. The days seem too short. But we praise the Lord for the way He has sent us "extra hands" to help us in the job. This past month, we've been busy typing and laying out our Old Testament stories in Macushi to be printed. Jane's mother and dad have been an indispensable help to us in many ways. Now the first volume, the stories of Genesis, have been sent to Jane's sister and brother-in-law in Florida, who will print it for us at cost. Again, we thank the Lord for these "extra hands."

Eventually, Miriam realized that the Old Testament stories were not enough Scripture for the Macushi and that if the Bible were ever to be translated into their language, she would be the one to do it. She began working with Macushi church leaders on the New Testament.

I'm working with Domingos and Iracema (Domingos' wife) every afternoon on 1 and 2 Timothy and Titus. We'll be doing this for two weeks. Domingos is a deep thinker. If I suggest something, he won't accept it unless it is absolutely right. And that attribute is really good for translation. We've been working on the word "patience." It depends on the context as to how we translate it. The verse where Paul says that he's the worst of sinners, but God had mercy on him in order to show His patience to others who would believe on Him? Well, we came up with two expressions. One is, "God didn't get fed up with me, but had mercy on me." The other is, "God didn't say 'tiwi,' (that is, 'Well, leave him be then!') to me, but had mercy on me." We used the last one. It has more of the idea that God didn't give up on me. That's just one example. Some verses take 1 to 2 hours to discuss, revise, and re-revise before Domingos is satisfied.

Miriam studied diligently and took as many courses as possible to help her in the translation work. In the fall of 1980, she traveled to Surinam for a linguistic workshop with several other missionaries.

I'm working on "narrative discourse." I hope to find out how the Macushi tell a story, how they refer to the actors in the story (by nouns or pronouns), and how they include background and parenthetical information, like:

"Walking down the street, I met Mrs. Brown (Remember that lady we met the day we went downtown?). She. . ."

This will be a big help in Bible translation. Remember the passage about Herodias's daughter asking for John the Baptist's head? The way it is written, it's an explanation of the reason Herod thought Jesus was John's ghost! So, it's sort of a parenthesis, and we have to know how to put it into the <u>main</u> events of that passage in Macushi. Well, it all gets <u>very</u> complicated, but I hope I can learn something during the weeks I'm here.

She did learn those things and more.

One example of the kind of things I studied in Surinam was the use of demonstrative pronouns in Macushi. The word "mîrîrî" that means "that" can be used in a story to take the place of a noun, verb, or adjective referring back to the place where that word was already mentioned, but it cannot refer forward to a word in the story. In translating "This is the condemnation. . .," where "this" refers to what comes after, we will have to turn that verse around and end with "that is the condemnation." So, that "that" will refer back to the right thing, as it can only refer backward in Macushi.

Miriam often said, "If you know "mîrîrî," then you know half of Macushi!"

Nearly a year later, Miriam was working on a different book of the New Testament.

I've finished checking Philippians with one language helper. I'm now making up lists of questions to ask about each verse so I can be sure of the impression the verse is giving. Sometimes we can have the right words, but they can transmit a different meaning than we want, depending on their usage. Just the other day, I discovered that the word "sit" is "ereuta" in Macushi, and it can be used in the following four ways:

1) Plain—I *sit*

2) The light *sits*—a'ka ereuta—This is when it's just beginning to get light in early morning. At first, it's just one spot that's light, and then suddenly, the world is lit up. That's "the light sits."

3) God *sits* your heart—This means God gives you peace

from anxiety.

4) We will *sit* down the singing—This means we will stop singing now.

So, you see, even though I think I know what a word means, it could also mean several other things that I don't know!

I've got to start preparing for James, too. I'm trying to memorize it before I start the exegesis. I read it at least once a day now. I only have one small commentary on it. I'll read that through and hope I can borrow some others.

Miriam found that a concentrated course of study on each book of the Bible with various Macushi church leaders proved to be an effective translation tool.

During this three-week course, I had an hour every day to teach the book of Philippians. I invited those from here (Manoá) who preach. We went through it verse by verse. I gave background (translated Acts 16 to do it), made a map to show them where Philippi was and where Paul was when he wrote it. Also, who the first Christians were in that church. Then we did some translation checking— all adding their opinions on terms to use for "believer," "gospel," "deacons," "bishops," "grace," etc. So, it included various word studies as well. Then I gave various sermon outlines and topics from the book for them and an overall outline of the book. I gave each of them a copy of the translation and had them underline all the times "joy" is mentioned—stuff like that which was entirely new. Well, five men attended every day! I wrote two songs in Macushi from it. Philippians 4:4, and a part in chapter two talking about Christ's incarnation and His exaltation. The church leader here was very interested. It's the first course he's attended like this where he could write down notes and keep up pretty well. (I kept notes very limited!) I gave a list of key verses they should memorize, too.

Oh, I was going to say about Abel, the leader here, he has made more progress in these two years than anyone else! When I first came to Brazil, he was only a nominal Christian and couldn't read a word! I spent time in his village in Napoleão, and he could have cared less. He was sick most of the time and had no interest. But the Lord used the sickness and really worked in his heart. Since we came here, he's taught himself to read and write. (He had studied with me before a bit but kept dropping out.) He's still a slow reader, but he's a very deep thinker and he really thinks about what he reads and comes up with good thoughts in his sermons. We've also seen progress in his wife.

Miriam pressed on with translation, even through the difficult places.

I battled today with "being born by the Word," and us being "first fruits!" How do you translate that understandably without writing a thesis on Old Testament sacrifices? Well, I decided the emphasis was that God made us His children through our believing His Word (which is truth), that we would be exclusively His out of all the ones (people) He made. Just like the old ones who worshipped God used to bring the first part of their crops to God because they were His. Well, that's sort of the way it reads now. Do you think I polluted it too much? It's really hard to try to put yourself into a "Macushi head" to think like they do!

God provided more helpers for Miriam along her journey of translating the New Testament. Waldemar, a Macushi believer and preacher, and Marge Crofts, a Wycliffe translation consultant, came to work with her for a time.

Miriam has invited Waldemar, the present pastor of the church in Napoleão to work with her full-time as assistant translator. He will be the expert in the Macushi language, and Miriam will be his commentary source (as she has the wealth of commentaries in her language). He will bring his family (7 children), build his house, and farm a piece of the land to augment his salary.

Waldemar and his family did move, which turned out to be a big help for Miriam in the translation of the New Testament.

It looks like we'll finish Acts! We worked on the first half of chapter 27 today. We are really fascinated by the ship wreck. I've been explaining all about ships, anchors, sails, lifeboats, wind directions, etc., to this land-lubber! He's had to come up with terms for everything, including ship—276 people in a canoe just wouldn't make much sense on an ocean! The word they use for ship means "a fire container." It comes from the old steamships. I guess their Macushi ancestors saw the smoke stacks on ships out to sea at Georgetown. So, the word has come to mean ship.

I'm traveling to Maracanã for clinics at the end of July. I want to go through what we've done on Acts and check it with several versions for omissions and additions. Also, I want one of the men there to write out for me a translation back into Portuguese—without looking at the Portuguese version at all. This will help me to see what kind of meaning he's getting out of it all.

Waldemar was reading it to his family at night, and he came back to me and said, "You know, even my kids are understanding it!" So, I think we're on the right track. If I can just keep on! I feed him all the helps, make the exegetical decisions that need to be made, and explain the meaning as clearly as possible—noting also grammatical things in Portuguese that are real problems in Macushi— that is, they have to be handled very differently.

For example—the word "personally"—talking to someone personally—Waldemar misunderstood and the translation came out "He talked as a person (or as a human)." So, he's learning Portuguese along the way, too! And I'm learning Macushi!

Jane also contributed to the translation of Macushi materials, even while she was on furlough.

Jane got 500 copies of the book of John printed. She's going to print the volume of various epistles (James, Philippians, Philemon, 1, 2, 3 John, and Jonah), 500 copies, too. Her dad is doing the songbook—1,000 copies for just the cost of materials. She's gotten three different ladies' groups at her church putting all the pages together and putting on cloth tape on the back of John. I told her she'll have to get the whole church together to package up the books for mailing!!!

You know she's bought us a computer and solar panel. It sure will save lots of work. We'll be able to get the translation— right to the final copy—all ready to be printed using that computer.

Indeed, their computer was the only one in the world that spoke Macushi!

By the spring of 1987, God began to raise up financing for the Macushi New Testament.

I've been hearing regularly from Collingdale Church about their project in raising funds for the Macushi Bible translation. Well, on April 12 they will introduce it. John Miesel will be the special speaker, and they want to show a video tape from here. So, if John brings a camera when he comes, we'll try and take a film to send back with him. The church has all sorts of ideas for publicity—posters, pledge cards, etc.

The further along the translation of the New Testament went, the more interruptions and difficulties Miriam and her helpers experienced. Computer problems, health issues, and various conflicts beset them, but they persevered in order to bring God's Word to Macushi hearts.

It's been a while since we gave an update on the translation project. Waldemar continues to work daily, even when I'm involved in other things. We are translating Revelation at present. Many have asked how many books have been completed to date. We praise the Lord that it is now easier to list those yet to be done: Romans, Galatians, 2 Corinthians, Hebrews, 1 and 2 Peter, and Jude. There are only seven more.

We are happy to report that the funds for printing the whole New Testament (possibly in 1990 or 1991) are being raised. One-third of it is in hand, and more has come in pledges. We praise the Lord for the faithfulness of His people in the First Baptist Church of Collingdale, PA.

Progress on this big project was slow but steady.

Well, seems like there are some big changes ahead. I want to get as much translation done as possible this year, but I doubt I can finish. I was thinking it would take two years anyway. We're working on 1 Peter now. Just finished Revelation. But even after this, I'll have all the revision to do, and I do need someone besides Waldemar to do it. I need to check each book with at least three other Macushi. So, there's a mountain of work to be done. We are praying about another family coming here and possibilities of me going elsewhere, too, to check some work.

As Miriam patiently continued working on the translation, she also fulfilled her other responsibilities to the mission and the Macushi. But God also was working behind the scenes to raise the funds for the printing of the New Testament upon its completion and to provide Miriam with the needed Macushi speakers for the checking and revision of the work.

God abundantly answered many prayers when the entire UFM Macushi team, which had grown to 18 members, devised a new plan to accomplish their goals and free up Miriam's time so that she could devote herself entirely to the translation project.

> *The Lord heard our cry for help and sent us a team of workers. This past month, we met together for strategy plans. Priorities were set, and the work divided up. It was agreed upon that the Bible translation was top priority. Therefore, Miriam has been relieved of all other responsibilities and relocated to Maracanã. There she will devote herself full-time to translation checking.*
>
> *Dave and Grace Crompton, located in Maracanã, offered to help in this task. They will include this in their language learning. Dave will check the Macushi text theologically. This is to make sure we are not teaching wrong doctrine.*
>
> *Miriam will be moving to Maracanã the month of April. She is very encouraged to have the Cromptons' help and is looking forward to getting a lot accomplished. They will begin with the gospels and hope to get a lot of feedback from the Indians. She is presently working with Waldemar trying to finish up the book of Romans before she moves.*

This plan helped Miriam move rapidly through the remaining translation and the checking of the New Testament.

> *Well, have been here in Maracanã for about a month*

now, and I feel I am getting a lot of work done. Am almost through Matthew with the first Macushi doing a comprehension check. I want to do it at least one more time with another person.

I also am doing an exegetical check with Dave. He tells me what the Greek is really saying, and I try and see if the Macushi word is anywhere near to that meaning. Sometimes it is!! Ha.

Then we are battling around key terms and what we will use for them—example: Kingdom of Heaven—we've decided to translate it differently depending upon the meaning in focus in that particular context. If it's focusing on Christ as King, it will be one way; if it's focusing on the blessings of the kingdom, being a part of it, we'll have to do it another way. In Matthew, we changed pearls to diamonds because the Macushi have no idea in the world what a pearl is—but most of them have mined diamonds! Again, this occurs in teaching passages, and the meaning is a gem of great value.

Well, this is what I'm spending my full time on. I think I'm getting to know Matthew quite well! I also have to check all the connecting words like for, therefore, because, and then, straightway, to make sure the clauses have the same type of relation in Macushi.

I'm making visits to non-Christian homes most afternoons and reading parts of Matthew to them to get their reactions. The reception has been very good so far, and as they relax more with me, I hope to get more feedback on some of the passages.

In 1992, while Jane was back in the States for medical tests, Miriam worked furiously on the translation. She was further "aided" when she slid down an embankment and broke her wrist, as she could no longer do any manual labor. Now she was free to focus solely on the Macushi New Testament.

> *In translation, I went through the book of Mark, checking for omissions and additions. Also, finished my checking of Matthew and now am on chapter 10 in John. I had passed out four copies of John to four different church leaders and asked them to check it. I had gotten them back with their corrections, so am going through it now to see if they are viable or not. It's amazing to me how many times I can go through a book and still find things to change!*

Even before completing the translation, Miriam began teaching the Macushi leaders how to use God's Word in teaching and application.

> *I'm teaching the leaders how to prepare messages in Macushi. Also, am working with some of them checking translation. I have the 5 T's (1, 2 Thess., 1, 2 Tim., Titus) in pretty fair shape now. 1 Thessalonians I sent to a Wycliffe consultant in Brasilia, and she sent back her comments and recommendations for changes. So, I worked through that, and I sent her Philippians now. Also, I sent out 5 copies of Mark I have finished revising to different Macushi pastors for them to read and send back their comments. I*

had already done that with John. So, now I'm trying to get my revisions of Matthew and Luke done and print out five copies of those to send around, too.

Have started the revision of Romans—which is hard, slow going! Paul's sentence structure is really complicated!

So—the present situation is that I'm fairly satisfied with the gospels. The 5 T's, James, and Philippians are good. I don't know how much more I can get done in the next 6 weeks—maybe 1, 2 Peter, Eph., and Col.—we'll see!

One more year to go on the revision of the Macushi New Testament for publication. It's still a question as to how much time it will take, but I plan to spend my entire furlough working on it with the help of a professional consultant.

Miriam and Jane spent 1994 in the United States, working diligently on the translation of the Macushi New Testament. They lived in Alabama, near Miriam's parents, in a house provided by Miriam's sister, Nancy. Miriam, of course, was involved with the actual translation, checking, and revising work. Jane was trained through Wycliffe on several desktop publishing programs, in order to print trial versions of the Scriptures for the Macushi to see.

Your prayers, support, and letters continue to be a real encouragement to us as we see the Lord work here in the North! (Alabama really is north of Brazil.) The love of many friends and family in helping us set up shop in this lovely home has been a special treat from the Lord. . .How wonderful to be so loved!

Since Jane was learning desktop publishing, the ladies' prayer letters took on a newsletter format, called "BurAbbott's Cabbage Patch News." In each issue, they would give an update on their translation work and the Macushi churches in Brazil, Jane's health, an interesting observation from their ministry to the Amerindians, and a question and answer section.

> More and more we realize the Enemy doesn't want the translation to be completed. There have been repeated interruptions and delays. We ask for your faithful prayers specifically in this regard.

> Miriam sent the manuscript of Matthew to be checked by a consultant in Brazil last September. She wrote about it and received no answer. We found out later that this consultant sent two letters to Miriam concerning this check, and the letters were apparently lost in the mail. We recently found out by fax that she referred it to another consultant in Dallas. . .a lot closer than Brazil. Pray that there be no more difficulties in checking the gospels.

> Miriam has confronted some difficult problems in Hebrews. She isn't completely satisfied with the word we use for priest. It means "One who prays." But how do we get a more meaningful term? "One who offers sacrifices" would be a good choice, but how do we say sacrifice? "Something given to be burned to worship God" would be good. But can that big phrase be used to translate priest? "One who offers what people bring to be killed and burnt in worship to God," what a mouthful! We don't want to have to provide a wheelbarrow for the Macushi to carry their huge Bible!

Jane began to introduce the manuscripts of various epistles into her new desktop publisher program. When she converted it from the program Miriam has been using, we discovered there is a problem. It is omitting the first letter of words sporadically. So, she had to get off a help fax to our consultant. We are waiting for an answer to the problem.

There were many other minor problems. But Miriam and Jane knew that the solutions were to be found in God, so they asked for prayers and trusted the outcome with Him. Their prayer letter informed their supporters of some of the struggles through which they had to work.

What makes Romans & Hebrews especially difficult to translate into the Macushi language?

In Romans, Paul talks much about the law and uses legal terms to describe man's position to God. Judgment, guilt, condemnation, justification, and reconciliation are difficult concepts for a people who have no legal system as we know it. Their chiefs do not convict nor condemn people of crimes. It's a matter of being accepted socially or bearing the brunt of gossip which brings shame or ostracism from society.

In Hebrews, the writer uses the Jewish religious system to explain the fulfillment and completeness of Christ's ministry. The Macushi have no priests and don't make sacrifices. But they do have a common practice of using a go-between to conduct business or gain favors.

Pray for us as we seek to make these most important teachings meaningful to the Macushi reader.

Through all of the ups and downs of ministry, God's sovereignty and grace shone through in Miriam's and Jane's persistence and joy.

"I have told you these things, so that in me you may have peace. In this world you will have **trouble**. *But take heart! I have overcome the world" (John 16:33).*

While we as Christians know the ultimate victory is ours in Christ, it is an encouragement to see day by day how the Lord is working all things together for our good and His glory. So, we thought we'd let you know the answers to your prayers.

Though *the enemy attacks and brings frustration by faulty machinery—as in the case of our new laser printer. And this didn't happen in Brazil! But it was a blessing to see how the Lord provided answers and helps from others to get it going again. Jane now has finished two Macushi tracts that will be sent to a Macushi pastor in Guyana.*

Though *the enemy attacks and Jane's health seems to go up and down like a see-saw, we praise Him for His strength and encouragement.* ***Though*** *she finds it difficult to sit and work at computer projects, we are grateful for the significant contribution she is making to the Macushi translation. Miriam is glad she finally has a "team."*

Though *the enemy attacks with frustration as Miriam checks translation, it is a joy to see how the Lord works* *in giving clarity of thinking and discipline in keeping at it. Praise Him that Hebrews is now in the hands of Miriam's consultant Catherine Rountree. Revelation and 1 & 2 Peter were checked. Dave Crompton (our coworker) recently sent his comments and suggestions for correction on 1 & 2 Thessalonians. They were very good ones, and those books are now much better for them.*

__Though__ the enemy attacks in the area of our computer software, we praise Him for the help Jane has gotten from Wycliffe and from her brother. She now has almost completed producing the epistles from Galatians to Philemon with various formats in one volume.

__Though__ the enemy attacks all who are serving the Lord, we thank each one of you who have been faithful in prayer and support these many years, in spite of all obstacles.

In 1995, with the trial version of the Macushi New Testament finally finished, the missionaries made plans to return to Brazil.

Jane and Miriam plan to stay in Brazil for six months to check the major revisions we have done in this past year and a half. We don't know how long it will take, but we've decided on this time period to see how Jane will do in Brazil now that she is taking medication specific for Lupus. Also, she needs to see her doctor every six months.

Pray for this trial version, that it may be used. As the Macushi have never been accustomed to reading the Word in their own language, pray that the Holy Spirit will teach them to use it—in church, at home, in personal devotions, at work, in evangelizing neighbors and relatives, in memorizing it, meditating upon it, and proclaiming it both near and far.

One very positive side result of our recent work was the formation of a translation committee. It was Raimundo's idea, suggesting we meet in the month of July at Maracanã, his village. We will invite a representative from each of the churches. There we hope to check some of the revision we have done, as well as make final decisions on various aspects of the translation.

Looking back, Miriam knew that the translation committee had been a key element in the Macushi New Testament translation.

At this point before getting into any final manuscripts, we needed input from people from various age groups, villages, genders, the people from mountains, the people from the plains, that spoke a bit different dialect because they were the ones that needed to decide how the language was to be written. We had explained to them how that even though they spoke differently, the language had to be written the same. Just like in Portuguese, people spoke differently in different regions, but the way it was written was the same. So, they were the ones that had to decide. It proved to be very profitable.

Day in and day out, in rain or shine, with helpers or alone, Miriam persisted in the translation.

I am busy getting ready for our encounter next week. On July 4, several men and their wives are coming to help check the New Testament.

When I get back to the States in September, I will have lots of computer work to do to add all the corrections that I've gotten here. I also have all the introductions corrected, and the glossary is almost all translated now. I should get it back on this clinic trip, as I left it in Napoleão for two men to work on there. Dave and Grace are on furlough in Tampa, Florida, so we can work together in the fall. They are doing a "read through" of the whole New Testament, and so I hope to get together with them one or two times during the fall to work on various problems. Then in January, I can start working with Catherine. I have Romans, Matthew, Mark, and Acts to check with her. And she said she'll stay with me to the bitter end. So, she'll probably help me with all the final decisions.

Well, this next month should tell me if I am anywhere near ready to publish. I think I am, and I want these checks to verify the fact. There is a certain aspect that it will never be "done." But I feel the next revision will have to be the Indians themselves. Maybe when we get the Old Testament done, we will be able to revise the New again.

The workload intensified as the time in Brazil grew short. Both Miriam and Jane threw their efforts into the translation. They were amazed and blessed by how the Lord directed and helped them every step of the way.

Our Translation Seminar has gone unusually well. We were surprised at the way the Lord has been in control over the ones He had planned to use. We had wanted to get checked the 7 books that I had revised in the US last year. Well, we've been able to check almost the whole New Testament. They didn't do it exactly like I wanted them to do it, but I feel that there is a large percentage of comprehension. We have changed many things to make it clearer and more natural Macushi.

It has cost us a lot though. As Jane says, if we keep their stomachs full, they will keep working.

Evangelista, who is a Bible school graduate, also is participating. It is amazing to us how much "church vocabulary" he uses fluently in Portuguese, but yet doesn't understand it. Portuguese is his first language, but he understands Macushi completely, though he just started speaking it since he's been grown. I have been pleased to see how they are understanding some of the most difficult doctrines of Scripture since it is in Macushi.

Valdisa, the pastor's wife said that a passage that Jane was checking in her group spoke to her heart how that she needs to leave behind the elementary things and begin to eat the meat of the Word. It's been a joy to work with them this month. Jane too has really enjoyed it, though it has been a very heavy workload.

We divided the group into two and she checks with one group, and I check with the other. In the afternoons, they are each assigned a book to check and they read it aloud to another and see if they understand it. Then they bring in their corrections and questions the next day, and we all meet together early to make the final decisions on their corrections as a group. We usually take a break about 10 o'clock for coffee and then divide into our two groups afterward until noon. In the afternoons, Jane goes over with me the things her group didn't understand, and I also put all the corrections in the computer. So, it's been a long month, but a good one.

We are getting anxious to return to the US. I guess we are both getting old and appreciate the conveniences more than ever. Jane especially, as she has so much arthritis now, appreciates warm showers and an inside bathroom. I appreciate the bright lighting.

Now in the final leg of this translation marathon, Jane and Miriam had earned a rest, by all human calculations. But they heard only the voice of their Savior, and they earnestly sought to bring praise and glory to Him.

We were challenged as we contemplated our recent trip to Macushi villages. It was filled with difficulties that gradually turned into complaints. Hotter weather, longer, rockier trails, deeper mud, peskier insects, and higher mountains used to be challenges to us in younger years.

We came to the conclusion that we were too old for this type of traveling ministry. However, opportunities presently abound in Macushi land. The churches need encouragement to reach out to neighboring villages, ranches, mines, and even other tribes.

Then we heard a sermon that challenged us to remember our Creator's Call as more important than our Creature Comforts. Pray for us as we seek to allow His strength to replace our weakness. "The one who calls you is faithful, and he will do it" (1 Thessalonians 5:24).

In early 1996, Miriam and Jane once again returned to the United States with a checklist of items to complete before the Macushi New Testament could be printed.

The Countdown Is Getting Lower. . .

10. Not only for the coming of the Lord but also for the publishing of the Macushi New Testament. We have been careful not to set dates for either, but we are closer now to setting one for the publishing date. The tasks yet to be done still seem numerous to us, but at least we are attacking them in manageable bits.

9. Comprehension Checks – testing with Macushi speakers to see if they are understanding the truths of the New Testament. (This was done last year in Brazil.)

8. Exegetical Checks – with a translation consultant (Wycliffe missionary Catherine Rountree) to see if it is accurate. Books left to do are Matthew and Mark.

7. Introduction Checks – a short paragraph of content summary for each book.

6. Glossary Check – an appendix explaining names, cultural aspects, etc. that are unfamiliar to Macushi culture.

5. Global Check – using a specially developed program by Wycliffe, we can make spelling changes, and check key terms and parallel passages for consistency.

4. Footnotes – these need to be keyed in as yet.

3. Typesetting – Ted Gollar at Wycliffe in Dallas will be doing this as his schedule permits. Probably this summer we will all be ready. This means a 2–3 month stay in Dallas to do the proofreading.

2. Publishing – Dr. Eugene F. Rubingh from International Bible Society will be seeing to this. We are now applying for the various permissions needed for the Portuguese version we want to use, as well as the pictures and maps.

1. Completed – ???? 1996!

We continue to count on your prayers, so pray us through each of these steps to the finish line!

On March 14, 1996, Catherine Rountree approved the New Testament for publication. On April 13, Miriam and Jane moved to Dallas for the typesetting to be done. Since they were the ones that knew Macushi, they also had to be the ones to proofread it. Despite their exhaustion, they were thrilled at the potential that finishing the New Testament held for the Macushi. The preface to the New Testament (below, translated back into English from Macushi) explains that beautifully.

A Word Beforehand

As we are here, there are a lot of messages on this earth, but this is the most important one of them all. They call it God's book. The Brazilians call it the Bible, and the reason we say it is the most important of them all is because human beings did not make it. But the Lord God himself made it. The reason I say that is His Spirit came upon people and caused them to write the things that are here. (2 Tim. 3:16) And those things that are in this book, they are not made-up things, but those things that God wants human beings to know, they are there in the book.

And this book you see here, this is not all of God's book because God's book has two parts. This is one of them only. The first big piece told things to us about the first message God made for human beings. The Brazilians call it the Old Testament. And that means the old agreement. And the second big piece tells us what is the new agreement with humans. Brazilians call it the New Testament and this means new agreement, that's what you have here in the Macushi language.

Finally, the big announcement came:

Did you hear about the big celebration? On July 18, 1996, we officially signed off the Macushi New Testament. That means we agreed to make no further changes in the text. (That's for this printing.) We were thrilled and encouraged as many here at Wycliffe congratulated us warmly. Then on Sunday, our Sunday School teacher made the big announcement, and we all stood and sang the doxology! We just wish we could share this joy with all of you, our partners and co-laborers in this project!

The New Testament is now being finished up at Wycliffe and will be sent in a few weeks to a printing company called "Clays" in England that specializes in the printing of Bibles. They should be done with it by mid-October or early November and then will ship them to Brazil. We can expect it there by the first of the year.

Rejoice with us that this huge project has been completed!

It seemed that Satan was not too happy about the Macushi New Testament reaching the villages and hands of the Macushi, but God's timing was just perfect!

Certainly your prayers were answered concerning the Macushi New Testament! The shipment of Bibles arrived in Manaus on January 25th, but it took a long time to get all the documents required to get them out of customs and trans-shipped by truck to Boa Vista. After two months of work and prayer, they arrived in Boa Vista. Here we had more paper work to do to get them out of customs. But finally, they were released on April 10th and we hauled two truckloads to Serra Grande for storage in the new hospital building. We rejoiced that they had been released in time for the dedication service on April 12th. So, we have tangible evidence of your prayers and faithful gifts over the years. Pray that these books will be used by many Macushi.

Many of you have asked us about the Macushi New Testament dedication ceremony that was held in Boa Vista. Many churches were represented, and the news of the publication has gone out in many different directions.

D-Day (Dedication Day)

Not many Macushi from the interior could come, but we did take the ones from around here at Serra Grande. They had prepared special music and sang in Macushi and Portuguese. The president of our mission, Edson da Silva led the meeting and gave a challenge for the work of translation, showing how many language groups in the world are without any Scripture and how many here in Brazil have no part of God's Word in their language.

Pastor Paulo Leite of the church in Rio de Janeiro was the special speaker. His church has prayed for years for the Macushi and will support a radio program in the Macushi language to be aired on Trans World Radio. Miriam's pastor of the church that raised the funds for printing gave the prayer of dedication and presented a copy of the New Testament to Waldemar, Miriam's co-translator for 5 years. We praise the Lord for His faithfulness through the years to bring this project to completion. You are a great part of this through your prayers and faithful gifts. Let's continue to seek the Lord's help and blessing as we now use this tool He provided.

Recently, Pastor Aluizio, one of our better preachers, told me how much he is enjoying the New Testament. He said,

"But sister, I now see how many lies I was telling in my preaching!" He meant that he was not understanding his Portuguese version very well, and now that he can read it in Macushi, he is seeing how often he misunderstood and misinterpreted the Scripture.

Another Macushi man commented, "Yes, my relatives and I have been reading this New Testament, and it is really clear. That old one we had was very difficult to understand, but this one is just the way we talk!"

Although the translating of the Macushi New Testament had cost thousands of dollars and untold hours of study and tedious work, no one doubted its worth. Miriam and Jane knew that its true value was eternal, measured only by their eternal Lord.

A note from Pastor Messick, First Baptist Lamplighter (the church that financed the Macushi New Testament Printing):

During the Centennial celebration of First Baptist Church in 1987, our church launched a major project. The Macushi Project set a goal to raise the funds needed to publish the New Testament in the native language of the Macushi Indians of Northern Brazil. Our missionary in Brazil, Miriam Abbott, had been working on the translation for many years. When the project was complete, First Baptist Church had raised just over $27,000. In the years while the translation was being finished, the interest brought the total to $40,000.

In April of 1997, I was joined by Esther Kamphausen and Betty Gerow in order to represent the church, and travel to Brazil to dedicate and present the Macushi New Testaments to the Indians. Upon arrival, Esther and Betty traveled to Serra Grande. At the same time, I stayed with a Christian family in Boa Vista to prepare to fly out to the bush villages the next day. With brand new Macushi Bibles in hand, the next morning we flew to three villages to present the New Testament to tribal leaders. What a privilege to present these brothers and sisters-in-Christ with God's Word in their own language for the first time!

This past December we received a ministry update from Miriam after her recent trip to Brazil. It was so exciting to hear what the Lord has been doing in the lives of the Macushi Christians. The older generation has remained faithful to Christ. And now the Lord has raised up new generations of Macushi Indians who are traveling to additional villages to share God's Word. In a direct quote from the update, Jane writes: "And so the work in which you have partnered with us continues on. . .generation after generation."

One day we will worship side by side with Macushi Indians around the throne of God. How blessed it will be to meet with those who came to Christ through Bibles that First Baptist Church helped to provide!

Chapter Twenty-Seven
God Uses the Macushi Church

And on this rock I am making My church; they are My people. The ones in My church are strong, greater than everything. They have become greater than death, even while Satan is persecuting them.
—Matthew 16:18, Macushi Back Translation

And I also say to you that you are Peter, and on this rock I will build My church, and the gates of Hades shall not prevail against it.
—Matthew 16:18

Macushi people began to be saved, and baby churches were started all across the savannah. While this was exciting in many ways, it also created a heavy load of work for the missionaries. Sin crept in easily, too, because the people were not able to read, nor did they have the Scripture in their own language at first. Several missionary families served the Macushi throughout the years, but none of the village churches had a full-time pastor.

Miriam and Jane chose to live in the Macushi villages to establish churches and help address these problems. At various times in their ministry, they lived in Maracanã, Napoleão, Manoá, Flexal, and many other villages. They taught the Bible regularly, often holding two or three Bible studies per week on top of the Sunday services. They taught the people Christian music and how to sing in parts. They taught the women how to teach other women and children. They even taught the men what and how to preach. Of course, this slow process required much patience.

One thrill we recently experienced was teaching a bilingual Bible study on the Church. At Napoleão, the leaders are continuing the study on their own, learning the key verses we had translated into Macushi. A young fellow from that church just got out of the army and wants to serve the Lord as a missionary. Pray for him, especially concerning his training. There is no Bible school close by, and to send him away is difficult because of the differences in culture. How can we train Macushi young people to serve the Lord and teach the Word to their own people? Pray with us as we seek the Lord to provide for them.

Another encouraging thing we've heard since being here is that the Christian men talk among themselves about what they would like to do. We heard that Waldemar (the leader here) desires to be a missionary, not just here, but in other places. He has a real thirst to study the Word. We started a New Testament survey course on Saturday nights. We have 17 studying. We need a Bible school. We need a Bible (in Macushi)!

Before long, the Napoleão church showed more signs of spiritual growth and fruit.

Today is Sunday, and comparatively quiet for a Sunday. We had church from 8 a.m. to about 10 a.m. We've started a Sunday school, dividing into two classes so far: men and women. I'm teaching Waldemar and his wife Josefa to teach. Waldemar has a natural gift, so he really doesn't need my help at all, but it helps me to have him here in teaching his wife. They study the lesson with me after church on Sunday and then study by themselves during the week. On Saturday afternoons, they come and give me the lessons they are going to teach. Josefa has never done this before, so is very unsure of herself. But she is intelligent and is catching on fast. Her reading is painfully slow though, so I have to work with her on that.

Then at 3 p.m. we have "choir practice." I'm teaching the Macushi to sing in two parts. We're going to work up some good songs for the Christmas conference. We also sing Sunday evenings in church.

Recently, we made a trip with several (about 12) of the believers to the village of Raposa, where many have relatives. We praise the Lord for the good reception we had. There were about 300 people gathered to hear God's Word. Though no decisions were made, many listened intently as Waldemar preached: "Come unto me all ye that labor and are heavy laden, and I will give you rest." The Christians were encouraged as they shared individually with their relatives what God has done for them. Pray for this village, that many will turn to the Lord.

No matter what new ways the missionaries used to reach more

Macushi, God seemed to always bless and prosper.

We had a youth retreat here at Manoá over Carnival (Mardi Gras). A new Brazilian pastor who recently arrived in Boa Vista is interested in working with young people. He brought 26 out here to have a retreat. A lot of them were not saved and seemed like a rowdy bunch. But he had excellent control over them. One was saved during the time here. However, they were all higher-class Brazilians—most from the south—and so were very different culturally from our Macushi young people. Our kids just sort of sat with their mouths open awed at this crowd!

However, since that time, one young fellow wants to start a youth group here for the kids. He started Saturday night and had four attend. He invited me to lead a Bible study next Saturday in Macushi. So, I'm real glad to see this started. As I said to Jane—there is some difference! When we arrived here last July, this same fellow was going to wild parties and drinking. Now he's the leader of the youth group! Domingos also wasn't even coming to church when we came. Now, since Christmas, he's been coming faithfully and participating.

Lionel Gordon and Joe Butler and three Indians took a survey trip on horseback from Macedonia up to Blue Creek, visiting many villages all along the way and preaching. This month we'll go to Mato Grosso where the men got a really good reception. The chief and all the people were enthusiastic about hearing God's Word. Waldemar will be going with us this month to preach there. Another village is

Flexal, where we'll probably go next month. Waldemar said he could hardly believe the reception they got there. One man there has been telling the people for years, "Someday the Christians will come here, and when they do, I want us all to receive their words well!" So, when the men went there, they all said they knew they would come. So, you see how the Lord is preparing hearts in the mountains. After Pat and June come back from furlough, Jane and I may move up to one of those villages with a Christian Indian family. They said at Flexal they already have a house that we could use if we wanted to stay there.

This week I'm going to start preparing sermons from Philippians for the men here to teach. It's hard work because they have to be so simple. I've usually made them too hard and complicated. Instead of the American three-point sermon, I have to reduce it to one point! And even then, it's hard to get that point across! If I were a man, I could just preach and be done with it—but since I don't believe in women preachers, I have to let them do it and teach them how!

As people began to be saved and grow in the Lord, various aspects of Christian living were addressed through the church. Miriam and Jane were thrilled to see God working in Macushi hearts.

Today we got news over the radio that Pat and June are coming Friday and so planned a wedding for Pat to perform while here. This wedding is important for this church, as it's the first Christian wedding to be performed here. After all the moral problems this church has suffered this year, we feel it's a victory. These Macushi will be married according to God's Word! We hope it will encourage the other young people to want to get married this way.

It seemed that Satan tried desperately to thwart the progress that was being made among the native people. Miriam, Jane, and the Macushi looked for the Lord to work in the midst of the trials.

A young fellow, 21, died the week before we came interior. He was a new Christian. They sent someone with a message calling the plane in for him on a Tuesday. The plane came on Friday, and he went unconscious that day and died on Sunday in the hospital. Sounded to me like he got hold of something poisonous. But he gave a real good testimony and pleaded with his wife to accept the Lord because he was sure he had found the right road!

So, we are still praying for her. She first went to live with some unsaved relatives but didn't like it because she didn't want her son to learn their ways. So, her sister-in-law invited her to live with them. She accepted (an unheard-of thing in Macushi culture), and she's living with a fine Christian family. Last night in church, after a long service, one of the men stood up and said he thought the church should give her 30,00 cruzeiros every month to help her buy things she needs for her children. We heard the "treasurer's report" yesterday, and they have 140,00 cruzeiros that they've collected since January! I was happy to hear they wanted to do that. They are all praying for her salvation. She's really listening and interested, but I don't know if she really understands yet what it's all about. She's a very sweet, quiet girl. Her name is Bem Bem. Her two children are a 3-year-old boy and a 4 or 5-month-old girl.

Somehow, amid the myriad projects, responsibilities, and difficulties, Miriam and Jane found time to make a Macushi songbook, with several songs written by the Indians. The number of missionaries working with Jane and Miriam rose and fell throughout the years, but God always provided just the right helpers at just the right time.

Our staff here is increasing. Ivo is in his second week of language study. I'm teaching him using the course I made up while on furlough. He's a big help here. We told him (he's single) that we would feed him and he wouldn't have to do the dishes if he took care of the lamp (filling it with kerosene), pulled up water from the well for us (2x per day), charged the battery 2x per week, and took care of the radio contact each morning. Yep, you guessed it. We gave him all the jobs we hate! Ha. But he seems to enjoy it. He's an electrical engineer and is very handy at mechanical things. He has also fixed our outhouse, so it doesn't leak inside everytime it rains. And he loves gardening, so each afternoon he's hoeing, planting, etc. He's showing us "how to do it!" He's sleeping with one of the Indian families and studies in the church. So far, we are really enjoying his help, and he is very enthusiastic about learning Macushi. He's had SIL (linguistic) training in Brasilia. He's one of 7 children and the only Christian of the bunch. He was saved when he went to São Paulo to study through a group of European missionaries (Swiss). So, he's even had experience working with foreigners!

Cecília is arriving tomorrow. She is at least six feet tall and makes Jane look like a midget! Jane really likes to feel small! Ha. Anyway, Cecília is a teacher and loves to work with children. We're going to have her give some children's classes for the two weeks she's here.

In the mornings, I'm finishing up the language course. It has 17 units. Eight of them are all done and mimeographed, and that's what Ivo and Jane are using now. Each unit is a week of study. So, I finished unit 9 last week, and am working on 10 this week, trying to do one a week till I finish.

In my "spare time" I'm trying to teach Sunday school teachers and preachers how to prepare lessons and sermons.

In the fall of 1982, Miriam and Jane turned their attention to the village of Maracanā. There they resumed their usual work of training and discipling the Macushi to become medical attendants and church leaders.

Nine men, some leaders of Macushi churches and some new Christians from our outreach in new villages, attended a short course in Boa Vista during the month of October. Some of our missionary men taught the course. On the weekends, they ministered in various locations, one of which is a Wapishana Indian village whose chief came to town and asked our mission to come. He and some of his immediate family are Christians and he is concerned about his village. Pray with us for an ongoing ministry in this new village of Truaru—only 59 kilometers from Boa Vista. We trust the Lord will continue to do His work in the hearts of these nine students as they have returned to their villages.

As 1983 began, the missionaries saw God expanding the borders of their influence. Jane and Miriam's ministry took on an itinerant flare.

Jane and Miriam—Where are they now?

In Maracanã?

From the beginning of December to the end of February, we spent working with the church in Maracanã. Jane taught various ones to teach Sunday school, which involved teaching some of them to read first. So, each afternoon she held reading classes and one day a week taught the Sunday school lesson so they could teach it on Sunday.

In Macedonia?

We spent two long weekends in Macedonia traveling by truck. We started the same type of program there for S.S. teachers.

In Piolho? (translated: lice)

Yes, we started visiting a new village on clinic trips, making a total of 12 villages now. A rancher's wife in the region was converted (she dates it back to the time our pilot and Jane were rained in and had to land unexpectedly at their ranch), and her life has undergone such a change that all her relatives are amazed. She's related to the chief of this village and several other people there. They are now wanting to hear God's Word because of what they've seen in the life of this woman. She used to fight with her husband using knives and pistols.

In Morro? (translated: hill)

Located on a hill near Maracanã, we are encouraging the believers to make regular evangelistic visits there. The chief is friendly and invited us to his house for a service. Pray for an entrance of the Word into his heart, as well as his home.

Jane's traveling medical ministry allowed her many opportunities for outreach and discipleship to both the lost and the saved.

The trip to Blue Creek in January was very successful. We visited Sun Mountain where about 500 Indians live. It's a beautiful spot, though hard to get to other than by plane. The people are a mixture, speaking Akrawaiyo and Macushi. However, they were very attentive to our Macushi preacher and said they would like to hear more. Pray with us for future follow-up work to be done and that the Lord will provide the necessary personnel.

Our monthly visits by car to Pium are being well-received. The people are warming up to us. They are begging us to learn their language, Wapishana. We're going to try and contact our missionary in Guyana among Wapishanas and have her send us some literature anyway, perhaps a Wapishana preacher, too. Pium is right along the border of Guyana. Pray for this outreach, too.

The Christians in the church here at Manoá seem to enjoy going out like this, but they are realizing they don't have a very good testimony. They are hearing what the non-Christians are saying about them. And, I'm afraid, they aren't "suffering for righteousness sake," but rather for their own wrongdoings. Pray that the Lord will bring real conviction to their hearts and they may make things right with each other so that this year may be one of real blessing to them.

Throughout the years, God grew and developed Miriam and Jane's vision for the Macushi.

Recruiting new missionaries is the burden on our hearts, but we have had little success with this. In 1970 when Miriam first came to Brazil, she was number seven on the team of Macushi workers. Jane and Miriam now are the "team" with Ivo Uchôa, who is presently on furlough.

The Lord has given us a real burden to train Macushi Indians as spiritual leaders and teachers of their own. This is a GROWING BURDEN as we see the Lord working in new villages and opening up new areas of service, making our contribution (two people with just two hands each) seem so little in the light of all the needs.

We have decided by faith to expand our ministry as the Lord leads and have invited some choice Macushi to join us full time in our work.

Vanda is the 26-year-old daughter of Messias, who lives

at Blue Creek, where we have been visiting for 15 years. Her older sister is presently in Bible school in Saõ Paulo training to be a missionary, and this is the GROWING BURDEN on Vanda's heart as well. Jane has invited her to work with her in a traveling ministry to our new villages. Vanda will be teaching the illiterate believers to read and write. Jane also hopes to teach her nursing, so she can help out in the growing medical work. She is presently studying a 3-year Bible correspondence course, and in addition, will be learning the Macushi language.

Waldemar has a GROWING BURDEN as well for the new Christians in the mountain villages. He wants to begin a tape ministry for them. He will make the tapes in Serra Grande and travel once a month as pastor of the clinic trips, taking the tapes with him to those villages.

Of course, there were still other challenges in the ministry to which they had been called. The village at Mt. Moria was a prime example of this.

To my way of thinking, open doors and adversity do not go together. They are a contradiction of terms. When adversity comes, I tend to think that the opportunity for effective work has gone. But that is not so, as Paul tells us of his experience in Ephesus.

Our trip to Mt. Moriá proved to be such an example of this. The chief met us as soon as the plane left Saturday afternoon and read us the riot act. Never in all our years working among the Macushi has anyone confronted us in such a way. Of course, the fact that he had been drinking gave him more "courage" to say what was on his mind.

On Monday morning, we went to have a talk with the chief and explained our work and "our talk." We explained that we don't enter into politics, that we just teach God's Word. That is why we don't tell them to fight against different people, as God's Word tells us to love our enemies and obey those in authority over us.

As a result of this talk, we received permission to hold services in the village each afternoon. The chief even attended the last meeting. During our week's visit there, we had an early morning service with the believers and an afternoon service in the chief's house with everyone attending.

These types of ups and downs in ministry were common, and Miriam and Jane were not immune to their effects. Yet for every discouragement, there was a greater encouragement.

Opposition or Opportunity?

Would you believe both? Where the Lord is opening doors of opportunity for work in new villages, His enemy is raising opposition. This was demonstrated dramatically this last clinic trip. Jane was unsure as to her reception in Camará, as she heard rumors of threats to the people if they should receive the "Evangelicals." A believer in a neighboring village received a letter saying the people there had decided they didn't want the mission to come. However, when the plane landed, they received a royal welcome. The chief insisted on taking Jane to the center of the village and made quite a speech describing his joy. He told his people (everyone was there) that he would not hinder anyone if they wanted to make a decision to accept the Lord, but that he personally wanted to hear more of the Word and understand and think about it for a while. Pray for these people in Camará.

Just before Miriam and Jane left for furlough at the end of 1989, they reviewed some of the great things God was doing in His Church in Brazil.

Discipleship Program: Four couples from three different villages up in the mountains have stayed with us for a year of study. They studied reading and writing, John and Acts, and had classes each afternoon with Waldemar. They are all back in their villages now helping in their local churches.

Congregation in Serra Grande: The Pereiras have joined us this term to begin a ministry in our own community here. We have seen interest wax and wane periodically, but there has been a consistent growth. One of our churches in Boa Vista has agreed to help us and the pastor has made several visits and has invited the young people to join his in special activities. Jane has a Bible study weekly with six young women with unsaved husbands. Four of these women have made decisions, and all are very excited about studying the Bible.

Once they returned to Brazil, they evaluated how the Macushi churches had fared in their absence.

It is good to be back in Macushi land again. We have had one clinic trip already in which we talked with some of our church leaders and believers in several different villages. Although the clinic work has expanded numerically, new villages have been visited, and dental assistance was given, we have seen a definite spiritual slump in some of the churches. Our clinic pastor, Waldemar, told us he cannot continue the present pace of being whisked away from village to village to preach. He feels he must spend more time on the ground to talk personally with people in order to have a spiritual ministry connected with the clinics.

At the same time we see these faults and discouragement, we see the Lord working in the lives of other Macushi leaders to help meet these needs.

Miguel, the pastor at Napoleão wants to go and encourage the believers in Flexal as well as help resolve problems in the church at Cararaua.

Sisi, the pastor at Maracanã, has an evangelist's heart and wants to visit other villages to preach. He plans to move his family and live near some relatives in order to do this. He told of a backslidden believer at Bala (where he wants to move) coming to him for reconciliation. He said to Sisi, "There are many of our relatives in these nearby villages who want to hear God's Word. I know the gospel, but I don't have the right to preach because I have been living wrong."

Well, it was good to see so many Macushi in different villages and the news we've heard—though there are problem situations, we felt encouraged at others who are seeking to follow the Lord. . .I visited the village of Santa Maria for the first time and felt like a celebrity! As usual, the people just fall all over themselves trying to please me, just because I can talk to them in their language. Right now, I feel they are friendly and accepting of us. So, we need to go slow and teach them just who God is to give the correct view.

Miriam and Jane could see the power of God at work in the lives of the Macushi as time went on.

When we arrived back from furlough in January, we were saddened to see the spiritual slump the Christians were experiencing in Flexal. One family decided to leave permanently because they felt they were not strong enough to stand alone and realized they too would soon be drawn back to their drinking habits. No services were being held as all were discouraged and were drinking more and more, even the children.

But in the last few months, we have seen the believers once again come back to the Lord, begin meeting together, and memorizing Scripture verses. And so, we saw 20 of them come to study the Word. What happened? Perhaps the Lord is using the Kalazar epidemic to speak to hearts. Several deaths have occurred in that region. Also, we have successfully treated several cases and they have returned to their villages cured.

Pray that the church leaders may be encouraged to continue meeting together with the believers and teach them what they know of the Word of God.

After the struggles of the previous year, 1991 was a time of new opportunities and open doors among the Macushis.

We've been here in Maracanã for a week having a course for medical attendants. We both have been thrilled to see the way this church has grown over the years. Evangelista has just arrived back from Bible school and is seeking the place and means to serve the Lord. We've invited him to preach on clinics this month. Also, he's trying to get back into the Macushi language, so I gave him the book of Matthew to back-translate for me into Portuguese. That way, he will learn Biblical language in Macushi—like how we've translated law and Son of man.

His sister is teaching the women's Sunday school class and also is trying to speak Macushi. Her husband, José Amazonas, is very shy, and Dave Crompton had been trying to disciple them. He told me yesterday that José wants to study nursing—get his documents and try to get hired by the health department, so he can go start a clinic in Santa Maria and reach that village for the Lord! All that came out of his own head!

So now we are beginning to see a new generation involve themselves in the work. I taught his wife's mother how to read years ago!

The UFM team laid out a plan to continue reaching the Macushi people all over the district. They drew up a map and assigned various workers to each region of villages.

> *"Paul and his companions traveled throughout the region of Phrygia and Galatia, having been kept by the Holy Spirit from preaching the word in the province of Asia" (Acts 16:6 NIV). We have definitely felt over the years led by the Spirit to different Macushi villages and away from others. In March of this year, the Macushi team set aside two days to seek the Lord's leading as to the future of the Macushi church and how we can best minister.*

> *Our goals for the Macushi church are: (1) an indigenous leadership, (2) to be self-sufficient financially, (3) to be able to train their own leadership and start similar churches locally.*

> *We've chosen key sites for these goals to be realized. Then, with the Lord's help, these churches will minister to the other already-existing congregations and evangelistic sites in their area.*

As the team began to implement that plan, Miriam and Jane recognized that even after 25 years of ministry to the Macushi, the people still had much to learn about God and His Word.

> *The church here is doing quite well. Lots of "growing pains" though. We have 17 more that have asked for baptism. Last Sunday afternoon, I taught them what a baptismal service was like and that they would have to give a testimony. I taught them what a testimony was. I asked*

the older Christians to tell how they were saved and then asked the candidates to tell their salvation testimonies. Went over much better than I thought. All of them gave their testimony. This week I'm going to teach them what a communion service is like. This is not only for the new Christians but also for the leaders, so they will be able to lead these services.

Last weekend I spent doing marriage counseling! The chief and his wife had a real rip-roaring fight and called me to help them. Actually, his wife called me to give him counsel! I didn't realize there were still so many words in Macushi I never heard before! I heard a lot! Didn't understand it all, but since arguments are the same the world over, it really didn't matter. Ha! All I did was listen (for about 2 hours) then I told them each one to get alone with the Lord and ask Him to show each his own faults. They had vividly clarified the "other's" faults, so I felt they needed to know their own and ask the Lord to forgive them for those. After that, go to the other and ask forgiveness for what they did, without going into the other's faults again. Then they could both come to my house, and we'd pray together. When I left, they both were still fuming.

The next day the chief came and told me they had made up the night before. Then he said he wanted me to read to his wife from Ephesians about a woman being submissive to her husband. He said, "I try to tell her that she needs to be submissive like the Bible says. But because she doesn't know that word in Portuguese, she thinks I'm making it up!"

Well, I read the whole passage and explained each one's responsibility toward the other. She had no trouble with the Macushi!

More and more I'm convinced of the need for Macushi Scriptures. Now she's started in my class to learn to read, and he will correct translation.

Never a dull moment here!

Each village seemed to have its own unique struggle in the battle for faithfulness to God.

Jane's at Mt. Moriá now, teaching her regular weekend classes. The people there are really doing well. Very anxious to study and seem more mature as a church. But they are still going through persecution from the other half of the village. One fellow especially, he's the converted catechist of the Catholic Church, and all his relatives are against him. But he's still faithful and comes and studies regularly and attends church with the Christians. Here in Flexal it's a different story. They have their ups and downs. They love to go from house to house drinking their "Casiri." It isn't as strong as it used to be, but the quantities they drink!! I'm teaching a young married fellow and his sister to be Sunday school teachers. They have a real desire to be used of the Lord. Both are fairly new Christians. They were baptized last October. Also, I am helping the "leaders" to prepare their sermons. Some do better than others, but not many want to take the time to study.

Still, all of the Macushi churches had some cultural obstacles to overcome. Miriam and Jane waited upon the Lord, for they knew He was the only One that could change Macushi hearts.

Because we have been working among Macushi Indians for over 20 years now, we have seen many changes. But there are some things that are very difficult to change, and one of these is the strong belief in their witchcraft and magic.

One of the church leaders asked prayer for his infant son who was sick and seemed to be getting worse. He said his mother wanted to use magic on him to cure this sickness. But he said, "Since I have studied more of God's Word, I know I cannot use magic anymore, so I told my mother no, and I surrendered my son to the Lord. The Lord can heal him if He wants. The Lord wants us to have faith in Him and ask Him to do things for us since we are His children."

Jane attended a difficult labor and delivery. The woman had been in labor for three days, but her pains just weren't very strong. Again, around her hammock as we prayed with her and talked with all the relatives, we praised the Lord for her sister, who was baptized just a week ago, as she told her sister's mother-in-law: "No, we don't want to do magic because that is not God's way. We will do like the doctor says." A few hours later, her sister delivered a healthy, but very large, daughter! Both are doing well.

Of course, the wisdom needed to deal with all of these issues can only be found in the Bible.

What equips the Church? The Word of God (2 Tim. 3:16, 17). Upon returning to Roraima, we have learned of many trials and hardships the Macushi believers have endured. Sadly, many have been infatuated with outward emotional experiences and have been deceived that these take the place of the Word of God. Several of the churches have been divided over these issues and others. This has confirmed even more to us the necessity of the Scriptures in their own language, teaching of the Word in a clear manner, and modeling the principles of Scripture in the lives of believers. The Word IS profitable for doctrine.

Despite the difficulties of life on the mission field, the ladies never failed to find something for which they could praise the Lord. His faithfulness was their constant companion; His presence, their guide. This perspective always shone through their prayer letters.

We have much to praise the Lord for these days. The first "Scripture in Use" seminar was a success. It had rained really hard for three days, the roads were a mess, and we knew if it continued to rain, people would not be able to walk to the meetings. We left right after the rain stopped, and it took twice as long to arrive at the church because of the roads, but people were waiting for us. From then until the time we left 3 days later, we had no rain. We were amazed at how many young people were there. We broke up into workgroups, one group of men, one of women, two groups of fellows, and one group of girls. Auxiliadora went with us and had something special for the children each day. We spent three days there, staying with the only family that has walls in their house. They treated us royally! They killed a chicken every day for us! But it was a bit difficult getting used to taking a bath in the creek again. As usual, Jane dropped the soap!!"

When the Macushi translation of the New Testament became available, the missionaries rejoiced in how God used it in the lives of the Indians. For those who have been taught the Bible and read it their whole lives, it is difficult to imagine life without it. But for those who have never read it or even held Scripture in their hands, the learning curve is steep. It was necessary for Miriam to teach the Macushi church leaders how to read, understand, interpret, and apply God's Word in their lives. They began working with the Macushi to find specific verses on a variety of topics for counseling purposes, using the Bible maps, learning unfamiliar vocabulary from the New Testament, and understanding the background material in the book introductions.

To date, we have held three seminars in three different churches. They were fairly well-attended and interest was high. The favorite subjects were: memorizing Scripture, preparing a Bible study, and preparing family devotions. At Mato Grosso, we were thrilled to have so many young people. We went there with 24 pounds of Bibles to sell, and we returned with 84 pounds of payment: farine, bananas, tapioca, manioc starch, cassava bread, and three chickens. Continue to pray that the seed sown will bring forth fruit for God's glory.

The work with the small local churches continued as well.

What a joy to see the groups of believers continuing to meet together even while we were gone. Miriam is beginning a Bible study at Quitauaú to help the leaders in preparing messages. She has 15 enrolled (not all leaders, but all can use this study to minister to others). We especially want to emphasize using the Bible in the home with the family.

Through the ministry of His faithful servants, God had been working spiritual changes in Macushi families for many years. He allowed Miriam and Jane a glimpse of the fruit.

We returned to some very sad news. Joventina, a Macushi who had lived with me and Isabel when I first came to Brazil, was very ill with cancer. Isabel had trained her and her cousin Raimunda to be school teachers, and they opened up the first schools up in the mountain villages of Maracanã and Macedonia. While we were talking with Dave and Grace, the phone rang, and they told us of her death. So yesterday, Friday, we went to her funeral. While it was sad, we were thrilled to hear of her testimony among all of her family. She and her husband are now grandparents, and they have been faithful believers all these years. The young Macushi pastor who had the service was a second cousin who has graduated from Bible school. He gave a wonderful salvation message and told what an encouragement Joventina had been to him. He said she told him before she died, "Eliseu, you keep on being strong in the Lord and in serving Him, because I have invested heavily in you. When you were in Bible school, I sent you money from my salary to help you. So, you keep on being firm and strong in the Lord!"

I remember Eliseu as a baby up in Macedonia. His parents were then living for the Lord. Later his mother died, and his father left the church and went back into the world. So, it was a joy to see him as one that Joventina had influenced, as well as taught. Her sister Levina (who had also lived with us later) told us of the testimony she was in the hospital. She could hardly talk because she was so weak, but she sang hymns in the hospital for all to hear. Levina said: "When I went to visit her, I never cried because she was the one who comforted me."

By far, our most joyous times are meeting old friends again and learning how the Lord has been faithful in their lives and seeing the spiritual growth that has taken place. Listen to some of our conversations:

Valdemir*: "When I went to Flexal and got married, I had only been a Christian a short while. I was scared to get up in front of people in church and speak and lead the singing. But the Lord has helped me. I know if I had stayed in my own village among non-Christian friends, I wouldn't have grown spiritually."*

Aluizio*: "When I went to the gold mines, all the people in my church got discouraged and gave up going to church. Upon returning, I visited them, and some were blaming me for not being there as their pastor during that time. I told them I had many places to go to minister to people in the mines, Guyana, and neighboring villages, and that they* *could carry on without me. I said, Look, when a rancher takes salt to his cows, they learn where the rancher leaves the salt lick. So, they don't go following after the rancher, they go to the salt lick. We have the church here and the Word of God; you don't need to come after me. You know where to go to get the help you need."*

The missionary ladies continued to evangelize, starting new churches wherever the Lord put them in Brazil.

Jane and I have been working with a little group in the village of Serra Grande, mixed Brazilian and Macushi. We are very encouraged. Last Sunday we had 11 decisions, several rededications, and several first-time decisions. Mainly young people. On Sunday night, we had 70 in church. We are teaching Galatians, and they are memorizing some verses from Galatians.

The other church in the jungle, at what they call Serra Grande II, is made up of mostly Macushi. They are doing quite well there. This week we are going to the leaders' meeting to talk with them about Scripture in Use and about the distribution of the New Testament. They have given us Friday afternoon to present this.

Even Macushi churches needed building projects from time to time, and these two small congregations were no exception. Miriam and Jane were thankful to see the Lord provide for the labor and the materials in answer to the people's faithful giving. An electrician volunteered his services as his offering to the Lord, and a widow made extra farine to sell so that she could contribute to the building projects.

While Miriam and Jane were out of Brazil finishing up the New Testament, several denominational groups came into the area and drew believers away from the Macushi congregations and from the Word of God.

If we were discouraged hearing all the problems upon our return, the Lord certainly gave us real encouragement at a recent meeting with the leaders of our churches. Our Brazilian mission called them together to discuss the problems of various denominations that have approached several of our churches and offered help. Denomination is an unknown concept in the Macushi culture. They are familiar with government organizations coming in and offering all kinds of things, also politicians. So many think that denominations are the same kind of things, organizations that give handouts.

As we discussed the problems and introduced new ideas, it was evident that the Lord was directing our thoughts throughout the day. We praise the Lord for the faith that was evident in the lives of many represented here. Here is an excerpt from the meetings:

Arcenia—a leader's wife from the church in Mato Grosso (a Bible school graduate): "When I think of how the Lord used the missionaries to bring the gospel to our village I am awed and filled with gratitude. Pastor Lionel Gordon, a Guyanese missionary now with the Lord, was the first to come through our village. Jane and Miriam were faithful in visiting for years, and the mission still keeps on helping us to learn more of the Bible. I was very sad to hear that some want a denomination for help. The mission has given us much help."

The discussion was chaired by a recent Bible school graduate, a Wapishana Indian who is now pastor of his church in Truaru. How we praised the Lord as we heard Nazário express his deep desires of serving in his community. He showed us a pamphlet he had made up with a sun on the front. Each of the rays led out to outlying areas of his community. This was their missionary program. He asked for pictures of each of the other churches so he could put them up in his church for his people to pray for them.

Boring Statistics

As each one was introduced at our Church leaders' meeting, it was a joy to see just how many there were and what areas were represented. 10 local churches were represented by their leaders. An extra blessing was to hear from the pastor of the Baptist church in Pakaraima, the frontier town near Venezuela. He married one of the girls we discipled! He is in charge of the Baptist work among the Macushis. His report told of 12 churches and their faithful leaders. And then I thought of the 15 Macushi churches in Guyana. What a wonderful faithful Lord we serve!

The local, New Testament church is still God's method for spreading His love and truth to the world. Miriam and Jane were blessed to be a part of that endeavor among the Macushi. The churches there continue to grow, reproduce, and thrive.

Chapter Twenty-Eight

God Uses Leadership Training

*Teach those men who make Him true without abandoning
Him, in order that they may teach others like that also.*
—2 Timothy 2:2, Macushi Back Translation

*And the things that you have heard from me among many
witnesses, commit these to faithful men who will be able to
teach others also.*
—2 Timothy 2:2

In March 1980, the UFM missionaries met for their annual field
conference. At this point, there were five different MEVA (a
Brazilian mission started by UFM) works among the tribal people
of Northern Brazil, with about 17 different missionary units,
including Brazilians and Americans. Information was exchanged
and plans were made. For Miriam and Jane, some very exciting
plans were put into the works.

*It was approved at this conference that we begin studying
the possibility of opening a Bible study and discipleship
center for the Macushi. We've got our hands full this year
trying to find out all the information we can on how to*

343

start. The way I see it, we'll have volunteer help from our churches to go there and build houses (mud and leaf-roof houses) and plant a field. Then students can study in the morning and work in the field in the afternoon. It would be a way of self-supporting. We would maybe give a day off now and then for them to go hunting. There's a new Brazilian couple coming who are interested in teaching. We want mostly Brazilian staff, although those of us knowing the Macushi language would have plenty to do.

In the past, most of our work was done in the Macushi villages. But we realize more and more the Macushi are leaving their villages for more study or better jobs. It is our desire to aid the Macushi church in training these. We will offer Bible courses, correspondence courses to finish junior high and high school, teachers' training courses, and nursing courses so that the students can better obtain jobs even in their own villages. Pray for us as we plan for this together with the Macushi leaders.

At the next year's field conference, the matter was again addressed.

Just this week, some of our men went to look at a piece of land that seems suitable. The price tag is about 12,000 dollars, about 9,000 more than we have, so we are looking to the Lord for His direction, and we pray that we may know His will concerning it. It seems to be sufficient for our use. Our students will have to use a piece of the land to grow their own food. Also, there is a lot of bush which still has some game there, as well as a creek with fish. So, it seems like an environment not too strange for Indian students. Pray with us about it.

Daddy, you would just go crazy seeing all the possibility for it and the crops we could grow and all. We really need someone who knows how to develop the land and make the best use of it. The Indians and students will supply the manual labor, but the overseeing and managing of it is where we are lacking.

Of course, Miriam's father, having been a farmer his whole life, would understand much about crop cultivation. Miriam felt this was a perfect opportunity and reason for her parents to finally visit her in Brazil.

A short time later, she reported the exciting news.

Oh, we bought the land!! We're trusting the Lord to send us the money. If I go there to teach, it will mean a house for us that we'll have to finance somehow, too. I'm too old to tie my hammock in the jungle! Ha. I am even going to start sleeping in a bed! Jane is buying a mattress for me now and will bring it in tomorrow. My bed is here waiting for it! Well, I'm not as young as I used to be!

She was 38 years old.

While Miriam took a short furlough during the summer of 1982, Jane, Ivo Uchôa, Joe Butler, and Lionel Gordon worked to prepare the land. Upon her return, the missionaries determined that they were ready to host the first Bible course for Macushi men.

Twelve or thirteen men from all our villages will be going for a month of study with several of our missionary men. We trust this will be a time of real encouragement and spiritual growth for them, and that they will be better equipped to minister in their churches. Some of these are men from our new villages where there are no established churches yet. Pray that these men will learn much from the older Christian believers during this month of living and studying together. But because no construction has been done yet, classes will be held in Boa Vista. They will spend 2 days a week out at the property building the classrooms. But we praise the Lord that enough food has been grown for them.

Miriam again suggested that her father was just the one to know how to get the most out of their land.

Saturday, I went out to the property for the first time since I've been back. To me, it looks like a whole lot has been done, and the space for building has been cleared off. I think we'll be starting to build our house soon.

This brings me up to my next point. Do you think you could swing it to come down in the spring? Because of your crops, what about April? The road is good now, so I feel rainy season wouldn't hinder our getting out there. Lionel is really the one who is dying to talk to you about the land, and I feel you could encourage him quite a bit.

Well, I know this seems like a lot of pressure on you. I don't know all your situation there, but I do know it seems like an excellent time here on this end. So, pray about it and let me know what you think.

Miriam and Jane built a house on the property, located near Serra Grande. When they were not ministering in other villages, Serra Grande was their home. As leaders of the Macushi church, Waldemar and Domingos moved their families there to help cultivate the land, to assist Miriam with the translation project, and to take over the bulk of the discipleship responsibilities. And apparently, the Lord agreed that Mr. Abbott would make a good land manager, as well.

While we were visiting Fran Tracy in Guyana, she told me that just that morning, she and Bev had decided to send a check to Mother and Daddy to help them come down to visit me. All told, it will be around $700.00 they will be sending to them! Can you imagine such a thing?? Won't Mother and Daddy be flabbergasted?

Our house on the property is now under construction. It was started this week. The well is almost finished—they should hit water tomorrow. The money I'm using is from gifts at furlough time—after my travel and baggage was all taken care of, I had over $1,000.00 left. I brought it back in traveler's checks so we can exchange it as we need it, to keep it from devaluating in Brazilian currency. Then on my last draft, the left-over furlough gifts that came through home office were over $1,000.00 also! So, that gave me $2,500.00. Jane had $2,000.00 left from her car fund— after exchanging the Chevy truck for the Toyota heavy duty truck. So, we feel we can get a pretty decent house for that! Also, we're going to put in some from our regular "housing *allowance" each month so we can finish up the house. I'm hoping it will be done by March. The Lord is so good!*

Miriam's mother, Mrs. Maude Abbott, recorded some special memories of their time in Brazil with the ladies:

"Have you been praying about going to Brazil?" These words rather startled me, as my husband came in with the mail one morning.

"Well, yes! But only if the Lord leads, as we agreed." This was met with a grin, as he laid an envelope before me.

Thus began a whole series of surprises from the Lord which enabled us to make the trip, which until recently, had been a far-off, vague "sometime" thing in our minds.

Miriam had often enough expressed the hope and desire that we might visit her there on the mission field. Our financial status kept us from even considering the enormous cost of such a flight.

But the children of one of our missionary sons in Mexico, Edward, began to save their tithes from their allowances to send Grandmom and Grandpop to visit Miriam. Since we had visited them in Mexico each year for a number of years, they realized what it must mean to Aunt Miriam to never have anyone visit her! So had accumulated $200.00, the beginning of our "Brazil Fund!"

After several letters in which Miriam shared the news of this special property being literally "hacked" out of the jungle—

and the need for advice concerning the growing of the food necessary for students and their families who would attend, the Lord really laid this need on my husband's heart. As Miriam suggested, we began to pray and seek the Lord's leading in it. Before very long, we saw the Lord answer and provide in many unusual ways.

Gifts came in from such "un-looked for" sources, that we could not doubt the direct leading of the Lord.

So we began to prepare things such as passports, visas, etc. A snag which hindered us was the need for our birth certificates to obtain passports. Years ago, I had tried to obtain mine, and there was no record. Therefore, I was forced to go a long circuitous route to answer my need of one. I was really discouraged.

We prayed and I wrote, asking what would need to be done in the event of not procuring one. The Lord worked a miracle in the Bureau of Statistics, for the mail brought both of them in time to receive our passports. Evidently, the records had been found since the earlier experience. Praise Him! All things are possible!

With these needs met, our luggage was packed (including numerous needs of Miriam's), and our arrangements for travel were made. The Lord had supplied every cent needed. Praise His Name!

When Miriam met us (their Jeep had conked out en route to town, causing a delay), we were quite tired, but happy to have arrived. She whisked us out to their mission headquarters in Boa Vista in the mission van.

We were treated to a delicious (though different) dinner at the hospitality house, hosted by Brazilian missionaries from southern Brazil. After a nice shower and rest, we left with the girls for the property, Serra Grande—Big Mountain, where Miriam's newly built home is located.

Work began the next day with Ed (my husband) and Jane making screens for the windows—the screen doors were already hung. Then the girls sanded and varnished <u>all</u> the woodwork, a monumental task, but satisfying in its beauty. And <u>this</u> was their vacation!!

Ed then began work on the land. A tractor was procured, which used diesel. Amid quite a few difficulties with it, he managed to disc a large section of land and proceeded to plant a variety of seed, seeking the ones which might be best fitted to the soil and climate.

I was able to be of some help by making up visual aids for teaching, cataloging medical books and language materials, as well as helping with the home chores.

Perhaps the greatest thrill for me was to meet so many Macushi (and missionaries at the base, as well) for whom I have prayed for many years—putting faces to the names I've known so long. It's a little foretaste of the experience to come when we meet such folk in heaven!

Time passed all too quickly until the day for our departure for home rolled around. What a wonderful delight as our feet touched once more the good ol' USA! But we realized keenly that we had left a part of our hearts there in Brazil with those whom the Lord is using to guide precious souls to that eternal Home, which will far exceed all expectations of any homecoming!

After more than fifteen years on the foreign field, Miriam's parents finally came to see her and her work in Brazil. God used the Abbotts to help prepare the Serra Grande property and to glean an eternal harvest, too.

Because we had decided to take our vacation in May, Miriam went on the clinic trips instead of Jane. (A vacation is a change!!!) She took her father along as the preacher for the services in our newer villages. (That's a change for a farmer!) It was a new experience for him to fly in the small aircraft, too. I'm not sure how he enjoyed that part, but the Lord blessed his visit, and in one village, Piolho, there were three people who made decisions for the Lord. Others are thinking seriously about it. Then in the village of Bananal, there were three teenagers who wanted to make their decision for the Lord.

On the third day of clinics, Miriam took her mother along to visit the villages she has been praying for these 13 years that we've been working here in Brazil. She met the believers she's been praying for by name, and now she has a face to go with them. In the village of Napoleão, she made a big hit as she gave out candy to every child who took their vaccine injections without crying! That even went over big with the medical attendants who were giving the shots!

The first classes were officially held at the Serra Grande property, beginning October 10, 1983.

Well, we finished up one week of classes, and everyone still seems to be in a good mood. Joe and Mr. Swain got the water hooked up but don't have all the "kinks" worked out yet. But we have a good rope and bucket now and plenty of water.

Mr. Swain got lights hooked up for the students so they can study at night. That's a big help. So now we're figuring a way to get lights here. We're not going to bother with switches. When the generator is on, the lights will be on; when the generator is off, they will go off!

We have nine men and four women. The women seem to be doing almost as well as the men.

Classes went well, but having enough food for the students was a struggle. Crops grown on the property were vital to sustain them.

The weather here is really hot now. It's dry season, and things are very dry. No rain for a long time. In all the villages, it's going to be a very tough year. All the rivers are very low in the whole territory! Everyone is saying there's never been a year like it.

Yet God provided enough, and classes continued. In the fall of 1986, the Lord sent Auxiliadora and José Carlos to help. They were a tremendous asset to the needy ministry. A Bible course was planned for October when Miriam would teach the book of Acts. The number of students coming was a concern, as Miriam relayed in her November letter.

The Lord brought us 32 students to our Bible school session this month. We trust the teaching and living together with other Christians will be a real help to each one as they return to their villages.

We almost stopped hoping for the dormitory to be built, but the Lord provided a mason at the last minute. The work was finished and the students moved in two days after school started. So, for one weekend, everyone was in cramped quarters.

Don't stop praying for the new work in the village of Serra Grande near our land. José Carlos has taken the students out each afternoon to do visitation. In this way, we're getting to know the people even better. Sunday services have been started—we've had four so far. Two of the services were attended by some drunks, so it's going to be a struggle.

God blessed, and by 1987 the ministry had grown both in size and in impact.

Bible classes started September 28 and ended October 16. It was our biggest year yet. We had 42 Macushi, 1 Maiongong, 1 Sanuma, and 16 Wai Wai. It was a grand time of fellowship for all of them.

Bob and Florine Hawkins were here to teach the Wai Wai,

and Dave Crompton taught the others how to prepare a message. Miriam taught the book of 1 Corinthians, and Pat had a practical question and answer hour, in which they discussed their own church problems.

Though Jane didn't teach a class, she was super busy organizing and directing the six women's teams for kitchen duty. She also divided the men into four work teams. Their projects included working on the new fence we're putting up for the sheep, hoeing in the field, making a new field, and building a work shed to replace the old one that was falling down. Many afternoons Jane was called upon to haul fence posts or leaves for the work shed. Many of these jobs, far from glamorous, contributed to a very positive attitude among the students. It was truly of the Lord, since we have so many from different cultures, dietary habits, etc. living together.

Other improvements were made to the program and the facilities at Serra Grande.

Discipleship Program: Each October we have taught Macushi church leaders as well as others, including Wai Wai, Maiongong, Sanuma, and Wapishana Indians. This past year, we have come up with a four-year curriculum for a diploma for these short courses. We are combining it with extension courses some of us are teaching in various villages.

Property Development: Two dormitory buildings (a total of ten rooms), clinic, tractor shed, airstrip, new bridge, and two new houses for our Macushi workers have been added here at Serra Grande during this term, as well as new fences for cattle, more cattle (a total of 12 cows now), and 20 pigs. The fields have been increasing in size each year, so we have been able to produce food for the students who have come.

Amid much spiritual warfare and opposition, discipleship and leadership development continued at the Serra Grande property. However, with Miriam trying to finish the New Testament translation and Jane keeping up with the demands of the medical ministries, the mission board relieved them of their obligations there. Pat Foster, Lionel Gordon, José Carlos, and others took over the teaching. But Miriam and Jane kept their home at Serra Grande, and eventually, God directed them back there for further opportunities of service.

Chapter Twenty-Nine
God Uses Project Bethel

Timothy, you are a young one. In spite of that, do it so that everyone can see your ways. By means of doing that, they will respect you. The believers in Jesus will see your ways, on account of your talk, on account of your ways, on account of your love for others, on account of your making God true, on account of your ways not being dirty, they will know.
—1 Timothy 4:12, Macushi Back Translation

Let no one despise your youth, but be an example to the believers in word, in conduct, in love, in spirit, in faith, in purity.
—1 Timothy 4:12

In 1997, with the New Testament completed and a burden to continue serving the Macushi people, Miriam and Jane planned their next project.

For years the Macushi churches have been seeking a solution for their children. Christian parents want their children to be educated, but many villages only have 4 grades of school. The young people themselves want to learn new skills and get jobs other than just subsistence farming in their own villages like their parents. With cultural change coming so fast and furious, Christian Macushi are faced with many decisions. Jane and Miriam have been sensing their needs over the years and now have decided to begin in a small way to try and offer a solution.

We started by inviting six students to the Serra Grande property, believers with recommendations from their parents and their pastors, to participate in Project Bethel, a discipleship program where we offer 5th to 8th grades by correspondence (provided by the government) for two hours and Bible courses two hours a day. The students are contributing to their support by working a half day in the fields with crops, fruit trees, cattle, and chickens. We are trying to get the land to support the students. We can support one student for $100.00 per month. Hopefully, this figure will decrease as the land produces more.

Pray for our students, 5 young fellows and one young girl. Pray for us that the Lord will give us strength to keep up with these young people. We were never mothers, and we feel it's a bit late to start now with teenagers, but the Lord gives grace.

Almost immediately, Project Bethel was beset with problems. Rumors of criminals in the area, a drought, and even the need for more workers threatened to discourage Miriam, Jane, and their students. In faith, they looked to the Lord for His help and guidance.

Since our area is "progressing" with new and better roads, communication, etc., we also are having problems with thieves in the area. And these are more sophisticated thieves from the south who don't feel badly at all if they rough up the people they steal from. (Recently the neighboring ranch was robbed of a chainsaw and shotgun, and the foreman was badly beaten.) So, pray that the Lord will give us His protection as He promises.

This is the worst dry season we can ever remember. Our water situation was critical, and we had to dig our hand-dug well deeper and install a new jet pump. So right now, we have enough water, more than many unfortunate people in our area. Because of the dry season, fires have been out of control. Many people are losing their fields, houses, and pastures to the fires.

As proud human beings, we don't like to beg, but we are begging the Lord for more personnel. We really feel it is too much for us to be teaching all the classes. Right now, we have temporary help. We praise the Lord for them, but we look to Him for permanent personnel. We feel the boys need a man to teach them, even though Pat Foster reminded us, "Remember it's a matriarchal society." We do really fit in as "mothers!"

In answer to their prayers, the school was never targeted for any crime, and the rains finally came, bringing much-needed relief to everyone. Miriam and Jane kept busy teaching at Project Bethel, discipling both their students and the new churches springing up nearby.

Our students are doing well, and we are pleased with the small signs of growth that we see. One of our students had invited two of his cousins to go to church with him on Sunday, and they both made a decision for the Lord. He said they told him, "Boy, you sure do know a lot about the Bible!" He answered: "Well, I should, I study it every day!!!" He also said he had a good opportunity to talk more with his dad about the Lord as well, and that he wasn't so hard-hearted this time. So, we rejoice.

One of our problems in the selling of the Macushi Bibles has been that the younger generation are our readers. The older generation, the ones longing for the Word of God in their own language, are illiterate or partially literate. We have tried to combat this problem over the years with literacy classes, tape recorders with Scripture portions, and other methods. But the problem still remains that the youth, now bilingual, have little interest in reading in their own language.

Sooo. . .we have started our own battle here at Bethel by teaching our students to read their own language. We're fighting a battle of age-long prejudices against Macushi. (They have been made to feel over the years by their Brazilian neighbors that their language isn't really a language, just unintelligible gibberish.)

Pray with us as they see that their language has grammatical structure, parts of speech, and rules of grammar, just like the Portuguese they're studying. Pray they'll begin to see that the God-given language they speak has value.

Miriam and Jane took a short vacation to Venezuela during the school's July break. The ladies enjoyed their time together, visiting the beach, shopping for truck tires, watching TV in English, eating at Wendy's and Pizza Hut, and just relaxing. But the vacation was quick, and the next school session began.

We have had quite a time with our students. But we feel the Lord is beginning to get through to them. Last week they showed a real spirit of repentance and confessed sin they had been hiding since last semester. So now they all seem to be really gung-ho in their studies, church, and even their work. Jane is also trying to keep up with them more and make sure they carry through with their jobs. To do that she gets up at 5 a.m. to get the group going. They work an hour before breakfast, milking cows, feeding chickens, and tending the garden. Then they have their quiet time and then their breakfast. After that, Domingos takes over and takes them to work repairing fences or weeding or any number of jobs that need to be done. So far this term it seems to be working better.

Jane was talking to them the other night and told them they had to confront temptations when they went to ball games or other places and learn to resist them in the Lord's strength. One of the fellows said, "Yes, we know. This semester we are really caught in Jesus!"

We praise the Lord especially for the spiritual growth we have seen in the students' lives. It is not easy, and we keep busy dealing with each problem as it arises, giving counsel according to the Scripture. This is the first time for all (I think) to realize that every aspect of our lives can be guided by the Lord through Scripture.

Are we training church leaders? We don't know the answer to that question, but what we hope to train are men of God who can be led by His Spirit into the work He has chosen for them, whether it be pastor, teacher, mechanic, or candlestick maker!!! We feel our churches need men of God, and of course, it is good if those men are in leadership.

We are talking about spiritual investments, treasures in heaven, wealth that endures for eternity. Here at Serra Grande, this is exactly what we are trying to do. We invest in the lives of young people of various tribes, becoming involved with them and trying to model the life that the Lord desires of us. Over the years, we have discovered that Indians do not learn well in the classroom, but rather by doing and imitating what their elders do. Paul speaks of this when he tells the believers to imitate him. Pray for us that our lives truly might be such that these young people can imitate and thus learn to live for Christ.

While Jane and Miriam returned to the United States for a short furlough, Miriam's parents both became ill with a serious virus. Her father's illness progressed into bronchitis, while her mother's progressed into pneumonia. She ended up spending three weeks in ICU, and needed several more weeks of help at home to recover. This delayed the opening of the next semester at Project Bethel, but all agreed that it was a necessary delay.

Jane and her sister Janet came to Alabama to help Miriam

with all the hospital visits and care for her dad at home. Because Jane could not return to our work in Brazil and carry on alone, she extended her furlough as well to continue physical therapy on her back and to help Miriam. This furlough, Jane has suffered much from degenerative arthritis of her spine. The neurosurgeon suggested physical therapy, and this is giving her some relief. She is learning to perform many tasks now without bending her back and actually becoming quite agile! She will return to Brazil with a back brace and portable electric current machine for pain.

In the midst of all this, Jane took Miriam to the emergency room in the middle of the night with gallbladder pain. Surgery was scheduled a week later, and Miriam had laparoscopic gallbladder surgery. This kept Jane busy running back and forth between Mrs. Abbott's and Miriam's hospital rooms. They both kept sending her to check on the other! The recovery time for gallbladder surgery is minimal, however, and Miriam was up and running again in a few days. The surgeon okayed her to return to Brazil one month after surgery, which will be in mid-May.

Plans to return to Brazil are in the works. We will leave the early part of June. We plan to open the school as soon as possible upon our return. We want to thank many of you who have prayed for us during these difficult weeks. It was wonderful to see the Lord answer prayer in raising Mother up again. None of us really expected it and we marvel at the Lord's grace on their behalf. Though difficult, it has been a privilege to serve in this way. Living so far away from our parents all our lives, it is truly a blessing to be able to minister to them in their time of need.

With this season of trials behind them for now, Miriam and Jane finally returned to Brazil and their students at Bethel.

As we sat down to breakfast this morning, eating our Serra Grande-grown grapefruit and papaya, and our cereal covered with Serra Grande milk, we thought of the time we've been back here, almost two months. It seems like yesterday that we arrived, but so much has happened that it seems like 6 months' worth of experiences!

Our students are required not only to attend the local church services, but to participate. Every Friday afternoon Jane takes them to Boa Vista to take their test for Jr. High at the school where they are registered. Then they have a class with Edilene (one of our Brazilian missionaries) to learn how to teach children in Sunday School. After that, they have music lessons, some on the guitar and some on the keyboard. With this knowledge, they are required to teach in two different congregations. Jane supervises them at the church in Serra Grande and Miriam takes 3 students to Quitauaú to teach there. They take turns leading the services, learning to pick out the songs ahead of time, or planning special music.

In between times, we make trips to Boa Vista to buy supplies for the school, food, fuel, and maintenance. When do we have time off? Every night from 9:00 p.m. till the next morning! We do try and take Saturdays off when Jane doesn't plan something else. Miriam tries to get the house cleaned on Saturdays with the girl students. They like some extra spending money, and Miriam likes the help!

Pray for more personnel. We would like to share the classes with others. We need coworkers who, Brazilian or American, have a vision of teaching Indian young people not only the Bible, but helping them get their education so they can go on to be pastors, teachers, nurses, mechanics, etc.

The return to Brazil was short-lived. In November 1999, Miriam was called home to help care for her mother. Mrs. Abbott was hospitalized once again with pneumonia. Miriam spent each day with her.

Because of her chronic lung condition, Mrs. Abbott is getting weaker and is now in a nursing home. Miriam goes every day to care for her. We don't know how long she has, but know her life is in the Lord's hands and that she is ready and longs to go home to be with Him. Pray for Miriam and her father and other family members caring for her.

The Lord shows Himself strong in our weakness, as Jane had to finish up the last six weeks alone. Coworkers José and Auxiliadora helped out with the teaching in Miriam's absence.

Jane witnessed the Lord's goodness to her during this trying time.

Despite the difficult end of the term due to Miriam's

absence, the Lord is good and provides even the extras. Due to a last minute canceling of a work team scheduled during this Brazilian summer, Jane found herself able to take a vacation. She got a flight at the last minute and came home for Christmas. She went to Alabama and helped Miriam with her mother over the holidays. Then on January 4th, she flew to Michigan to be with her family. It was such an encouragement to Miriam to have her there for even a short time to help.

Project Bethel will be opening again on the 13th of March, the first week after Carnival. (From Christmas to Carnival is the normal summer holiday.) We have seven new applicants for next year: four from Napoleão, one from Flexal, one from Mapuera, and one from Truaru. Pray as these candidates are interviewed and prayed over, that the Lord may show us the ones of His choice.

In mid-January, Miriam's most faithful prayer warrior, her mother, left this earth to meet her Savior and God.

Jane was there with Miriam when her mother passed away on the 17th of January. What a blessing of the Lord to allow her to be there for Miriam. All seven of Mrs. Abbott's children were able to attend the funeral and about half of the grandchildren were there. The Lord's timing is perfect, and as we gathered together, we found great comfort in each other and in the Lord we all serve. Jane left shortly afterward and met the Drummers in Miami and traveled with them to Boa Vista. Drummers are from our supporting church, Talbot Bible Church in Easton, Maryland. So, Jane has been busy orienting them and putting them to work in all kinds of fix-it jobs. Because of the language problem, she's had to interpret for them in offices, stores, and on the street, which has kept her very busy. So, she was very happy when Miriam returned in February.

We want to express our appreciation to all of you who prayed for us at this difficult time. Miriam was thankful to be able to spend the last 2 1/2 months of her mother's life caring for her, but it was also a very difficult thing to watch her mother grow weaker each day. Thank you for your prayers and especially for your cards and gifts. She received so many, and she cherished each personal note. The Lord used many of you to bring comfort to her heart at this time.

More trials invaded Miriam's and Jane's lives. Jane's dad was put in the hospital with a life-threatening abdominal infection. Jane had a scratch, which turned into blood poisoning in her leg, and later she was gored by a cow. Miriam had a small accident in the truck as she crossed a dangerous bridge. Although their faith was tested, they stayed true to the Lord and His calling on their lives. God had seen them through their darkest days; they knew He would not fail them now.

Both ladies returned to Serra Grande and Project Bethel, encouraged to see how God was transforming the lives of their students. Flavio, who spoke six languages, was eager to preach to the people of his native Guyana. Josevaldo and his wife Antonia were effectively witnessing to their unsaved families. Delio, a new Christian, was growing in his walk with the Lord. On and on the list went, evidence that God was changing each life.

> *The highlight of this past year was the 8th-grade graduation. Debrão was the only one who stuck it out and finished 5th through 8th-grade work. At the same time, he finished Bible courses that took him through the whole Bible. Sharing the celebration with him was his new wife, a sincere believer who loves the Lord and wants to serve Him together with Debrão. We had the privilege of helping them get the proper document so they could be married legally, a real rarity among Macushi young people. Pray that this marriage will be an example to many.*

A Macushi being accepted as a leader among Brazilians is a rare thing indeed. However, Debrão went on to study at a formal Bible school in Manaus, where he became a student leader. God used him to lead his entire family to the Lord and to help plant a couple of churches. Several of the students who came to Project Bethel went on to serve the Lord with their lives. Miriam and Jane referred to them as "diamonds in the rough." Indeed, God's transforming power was evident for all to see.

Chapter Thirty
God Uses the Radio Ministry

Because by means of you, people in the grace place have heard God's Word and also the Macedonia people and again more places. Many others have heard the news of you making God true.
—1 Thessalonians 1:8, Macushi Back Translation

For from you the word of the Lord has sounded forth, not only in Macedonia and Achaia, but also in every place your faith toward God has gone out, so that we do not need to say anything.
—1 Thessalonians 1:8

An effective tool for reaching and teaching the often-illiterate Macushi people was cassette tape recordings, which Jane made for them.

We started a tape ministry in the early days to help the churches with music. We had composed quite a few hymns, but we didn't know how we were going to get everybody to sing them exactly the same when we didn't have music for them to listen to. There were no guitars or keyboards in the beginning. Most songs weren't written with music, and the Indians didn't know how to read music. We had our most gifted people sing through the hymn book. They would sing straight through, and we'd record it. That worked out well and became popular. We had hand-wind tape recorders from Gospel Recordings that the Macushi would use to listen to the tapes.

Then we began to record and include sermons with the songs, like a mini service. We started a lending library, and when I went around on clinics, I'd let them borrow tapes for a month. Then the next month, they'd borrow a couple more tapes.

Of course, that was together with any literature we had. I started traveling with hymn books and anything that Miriam had produced in the Macushi language. We wanted to encourage them to read in their own language, and there wasn't anything else readily available. We charged a small fee for them to buy the literature. That went on for some time.

Miriam and Jane would often host Macushi preachers at Serra Grande, who recorded more of these tapes.

The Bible course finishes November 2nd, and on November 5th a missionary named Nathan is coming to record messages on tape in Macushi to help us. He is being sent by Gospel Recordings. Waldemar is coming to do the preaching. That should take a couple days.

Jane shared how the tape library evolved into the radio ministry.

Trans World Radio aired many Christian programs in Portuguese, and their board desired to begin airing gospel programs in an Indian language of northern Brazil. They came to our mission and asked for volunteers to do something like this. God burdened our hearts with it. We thought, since we were already doing the recorded tapes, it wouldn't be too much trouble to also prepare a radio program.

We used the space where I kept our medicines. It was typically empty, except when the clinic was open. There was a lot of noise around, the usual dogs and chickens in the background. We would invite one of our Macushi leaders to preach, suggest a passage of Scripture, and give him an idea for an appropriate application. He would prepare it. Finally, we would listen to ensure that it filled the allotted time slot. We followed that protocol for a good number of years.

Eventually, it became feasible for the radio program to be done more professionally, a move that improved and expanded its reach.

Trans World is requesting more professional recordings. Therefore, from June 4 to June 18 we are having a training course for 12 Macushi (chosen by their churches) to produce programs for radio. Al Bachman of Trans World Radio is coming to teach for a week, and Paulo Sergio is coming to record the programs. Pray for this endeavor, as it is so new to all of us. We want these programs to be used of the Lord in many villages we can't reach. We want to "advertise" the Macushi New Testament by reading portions of it on radio.

After the recording sessions, Miriam and Jane saw how God had been at work.

We know that the Lord will certainly use these programs because Satan was working overtime! A week before the course, one of the leaders who was coming lost his wife in childbirth. So, he couldn't come. Many of the others backed out because it's a bad time of year for their field work. They have to get things planted and weeded. The day before the ones in the mountains were to leave to come, the buses stopped running for the rest of the rainy season. Then Dan Teeter went to pick up another pastor and his wife and arrived at their house just after the father had taken their two-year-old to the hospital. So, Dan took his wife to the hospital, where they stayed for 4 days until the baby died of cerebral malaria. So, they couldn't come.

We started with just two people, and then others came two and three days late. But all in all, we had a good group, and I think they learned something about preparing sermons. Each of the five men prepared four sermons, each ten to twelve minutes long. The women were used in interviews and also in telling Bible stories about women. One interview was with two women who each had lost a child. So they shared how the Lord helped them in their grief.

The technician with Trans World Radio came from São Paulo for two days and helped Jane learn to do digital recording. He was very impressed with the quality of tapes we were getting, though it was very frustrating to try and maintain quiet with both Indians and our dogs!!!

Needless to say, we both were very busy. I was helping each one individually to prepare their sermons and oversee the lady in the kitchen. Jane and I ate beans and rice and farine with the Indians every day for two weeks. So, I am not on speaking terms with beans right now! Jane did all the recording and tried to keep the classes going for our school. Well, we got 6 months' worth of programs taped. Sermon tapes, music tapes, Scripture reading tapes, and a tape of the beginning and ending of the program. The name of the program in Macushi is: God Speaks to Us. And it starts with a greeting saying, "We are happy that you have received us into your house. God is wanting to speak to us in our own language. Let's all listen."

By the way, the Macushi radio program is aired every Sunday morning at 4 a.m. That may seem like a horrible time, but actually, that is perfect timing for the Macushi. They go to bed when it gets dark, which means about 6 p.m.. But 4 a.m. is about the time they wake up, and so we are able to participate in their family devotional time on Sundays at 4 a.m.

Again, Jane explained further about the recording ministry.

Eventually, Trans World told us that they were trying to improve the quality of their recordings even more, and they wanted us to start taping in a regular studio to clean the background noise out. Initially, they had suggested certain machines that would be helpful in cleaning up the recordings. They also had a certain format they wanted us to follow to make sure we left time for their advertising. Additionally, they offered to train us to do this professionally in São Paulo. We determined to bring a couple of Indians and do as many programs as possible while we were there.

So we took two Indians, Abel and Aluizio, with us to São Paulo. Basically, I was the technical person. Miriam taught the Indians to time their sermons down to the second. We made a year's worth of programs in a couple of weeks.

At that time, I believe our trainers weren't sure that I could learn to use all of that equipment. But I did! We started out renting two different studios. There was one from a secular radio program. The conditions for that were quite primitive. The studio was the size of a telephone booth. You locked yourself in there to keep sounds out. There was no air conditioning or anything, just you and the microphone. The Macushi pastors didn't like that too much, but they cooperated.

Eventually, we realized that we needed our own studio. So, under the tutelage of Trans World Radio, we figured out exactly what we needed. Eric Shrift, a fellow missionary who was starting to take an interest in the radio program, built a noise-proof studio for us. While he worked on that, we went on deputation raising money for the equipment that was needed. Thanks to the Lord's people, the funds for the necessary equipment were raised. We installed it in *our brand-new studio and started producing professional recordings.*

In 2005, Miriam and Jane brought two young ladies from South Carolina to Brazil to help with the music in these radio broadcasts.

Thank you for your prayers concerning the recording of sermons and music for the weekly Macushi radio program. The Lord went before us and though "our plans" didn't quite work out, we praise Him for leading us in His direction.

Week 1: We made trips to villages, inviting Macushi pastors to come to town and record in our new studio in Boa Vista. Good contacts were made in Guyana.

We arrived there at the time of their bi-annual Bible school, so we met several pastors. Brother Desmond Michaels promised to come and record messages. We also talked with the pastor there, and he told us how his church is growing. They now have 180 in their Sunday school. It seems the Lord has done a special work in the pastor's heart, using trouble in his family to draw him closer and make him more compassionate. We praise Him for what He is doing on that side of the border.

Week 2: The pastors from Serra Grande and Fonte Nova arrived as promised. Hannah Aiken and Emily Danuser, the girls who traveled with us, were kept busy accompanying those singing Macushi songs. Jane began training our missionary colleague, Eric Shrift, in the computer program for recording. We praise the Lord for the new studio Eric helped build last year. It really is a wonderful facility and served us well.

Week 3: Though we had scheduled pastors for this week, no one came to record. But we were kept busy, Jane working with Eric editing the work done in week 2, and Miriam making contacts for the next week.

Week 4: Pastors who had been scheduled for week 3 arrived, as well as others we had scheduled for week 4. Feast or famine!! We roll with the punches, so this was a very busy and exhausting week recording both messages and music. Hannah's fingers were very sore from spending so many hours strumming the guitar accompanying the singers.

Once again, Jane explained.

After recording enough sermons for a year, we returned to Pickens, SC. There I would clean the recordings up, check them doctrinally, and prepare them for the radio program. I then sent them over the Internet to Trans World Radio in São Paulo. In turn, they were sent to Bon Aire, Netherlands, Antilles. So right from Pickens, South Carolina, someplace you've probably never heard of, we were running a little radio studio and putting out programs.

This radio program, produced in Macushi, reached hundreds of people across the Brazilian savannahs, as well as into Venezuela and Guyana. The eternal fruit from this labor of love will not likely be known until Miriam and Jane reach heaven.

Chapter Thirty-One
God Uses the Luke Film

To my relative, Theophilus, many people are writing Jesus'
story, to tell what's happened among us. . .I am writing it in
order that you know what you've studied is right.
                    —Luke 1:1, 4, Macushi Back Translation

Inasmuch as many have taken in hand to set in order a
narrative of those things which have been fulfilled among
us. . .that you may know the certainty of those things in
which you were instructed.
                                        —Luke 1:1, 4

In 1995, Miriam and Jane began yet another new project, the Luke
Film (the longer film from which the Jesus Film was taken). They
hoped it would assist them in reaching new villages with the gospel.

We finally finished the Macushi film of Luke. I have worked
on that script since before coming back here to Brazil, so
I am thoroughly sick of it! But. . .there have been many
blessings along the way as we worked with our taping crew.

João Salty Peter, the pastor of the church at Patativa did
the voice of Jesus. We found out after working with him for

a week that it was the first time he has read Macushi. We wondered what his problem was!

He did have a difficult time with his part at first. He felt that he was being oppressed by evil spirits, and he was having nightmares. We prayed for him one morning before work, and he seemed to calm down and ended up doing a fantastic job.

Valdemir, from Napoleão, was our narrator. These two parts were by far the heaviest. He also hadn't read very much Macushi, but he rapidly improved. He said: "Sister, you taught me to read Macushi in 1991, but since then I haven't read Macushi at all. But now, I will never leave it again." So, even though I've taught people to read Macushi through the years because they haven't had much at all to read, they just didn't read. He too did a fabulous job and is really excited about the finished product.

Raimundo, the pastor from Maracanã, did some of the other male voices. But he was an excellent help in correcting the script and making sure no one said anything that wasn't natural or grammatically correct.

Âluizio from Mt. Moriá did the other male voices: Peter, John the Baptist, etc. He too was very good and wants to use the film in his area.

Nathan Burgess, the technician who came from the south of Brazil to record for us, has been great to work with. It's been a busy time for all of us.

God Uses the Luke Film

In June, the film was released.

For the first time ever in this world, a film portraying the life and teachings of Jesus, as written in the book of Luke, is narrated in the Macushi language. In all of this, we feel the Lord will use it, not only in conveying this most important message but also in preparing the way for the acceptance and use of the Macushi New Testament.

While Miriam had written the script in Macushi, it was Jane who traveled to each village to show the film.

Lots of different groups chose to do the Luke Film. It took at least 5 hours to run, but the Indians loved to sit there that long and watch it. Let me explain to you how difficult it was to show the film at times.

It took at least two men to carry the generator, and another to carry the electrical cord. We had to make sure we had plenty of cord. Otherwise, the sound of the generator drowned out the sound of the film. And I always had to go along, because I was the only one that knew how to operate the equipment.

It just so happened that I was having quite a lot of trouble walking. (It turned out I had a slipped disc.) So, we'd walk a short distance, and then the pain became excruciating. I would lay down on the ground, and the Indians would pull on my leg! It must've worked like traction, and would temporarily relieve the pain. Then I could get up and walk some distance again.

A lot of times we were going on footpaths over mountains, and we did it in a lot of places that had never even seen a car come into their village. It was quite an experience, all to show how Jesus really did walk here on this earth.

In one village, after we'd shown it, a woman came to me and said, "Now I want you to show how God created the world, so we can understand that!"

I thought to myself, "That really would be a film!"

During this time, the ladies welcomed Miriam's niece, Ann Abbott, a nursing student who was considering God's plan for her future. They put her to work, as well as gave her an authentic missionary experience.

We did decide to do something special with Ann. We took a trip to Venezuela. The road is now paved all the way and there are nice comfortable buses that go 5 times a day. So, Debby, Auxiliadora, Ann, Jane, and I all went on Tuesday. We had a good time shopping there in Santa Elena on the border.

We left to return home on the 5:30 p.m. bus. We got to the border and were delayed a bit while the Federal police checked passports, etc. Then we went on about 20 minutes. It was dark by then, and a big tanker truck flagged the bus down and told the driver that a big piece of road had washed away. He had just gotten across it when it gave way. One of those huge culverts had been swept down the mountain. Well, we all got out and went to the edge of the abyss, and sure enough, a huge section was missing. There was a piece of roadway about 4 feet wide that was left, and would you believe, a Volkswagen crossed on that piece! Well, we (the bus load of people) waited until the other bus came from Boa Vista, and we all crossed on foot to the bus on the other side, and they did the same to get to Venezuela. We didn't get into Boa Vista until midnight, and then we drove on back here to Serra Grande. Ann sure got her hair-raising experience that night.

The Luke Film required a great deal of work to bring to the Macushi. Miriam and Jane happily invested themselves into this project because they believed its impact would be great. And they were correct! The Lord greatly used this form of sharing the gospel to bring people to Himself, to burden their hearts for sharing the gospel with others, and to teach them how to live their lives for Him.

Ann Abbott Covey, Miriam's niece, learned much from the veteran missionaries during her visit. A note from Abbot Covey:

Breathtaking, enlightening, strengthening, amazing. . .these are a few words I would use to describe my time in Brazil. It was an experience that revealed God's will in how I would serve Him. I went with an open mind for missions and had always desired to go to Brazil. Aunt Miriam was always an inspiration to me to become a nurse, and I wanted to see if God was calling me to follow in her steps. I wanted to see firsthand how she served God.

In a time of religious warfare in Brazil, Miriam, Jane, Debra and I flew with Tim in a small plane to multiple villages, spreading God's Word and vaccinating the Macushi against tetanus, polio, and yellow fever. We also went to a village with a mixture of Macushi and Inkarikó people. We administered about 750 vaccines to men (including the witch doctors), women, and children. The natives were very receptive to medical attention, as well as listening to God's Word and our testimonies. New churches were being established, and villages with established churches were being maintained with pastors training new pastors. There were medical posts where trained technicians were treating people with a variety of illnesses, many with malaria. Jane had started training these techs years earlier and established some healthcare to continue independently. It was clear that God could use all of our talents in opening doors to spread the message of salvation.

Miriam and Jane had recently introduced the first rough copy of the Macushi New Testament. In many of the villages we visited, we called a service together and showed the Luke Film. Miriam and Jane would read from the New Testament and then would invite the Macushi to come forward and read a passage. If they were able to read the passage, they received a copy of the New Testament for themselves to keep. It was seen as an honor and privilege to receive "this book." It was a wonderful feeling when the people were so excited to hear God's Word.

The thing that kept nagging at my heart the entire trip

was the thought of why so many Americans were closed-minded to hearing the gospel of Christ. Many think they have everything and want to be in control of their own lives. They think they don't need Christ, but where will they be without faith, hope, and love? I was heartbroken for my own country and felt a calling to use nursing as my open door to be a living testimony for Christ. When I look back on my journal entries from my time in Brazil, it is evident how God used every step of faith and every person along the way to reveal His calling. Great is Thy Faithfulness!

Chapter Thirty-Two
God Is Still Working

My relatives, I have not done everything that God has wanted; therefore, I continue at it, not thinking of what has already passed long ago. But I remain thinking about what is to come later.
　　　　　　　　　—Philippians 3:13, Macushi Back Translation

Brethren, I do not count myself to have apprehended: but one thing I do, forgetting those things which are behind and reaching forward to those things which are ahead.
　　　　　　　　　—Philippians 3:13

With Mrs. Abbott's declining health and eventual passing, the letters from Miriam slowed and finally stopped. But prayer letters still continued, as did the work!

Jane continued to teach at Project Bethel and helped the students participate in the two local churches. She also directed construction projects and cared for the animals which provided food for the students and staff. But her arthritis was getting worse. At the beginning of 2002, both ladies planned to return to the US. Miriam hoped to report to her supporting churches, and Jane planned to visit her doctors and have surgery to help with the pain in her joints. They were both thankful to know that the Lord always had and always would direct their paths.

Upon returning to the States, Jane endured three surgeries. As the doctors continued to treat her auto-immune diseases, the mission concluded that it was not feasible for her to live full-time in the tropical heat. Therefore, the Lord seemed to be preparing a change for her, for Miriam, and for their ministry.

> *After over thirty years living on the equator, how and where are we to live anywhere else? We were concerned about all the logistics of moving. And many are saying, "Aren't you retiring? You've put in enough years!" But our concern is, "What does the Lord have for us?"*

> *The Macushi church still needs some help. We are producing literature: tracts, Sunday school lessons, devotional books, etc. We need to do more in training teachers of both children and adults. Therefore, we feel the Lord would have us in a place where we can continue to help with the ongoing needs of the church.*

> *We are humbled and ecstatically grateful for the way He is providing for us through friends and relatives. We are seeking to purchase a home in South Carolina. Jane has an uncle and aunt who live there, so she will be close to family. Her 5 cousins and their families are all in the area. We feel it will be a lower cost of living there so that our support will go further.*

> *We covet your prayers during this transition.*

David and Eddie Hutton, cousins of Jane's, helped to make it possible for the missionaries to purchase their first home in South Carolina. They both had taken several trips to Brazil, and their time with Miriam and Jane had deepened their love and burden for the missionaries.

These men set out to help in any way they could. The house itself was financed by David and built by Eddie. With their support's housing allowance, Miriam and Jane paid for the house a little at a time. Other cousins donated toward the house through gifts of appliances, blinds, and finances to allow Miriam and Jane to furnish the house and make it a comfortable home. The church family welcomed them with a "pounding," where many donated a pound of food to stock the pantry.

Before they completed their move to South Carolina, the station at Serra Grande had to be closed, a bittersweet moment for the ladies.

After Miriam's first term in Guyana, she had to close down the mission station, pack up, and move everything across the border to Brazil. Now after 30 years, we are doing the same thing. In late September, our administration finally told us that we needed to sell out everything in Serra Grande, as they had no immediate plans for the use of the property. So, we had to scramble and try to find buyers for the equipment, vehicles, and personal effects. Needless to say, it has been a busy time since we had to keep working as well. But we praise the Lord for all He has done. All was sold in time (even if the Volkswagen van didn't move until 2 days before we left).

We give God the praise and glory for all He has accomplished in that location. What we sold and got rid of were just temporal things, the real value continues in the hearts and lives of young people who were trained and discipled in the Word of God, which does not pass away. Pray for these "products" of the Lord's grace during these past few years.

As the ladies arrived in South Carolina before the holidays, they enjoyed hosting several relatives through the season. They were blessed and encouraged to be able to fellowship with so many in a short period of time, especially in their own home! But Miriam and Jane did face a few struggles in returning to the US full time.

In Brazil, when presented with a gift, it is poor taste to open it then and there. What do we do here?

In Brazil, one must eat a sandwich wrapped in a napkin. I have seen many Americans in fast-food restaurants eating burgers with their bare hands!

In Brazil, one does not put their purse on the floor. Many times here in the US, that is the only place to put it!

In Brazil, one greets a person with a hug and two kisses, one on each cheek. Here, one is lucky to get a handshake!

We naively thought that life in the good ol' USA would be a lot easier. What a culture shock! Things have changed dramatically over the years we've been gone! But what a blessing it is to know that God does not change and that He will work in any society, any culture, any tribe. Pray for us as we seek avenues of witness here. We won't go on about language differences and dress styles, but pray for us as we try to adapt to this "new" culture.

When they arrived home from Brazil, Miriam and Jane were met with a great welcome, and they entered wholly into the seasonal celebrations.

What a wonderful loving homecoming we had as we arrived back in South Carolina. Jane's cousin met us at the airport and took us out to dinner and then home. His wife and another cousin had brought in food and stocked our refrigerator. Then on Wednesday night, when we went to prayer meeting, we had almost a standing ovation as we entered. What a friendly bunch of people. And they all speak English!

Thursday morning the pastor's wife brought some of the AWANA children to our home to decorate a tree (we haven't had one before). The kids made popcorn and cranberry strings, paper chains, and all sorts of ornaments. Of course, the highlight was putting on the gobs of tinsel! They also brought a big box of canned goods and a gift card for the grocery store! What an abundance of love. We just praise the Lord for our loving church family!

Although they set up base in South Carolina, they still worked full-time to help the Macushi churches and their mission board in Brazil. They traveled to Brazil twice per year, as the Lord had plenty of work for them to do!

But the Lord also had ministry for the ladies close to home.

We praise the Lord for the opportunities He gives from time to time to share our work with others. It was a real blessing to us to visit and speak at a Mother-Daughter luncheon in North Carolina recently. We will be helping teach Vacation Bible School next week in our church. Other opportunities abound in our neighborhood, and this week we set up a table at the local Flea Market, giving out drinks of cold water, tracts, and taking blood pressures. We took several children from the church to help, and they really enjoyed walking around and handing out tracts and balloons that said "Jesus Loves Me." Surely there are opportunities all around us. Pray we may be sensitive to the Lord's leading.

Even though our full-time ministry is geared to the Macushi of Brazil, we dare not neglect the people living around us. This has been true for us wherever we lived. We felt responsible for Brazilian ranchers and miners who were our neighbors, and as a result, the Lord blessed in various ways through the years. He has us living among a different people here in South Carolina who look like us (even though their speech is different), and we feel a burden towards them. Our pastor asked us to consider teaching a Ladies' Bible study, so we thank the Lord for this opportunity. We are including our neighbors, as well as those in our local church. So far we have 4 from our immediate neighborhood, as well as several from the church. We are meeting in different ones' homes each week. Jane and I are humbled to think the Lord may use us right here where we are. After spending so long in the boonies of Brazil, we are now learning how to relate to people here (as well as how to wear shoes!).

The end of 2004 brought difficult news. Jane's mother's health declined quickly. After she suffered kidney failure and a heart attack, the family had to move her to a nursing home. This was difficult for them all but was especially hard on Jane's father as it meant he was living alone. Jane traveled to Michigan to help her siblings and parents, thankful that her work could continue with the help of technology.

Miriam was involved in checking Bible translations for at least four groups, while Jane was charged with the desktop publishing for several of these projects.

Translation continues in 4 Yanomami languages. Miriam checked passages done by Patricia Rocha, a new translator with our mission. She learned a lot about the language and culture during her stay in Brazil this time. Isaque, the language helper who worked with them, has given his heart and life to the Lord and is anxious for more Scripture to teach to his people.

Carole is translating the book of Ephesians. What a challenge to properly understand all the abstract truths and put them into comprehensible language for the Ninam, another language of the Yanomami. She is an experienced translator and has worked with these people for almost 40 years. Pray for her as she grapples with Paul's logic in presenting God's truth.

Miriam came home with a lot more projects to work on. The Macushi team told us the hymn books are all sold out. They want us to do a new edition. The translators want us to publish the books that Miriam checked, complete with pictures. The administration wants Jane to work on an orientation course for new missionaries (mostly Brazilians) with respect to the special needs for jungle living and ministering medically to the Indians, as well as their own families. The administration wants Miriam to follow up and evaluate the new missionaries who are learning Indian languages.

Looking back upon the years of ministry, God's direction and help were clear through them all.

Dearest Mother,

God answered your prayers! Here I am in the country of Guyana to serve Him. The Macushi language is difficult, but by His grace and help, I'll soon be able to communicate.

Thirty-four years ago, when I wrote this letter to my most faithful prayer supporter, I had no idea of the ways God would work. After just one year in the country, my hopes were dashed as the failed revolution worked havoc in the interior—in Macushi land. Two years of frustration followed as we tried to get permission to work among Amerindians. Why did the Lord call me to a life-work, only to be expelled after a few short years? But He had a perfect plan in motion. Doors opened to minister among the Macushi in Brazil. Freedom to travel and work in

Brazil's hinterland, God's provision of a coworker in Jane Burns RN, and much support from Missionary Aviation Fellowship were the means God used in answer to your prayers for ministry among the Macushi.

The years of medical-evangelistic trips, linguistic analysis, literacy classes, teaching, and Bible translation have passed quickly. And now that you, my most faithful prayer warrior have gone on to your reward, the Lord is still answering your prayers. You who have been faithful in praying over the years for this ministry share in the fruits of it.

And so it has continued, day in and day out, year after year. Miriam and Jane live in Florida now, but they are as busy as ever serving the Lord. They minister to the elderly that live nearby, to the neighbors of their community, to the poor and needy among them, to the ladies in their church, and to anyone who crosses their paths. They continue to have an influence upon the Amerindian tribes of Brazil through computer projects, yearly trips, and translation consulting. Their lives and testimonies are a tribute to God's great power and grace to accomplish His extraordinary work in the souls of men through the means of His humble, submitted servants.

Acknowledgments

We extend a big thank you to those who helped make this book possible!

—Miriam Abbott and Jane Burns, for sharing their many years of experiences, letters, memories, stories, and more

—Mrs. Heidi Coombs for permission to reprint her poem "Beginnings"

—Mr. Jim Bjur for permission to use his poems "Get Involved" and "Not Home Yet"

—Ruth Sharp Cochrane, DiAnne Butler, Elizabeth Kereji, Ann Abbott Covey, Melody Smith Bjur, and Carol Morrill, for their testimonies and memories of their friends

—Elyse Coleman, Brenda Coats, Becky Smith, Jann Loderhose, and Matt Johnson for their time to read the rough draft of this book, to make editorial corrections and suggestions, and to share their thoughts

—Julie Chappell for her expertise and help with the photographs

—Jared Smith for his design of the map and timeline

CPSIA information can be obtained
at www.ICGtesting.com
Printed in the USA
FFOW02n1120011117
41760FF

9 781632 961594